Rethinking Power Relations in Indonesia

Since colonial rule, the island of Java served as Indonesia's imagined centre and prime example of development, while the Outer Islands were constructed as the state's marginalised periphery. Recent processes of democratisation and regional autonomy, however, have significantly changed the power relations that once produced the marginality of the Outer Islands.

This book explores processes of political, economic and cultural transformations in Indonesia, emphasising their implications for centre–periphery relations from the perspective of the archipelago's 'margins'. Structured along three central themes, the book first provides theoretical contributions to the understanding of marginality in Indonesia. The second part focuses on political transformation processes and their implications for the Outer Islands. The third part investigates the dynamics caused by economic changes on Indonesia's periphery.

Chapters written by experts in the field offer examples from various regions, which demonstrate how power relations between centre and periphery are being challenged, contested and reshaped. The book fills a gap in the literature by analysing the implications of the recent transformation processes for the construction of marginality on Indonesia's Outer Islands.

Michaela Haug is Assistant Professor at the Department of Cultural and Social Anthropology, University of Cologne, Germany.

Martin Rössler is Professor at the Department of Cultural and Social Anthropology, University of Cologne, Germany.

Anna-Teresa Grumblies is an anthropologist who is currently working for the German Academic Scholarship Foundation.

Routledge Contemporary Southeast Asia Series

Rethinking Power Relations in Indonesia

Transforming the margins

**Edited by Michaela Haug, Martin Rössler
and Anna-Teresa Grumblies**

Routledge
Taylor & Francis Group

LONDON AND NEW YORK

First published 2017
by Routledge
2 Park Square, Milton Park, Abingdon, Oxon OX14 4RN

and by Routledge
711 Third Avenue, New York, NY 10017

Routledge is an imprint of the Taylor & Francis Group, an informa business

© 2017 Michaela Haug, Martin Rössler and Anna-Teresa Grumblies

British Library Cataloguing in Publication Data
A catalogue record for this book is available from the British Library

Library of Congress Cataloging-in -Publication Data
Names: Haug, Michaela, 1976– editor. | Rèossler, Martin, 1956– editor. | Grumblies, Anna-Teresa, editor. | Ziegenhain, Patrick, 1969–
Decentralization and its impact on the democratization process. Container of (work):
Title: Rethinking power relations in Indonesia : transforming the margins / edited [by] Michaela Haug, Martin Rèossler and Anna-Teresa Grumblies.
Description: New York : Routledge, 2016. | Series: Routledge contemporary Southeast Asia series ; 82 | Includes bibliographical references and index.
Identifiers: LCCN 2016005954| ISBN 9781138962781 (hardback) | ISBN 9781315659190 (ebook)
Subjects: LCSH: Central-local government relations–Indonesia. | Decentralization in government–Indonesia. | Power (Social sciences)–Indonesia.|Marginality,Social–Indonesia.|Indonesia–Politicsandgovernment–1998–
Classification: LCC JQ766.S8 R48 2016 | DDC 320.9598–dc23
LC record available at http://lccn.loc.gov/2016005954

ISBN: 978-1-138-96278-1 (hbk)
ISBN: 978-1-315-65919-0 (ebk)

Typeset in Times New Roman
by Wearset Ltd, Boldon, Tyne and Wear

Contents

Contributors

Laurens Bakker is Assistant Professor at the Department of Anthropology at the University of Amsterdam. His research focuses on land law and land conflict in Southeast Asia, as well as on the influence of informal militias in Southeast Asian local politics, society and economy. His publications include *Who Owns the Land? Looking for Law and Power in Reformasi East Kalimantan* (Radboud University Nijmegen, 2009) and a wide variety of contributions to edited volumes and journals.

Michael Eilenberg is Associate Professor of Anthropology at Aarhus University. His research is based on serial field visits to Indonesia and Malaysia from 2002 to 2013 and deals with the particular social and political dynamics taking place along the Indonesian–Malaysian border on the island of Borneo. His recent monograph entitled *At the Edge of States*, first published by KITLV Press (2012) and later reprinted by Brill Academic Publishers (2014), deals with the dynamics of state formation in Southeast Asian borderlands. His recent articles have appeared in *Modern Asian Studies, Identities: Global Studies in Culture and Power, Journal of Peasant Studies, Journal of Borderland Studies* and *Asia Pacific Viewpoint*.

Anna-Teresa Grumblies studied Social and Cultural Anthropology, Gender Studies, History and Philosophy at the University of Göttingen and at the University of California in Santa Barbara, and graduated in 2010. Her PhD thesis, which she successfully defended at the University of Cologne, is based on 14 months of field work among the Wana of Central Sulawesi, where she investigated marginalisation processes among upland groups. She is currently working for the German Academic Scholarship Foundation.

Michaela Haug received her doctoral degree from the University of Freiburg and is currently Assistant Professor of Cultural and Social Anthropology at the University of Cologne. Her research focuses on human–environment relations, processes of political, economic and social change, social inequalities, gender, and rights to land and forest resources, with a regional focus on Indonesian Borneo. Her monograph entitled *Poverty and Decentralisation in East Kalimantan: The Impact of Regional Autonomy on Dayak Benuaq Wellbeing*

(2010) analyses the dynamics of the political reform process in Indonesia on the village level and shows how decentralisation has been intertwined with other processes of change. Her recent publications explore local responses to decentralised forest governance and the expansion of oil palm plantations in East Kalimantan.

Kirsten Jäger studied Social Anthropology, Political Science and German Philology at the University of Münster, where she also received her PhD in Social Anthropology. Her dissertation deals with the revitalisation of traditional polities in the Sultanate of Jailolo, North Moluccas. Her research has focused on political anthropology in Southeast Asia, in particular Indonesia. She is currently teaching at the Institute of Social Anthropology at the University of Münster.

Nicholas J. Long is Assistant Professor of Anthropology at the London School of Economics and Political Science. He is the author of *Being Malay in Indonesia: Histories, Hopes and Citizenship in the Riau Archipelago* (NUS Press, NIAS Press and University of Hawai'i Press, 2013), and co-editor of *Southeast Asian Perspectives on Power* (Routledge, 2012), *Sociality: New Directions* (Berghahn, 2012), *The Social Life of Achievement* (Berghahn, 2013) and *The State We're In: Reflecting on Democracy's Troubles* (Berghahn, 2016).

Martin Rössler is Professor and Chair at the Department of Cultural and Social Anthropology at the University of Cologne. Based upon several years of fieldwork in Indonesia since 1984, he has published extensively on the Makassarese of South Sulawesi. In addition to his theoretical work on economic anthropology, his research has focused on kinship and social structure, political organisation, religion and ritual, the revitalisation of Islam and transformations of the rural economy in Indonesia.

Patrick Ziegenhain holds a PhD in Political Science from the University of Freiburg and is currently Visiting Professor at the Department of Business Administration at Atma Jaya University in Jakarta/Indonesia. Previously, he had been an Interim Professor at the Department of Southeast Asian Studies at the University of Frankfurt (2015), Visiting Professor at De la Salle University Manila in 2014 and Assistant Professor at the Department of Political Science, University of Trier (2007–2014). He has published numerous academic articles and is the author of the monographs *Institutional Engineering and Political Accountability in Thailand, Indonesia, and the Philippines* (2015), *The Indonesian Parliament and Democratization* (2008) and co-author of *Parliaments and Political Change in Asia* (2005).

Acknowledgements

This volume emerged out of the workshop 'Transforming the Margins: Contesting and Reformulating Centre–Periphery Relations in Post-Suharto Indonesia', which was organised by the editors at the Department of Cultural and Social Anthropology at the University of Cologne, from 31 January to 2 February 2013. The interdisciplinary workshop was triggered by our common interest to explore social, political, economic and religious transformation processes in post-Suharto Indonesia from the perspective of the archipelago's peripheral regions, and to initiate a debate about how these changes have altered centre–periphery relations. For this purpose we brought together senior and junior researchers from Europe and Indonesia, with backgrounds from anthropology, history, geography and political science. All of them look back on intensive research in different locations in Indonesia's so-called 'Outer Islands', covering such diverse regions as the Riau Islands, East and West Kalimantan, South and Central Sulawesi, Sumbawa, Flores, Timor, the North Moluccas and West Papua.

We are very grateful to the Fritz Thyssen Stiftung for generously funding the workshop. Chairing the respective panels, Christoph Antweiler, Birgitt Röttger-Rössler and Judith Schlehe contributed much to stimulating discussions in the course of the workshop and simultaneously helped to formulate a useful analytical framework. Our deepest thanks go to all participants who presented papers at the workshop and thus helped to strengthen our perspective on Indonesia's 'margins'. For various reasons not all of them were able to contribute to this book, which therefore does not cover the regional breadth as originally intended. However, we believe that the case studies represented here sufficiently demonstrate the far-reaching changes of power constellations, which altered the various ways through which marginality has been constructed on the islands beyond Java, and that the book makes a valuable contribution to the ongoing effort of rethinking power relations in contemporary Indonesia.

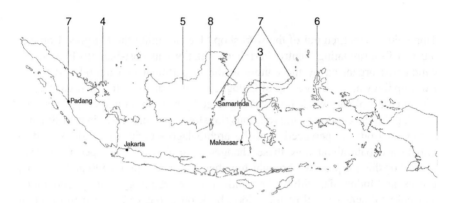

Map 0.1 Map of Indonesia (source: 123rf, adapted by Martin Rössler).

Note
Numbers indicate chapters addressing the respective regions.

1 Introduction

Contesting and reformulating centre–periphery relations in Indonesia

Michaela Haug, Martin Rössler and Anna-Teresa Grumblies

On 4 November 2004 hundreds of people gathered to celebrate the ceremonious inauguration of the new government building complex of West Kutai in East Kalimantan. The celebration marked the fifth birthday of the new regency, which had come into existence in November 1999 when the former regency of Kutai was split into three parts. The new government complex consisted at that time of eight[1] spacious buildings whose construction had swallowed up an entire annual budget of the regency. During the dedication ceremony, the governor of East Kalimantan could not help hinting at the extraordinary dimensions of the new building complex as he opened his speech with the comment that he felt jealous, comparing the new government buildings of Kutai Barat with the cramped and comparatively simple building of the provincial government in Samarinda. Why does a regency in the forested interior of East Kalimantan with roughly 150,000 inhabitants erect such a splendid building complex?

In many respects, the impressive buildings reflect the far-reaching changes that the reform era has brought to the regions beyond Java since the end of President Suharto's New Order regime in 1998. After 32 years of authoritarian rule, the archipelago has become one of the world's largest democracies. Regional autonomy, initiated in 2001, transferred much of central government's authority to the regions and replaced a previously highly centralistic system with one of Southeast Asia's most rigorous decentralisation reforms. Regencies (*kabupaten*) have become the main recipients of new authority, turning the institutions and procedures of the centralistic state into a highly diverse array of new regional centres. In some of them, previously marginalised ethnic minorities have become local majorities (Haug 2010), and people formerly excluded from power have (re-)turned into ruling elites (van Klinken 2007a; Vel 2008; Eilenberg 2009), while shifts in capital have brought about an extreme rise of income in some resource-rich regions beyond Java. The *era reformasi* has thereby set off processes of change all over Indonesia. However, we argue that these developments had particularly profound impacts on the state's periphery, bearing far-reaching implications for local power constellations. The government complex of Kutai Barat is an apparent manifestation of these changes. Its extraordinary dimensions mirror a new local elite's ambitions, as well as the pride and self-esteem of a previously remote area that is now brimming with enthusiasm to challenge its alleged peripheral status.

The Indonesian archipelago has a long history of emerging and declining centres. With the rise and fall of kingdoms and sultanates, some places have been temporarily constructed as centres and others as peripheries. But it was not until colonial times that a single centre, Java, was established and the surrounding islands were transformed into the state's periphery. After independence, the central position of Java and the capital Jakarta was further strengthened, a process which finally culminated in the highly centralistic organisation of Indonesia during the *Orde Baru.*[2]

The 'big bang' decentralisation reforms which overturned this strictly centralised system have been intensively studied (e.g. Aspinall and Fealy 2003; Erb and Sulistiyanto 2009; Hill 2014) and stimulated debates about the (in)stability of Indonesia (Kingsbury and Aveling 2003) and the prospects for democratisation (McLeod and MacIntyre 2007). With regional autonomy, scholarly interest has shifted toward 'the local' in Indonesia. Small communities, religious and ethnic organisations, local elites as well as mid-sized towns beyond Java receive new attention as important sites of regional power struggles, quests for identity and networks of patronage (Sakai 2002a; Erb *et al.* 2005; Schulte Nordholt and van Klinken 2007; Holtzappel and Ramstedt 2009; van Klinken and Berenschot 2014). This new interest in contemporary local politics has shifted attention away from predominantly grand narratives and stimulated much more nuanced accounts, which reflect the diversity of political and economic processes as well as identities on the islands beyond Java (Sakai *et al.* 2009). Research on the proliferation of new provinces and regencies (Kimura 2012) and the creation of new centres (Sakai 2009) further opens new perspectives on centre–periphery relations.

This book explores the recent transformations in post-Suharto Indonesia from the perspective of the archipelago's peripheral regions and shows how they have provided the margins with new opportunities to challenge and alter their position vis-à-vis the centre. We argue that processes of democratisation and regional autonomy have significantly changed the power relations that produced and maintained the marginality of the so-called Outer Islands since colonial rule. The case studies presented in this volume comprise examples from various regions, demonstrating how local actors become actively and creatively engaged in creating new centres and new peripheries alike, contributing to a much more complex political landscape in which power relations between centres and peripheries are constantly challenged, contested and reshaped.

Historical dimensions of changing centre–periphery relations

A historical perspective on the rise and decline of centres and peripheries in the Indonesian archipelago over the course of time pinpoints some aspects which are of central importance for the subsequent case studies by illustrating the temporality of centre–periphery relations, the fluidity of borders between different spheres of influence, the fragility of power constellations that construct certain places as centres and others as peripheries, and the multiple links between them.

The following overview, while focusing on some of the most important historical trends on a more general level, will necessarily neglect many others.

Examining the historical development of centres and peripheries in Indonesia
first of all requires one to distinguish between coastal port-states and inland agrarian states. While early examples of the latter, which in the archipelago were mainly
located on the island of Java (Schutte 1994: 3), were centres of Hindu–Buddhist
culture, most states which later emerged along the coasts of Java, Sumatra, Borneo,
Sulawesi and eastern Indonesia were strongly shaped by Islam, which for centuries
was spread along the trade routes and in many cases helped to strengthen the local
rulers' legitimation (Reid 1993a: 16; Andaya 1993: 34). The rise and decline of
historical centres in the archipelago, particularly during the 'golden age' of maritime commerce between the fifteenth and the seventeenth centuries, is above all
linked to the expansion of long-distance trade, which gave rise to powerful centralised states, social stratification, urbanisation, and the spread of rich scriptural traditions of which in the long run Islam should prove to be the most important one (cf.
Selling 1981). While for centuries Chinese, Europeans, Arabs and Indians were
competing in the trade of products such as pepper, cloves, cinnamon and nutmeg,
the rise and decline of various concentrations of power was crucial for the emergence of socio-economic and political patterns among the indigenous societies all
over the region. The fluidity of the relations among these centres as well as
between them and their peripheries was an important feature of the historical
development of what is now Indonesia.

In contrast to the agrarian states on Java, in particular on Sumatra and Borneo,
many power centres relied on upstream–downstream relations linking the coast
with the sparsely populated hinterland. The interior provided trading goods
ranging from forest products to slaves, whereas the coastal centres exercised
political and economic control over the people living along the rivers (Reid
1993a: 5, 1993b: 207; Watson-Andaya 1993). On a more general level this
upstream–downstream dualism, structurally equivalent to upland–lowland
dichotomies, centuries ago established a social and cultural distinction which is
still symptomatic for many parts of present-day Southeast Asia, namely a contrast which in the eyes of the elites is one between the primitive and the civilised
(Li 1999; Scott 2009). In terms of ethnic categories this contrast, in the Borneo
example, was one between the Dayak hinterland population and Malay rulers of
the coastal trading centres. Malay traders from Sumatra and the Malay peninsula
had long since been migrating eastwards, often establishing trading posts at strategic places along the coasts, which later developed into political centres (Ismail
1994). It should be noted that these small kingdoms never gained power equivalent to that of empires such as Majapahit on Java, and that the states along the
Borneo coast, for example, exercised but limited influence on neighbouring
regions (Cribb 2000: 100). Yet, around 1600, most of the substantial political
centres in the archipelago – Aceh, Melaka, Johor, Banten, Mataram, Demak,
Banjarmasin, Brunei, Makassar, and Ternate – had risen to power through maritime trade and were located on the coast, some of them having a population of
100,000 or more (Reid 1988: 9, 1993b: 76).

Early centres

As early as in the eighth century, three major centres of political and economic power emerged in the archipelago: the Melaka strait, which was of crucial significance for the trade route between India and China, the Buddhist kingdom of Srivijaya in Sumatra, with its capital near present-day Palembang, and the empire of the Sailendra dynasty in Java. While the latter's dominance may be regarded as a starting point of Javanese cultural dominance for the following centuries, it was above all the Javanese empire of Majapahit which later exerted considerable Javanese influence on Sumatra.

In the fifteenth century the most powerful centre in the region was Melaka, at that time a new type of state, which due to its strategic location owed its rise largely to long-distance trade across the whole Indian Ocean, and hence became the 'port-state par excellence' (Reid 1993b: 208; cf. Thomaz 1993: 71). After Melaka was conquered by the Portuguese in 1511 – one of the most prominent incidents in Southeast Asian history – many of the local traders migrated to Aceh, which, however, lost power in the seventeenth century because the southern kingdoms of Jambi and Palembang, both strongly involved in the pepper trade, had regained new strength through their alliance with the Dutch East India Company (Vereenigde Oostindische Compagnie [VOC]) that had meanwhile entered the scene.

Partly due to ecological and demographic factors, the development on the island of Borneo took a different course. Sparsely populated and largely covered by rainforest, the interior never saw the emergence of empires such as arose in Sumatra or Java. Instead, the island's political centres, such as Banjarmasin and the Malay kingdom of Kutai, were confined to the coasts. On the southwestern peninsula of Sulawesi, the centralised states of Luwu and Soppeng appear to have been formed in the fourteenth century. After the power of both began to vanish in the fifteenth or sixteenth centuries, the Buginese kingdom of Bone and the Makassarese kingdom of Gowa began to emerge as the new major empires on the peninsula. Alongside with the rise of Gowa, the port town of Makassar became the most important centre of trade in the region, reaching its peak in the seventeenth century. The empire of Gowa extended its influence to much of eastern Indonesia and became the most significant centre in the eastern archipelago until its defeat by the Dutch in 1669 (Rössler 1987: 24f.).

In the Moluccas (Maluku), the archipelago's most important centre of clove trade, the kingdoms of Ternate and Tidore rose to power in the fifteenth/sixteenth century (Cribb 2000: 103). The expansion of their sphere of influence was the result of an increase in the trade of cloves because of rising European demand. Another important factor was their role in the import and redistribution of Indian cloth and – above all – iron, most of which originated from southeast Sulawesi and 'became a crucial element in forging links between the centre and the periphery' (Andaya 1993: 33). Yet it has also been argued that the Moluccas remained a loosely structured alliance of communities (Andaya 1993: 40). In the middle of the seventeenth century, Ternate and Tidore lost their status as trade centres when the VOC by military means enforced their claim for a monopoly of the clove trade. The shift of the centre of clove trade to Ambon contributed not only to the decline of Ternate and Tidore, but also to the absolute dominance of the VOC as the major commercial power in Southeast Asia. On a more general level, the monopoly of the VOC at the same time weakened not only indigenous commerce but, with the exception of Makassar, also the political stability of many maritime states in the archipelago (Reid 1993a: 18, 1993b: 278, 319).

The formation of a single centre

It has been mentioned above that the Portuguese conquest of Melaka in 1511 was one of the most crucial incidents in Southeast Asian history. Another decisive event, 100 years later, was the foundation of Batavia in 1619. With the expansion of the spice trade all over the archipelago, the VOC decided to replace their base on Ambon with a headquarters in a more central location. In fact, this was the starting point of a far-reaching political and economic transformation process. It comprised increasing commercialisation, urbanisation and, above all, centralisation focusing on Java, which was going to be characteristic for Indonesia until the twenty-first century (cf. Reid 1993b: 327; Vickers 2005: 10).

Except for the political control which the Dutch effectively exercised on Java and some scattered spots in the archipelago by the late eighteenth century, most indigenous states (e.g. the powerful sultanates of Aceh, Banjarmasin and Gowa) at that time were still largely independent. It was beyond Dutch political concerns to conquer such polities in the Outer Islands. But after the VOC had been dissolved in 1799 and other nations exerted increasing imperialist pressure, the Dutch during the nineteenth and early twentieth centuries accelerated their conquests and strived harder to strengthen their hegemony and to establish an integrated empire (Locher-Scholten 1994; Cribb 2000: 114). Rising demand for colonial products in industrialising Europe required more effective control of both economic and political affairs. The most important strategy to achieve this aim was the creation of a rigid, hierarchical administrative structure the centre of which was located in Batavia. It was an arduous process, because for long periods in the late eighteenth and nineteenth centuries Dutch presence in places such as the Sumatran west coast, Borneo or South Sulawesi had basically been limited to some fortified trade offices situated on the coast, while they had almost no access to the interior of the islands (Rössler 1987: 26; Cribb 2000: 115). During this period resistance movements arose in the indigenous states on most of the Outer Islands, and it was only through military force that the Dutch were able to subdue them in the end. North Sumatra was conquered by the end of the nineteenth century, and Gowa as late as in 1906.

These military efforts came along with changes within the administrative system, which became increasingly centralised. In the Outer Islands, the prevailing governmental principle was often one of indirect rule, owing to the fact that the indigenous population would rather follow their traditional elites than colonial officials. But by and large, continuous modifications resulted in a very complicated and heterogeneous administrative structure, within which territorial boundaries (between *afdelingen* and *onderafdelingen* for example) were repeatedly redrawn, increasingly less corresponding to the boundaries of the former indigenous states and principalities (cf. Cribb 2000: 124ff.).

On a general level, it is obvious that Indonesian history consisted of an ever-changing pattern of emerging and declining centres, accompanied by continuous shifts in economic dominance and political power across the archipelago. Indigenous rulers as well as multiple external powers played important parts in the development of highly complex economic and political networks, which over the centuries always created disparities between different regions. These disparities appeared within a constantly changing seesaw of centres and peripheries, with one notable exception in colonial history. The emergence of Java as the archipelago's heartland, surrounded by islands of somewhat minor importance (as mirrored in the term *Buitengewesten*, i.e. Outer Areas) and reflected in the implementation of a centralised administrative structure focusing entirely on Batavia, was doubtless a product of colonial policy. With respect to the economic realm, the pivotal role of Batavia was further fostered when in the 1920s its harbour Tanjung Priok became the central nucleus of a network of ports set up by the royal shipping company Koninklijke Paketvaart Maatschappij (KPM). Through its focus on Batavia, the KPM, founded in 1888, contributed much to the integration of the Dutch colonial empire. After independence the status of a commercial network's core was passed over to Jakarta, as the capital was renamed in 1950 (Vickers 2005: 20). Nevertheless it must also be emphasised that, besides Batavia, various regions in the Outer Islands have repeatedly acquired the status of prosperous centres even in the late colonial era. Striking examples are provided by the plantation areas in eastern Sumatra or southeastern Borneo (Lindblad 1988) – regions which for centuries had been typical representatives of the 'periphery'.

Yet the focus on Java was going to shape the archipelago's political history well until the end of Dutch rule and the emergence of the Indonesian nation, which brought about a new dimension of centricity. Concerning the concept of the political centre as emphasised in the last paragraphs, it has to be underlined that the attributes of 'centres' may vary considerably. This holds in particular if we compare the early states (kingdoms, sultanates) in the archipelago with the features of a modern nation state such as Indonesia. Both agrarian and coastal port-states in the archipelago shared, to varying degrees, typical features of the early state (cf. Claessen and Skalník 1978), particularly in that they revealed a more or less centralised structure. In some instances, and most notably in Java, this implied a focus on sacred centres occupied by divine rulers, while in the case of coastal port-states, and particularly after the rise of Islam, kings and sultans tracing their descent back to the Prophet were considered the hub of the universe. Although few of these polities in the Outer Islands were as complex as the great Javanese empires, many of them exercised considerable power that rivalled European countries for economic and political control, and aimed at territorial expansion. Another important feature shared by all of these states was that they were to a great extent ethnically homogeneous, regardless of the Arab,

Indian or Chinese populations especially in the trade centres. Alongside the development of various economic and political centres in the region, the multiplicity of the archipelago's cultures in the course of time witnessed the emergence of two large and dominant ethnic groups: the Malays and the Javanese, whose cultures centuries ago accounted for the division of the archipelago into a 'Javanese world' (*bhumi Jawa*) and a 'Malay world' (*bhumi Melayu*), a division that was overtly connected to the dominance exerted by the empires of Majapahit and, respectively, Srivijaya (Andaya 2014: 270).

Structural features, the idea of power and, most notably, political ideologies underlying all of these empires (for the Javanese example, see Anderson 1972) differed considerably from those typical of the modern nation state. While a state is basically defined as a centralised structural order holding a monopoly of legitimate violence, a 'nation' additionally presupposes an envisioned order of belonging. It constitutes, in the words of Anderson (1983), an 'imagined community', which also conveys a sentiment, or an artefact of 'men's convictions and loyalties and solidarities' (Gellner 1983: 5). Such imaginations, centring on the idea of a new national community which up to that time had not existed, were an important part of the early Indonesian nationalist movement before independence. As with most former colonies, European models of the nation state, including political ideals and bureaucracy as heritages from colonialism and expanding capitalism, were adopted (Owen 2014: 55f.). But at the heart of the nationalist movement lay belief in the new nation, a belief which was ultimately based upon shared cultural features such as language, common descent, religion and an association with territory, features which Clifford Geertz (1963a) subsumed under the label of 'primordial sentiments'. It goes without saying that in Indonesia, under the conditions of pronounced ethnic heterogeneity the idea of a nation that was expected to unify approximately 250 different cultures faced enormous difficulties.

While ethnicity had not been a significant factor for the successful functioning of polities under pre-colonial conditions, the pooling of power in the centre of a newly created nation state often resulted in the consolidation of a single ethnic group's domination (Andaya 2014: 275). Accordingly, and paralleling other Southeast Asian nationalisms, in the Indonesian case early nationalism as put forward by Budi Utomo, the first national party founded in 1908, focused heavily on a dominant ethnic culture, which as expected was the Javanese. Yet to foster the idea of a national community not built around Javanese culture in the sense of a 'Javanese nation', which non-Javanese communities would have resisted, such an image of ethnic nationalism had to merge with state nationalism encompassing all indigenous communities (Owen 2014: 61). By utilising an educational system, media and a variety of symbolisms, Indonesian state nationalism was expected to integrate all regional identities into an encompassing national image – a vision that has been thwarted by many separatist movements from independence to this day, because some regions and/or societies (Aceh or Papua, for example) have continuously articulated their unwillingness to associate themselves with an 'Indonesian nation'. Such explicit expressions of 'ethnie nationalism' (Reid 2010), generally emphasising myths of common descent and other shared cultural features, have always been closely connected to centre–periphery relations. It is also evident that against this background, the relations between centre and periphery have different implications in the context of a modern nation state as compared to pre-colonial polities. Although the latter were often arranged in dense political and economic networks, there was never a common bond uniting them under a superordinate centre as required by a nation, and which after independence would radically redefine centre–periphery relations.

Separatist movements have not only marked Indonesia's recent history but also were a component of the young nation's birth. When the Dutch returned after the war, they counteracted nationalists' efforts to create an independent republic, by establishing the federal State of East Indonesia (Negara Indonesia Timur, NIT) in 1946, which comprised all islands east of Java and Borneo and was centred in Makassar (Vickers 2005: 99; Bräuchler and Erb 2011: 116). In 1949, NIT became part of the 'United States of Indonesia' (USI), which also constituted a federal state additionally comprising some territories in Sumatra and Java, before it was dissolved in 1950 by Sukarno, who rejected the idea of a small republican core linked to the federal states generated by the Dutch. Although the NIT was broadly considered an illegitimate neo-colonial construction, it was actively supported by many East Indonesian regions, which strictly opposed a unitary and Java-centred republic. Religion, notably Christianity, which dominated many parts of Eastern Indonesia, also played an important role. A case in point was the proclamation of the Republic of the South Moluccas, which led into a short-term rebellion after the USI was dissolved in favour of a unitary nation.

It is evident that throughout colonial history, the rise of the nationalist movement in the early twentieth century, the struggle for independence and through various governmental scenarios after 1945, Javanese hegemony has in the end survived into the twenty-first century. Beyond the political and the economic dimension it was further boosted in the late colonial period by many young people from all over Indonesia who migrated to Java for the purpose of higher education (Vickers 2005: 59), and was later perfected under Sukarno. Indonesia's first president contributed particularly to the planning and design of Jakarta, which under his guidance aimed to develop a capital that was 'more than just one of the regions' (Vickers 2005: 147). Under Sukarno, Jakarta's position as the national centre par excellence was enhanced by a variety of symbolic means, such as monumental architecture and memorials reflecting the pride of a young nation. Symbolism as a means of representing the core values of political principles was later also utilised by Suharto, who explicitly referred to Javanese culture and mysticism in order to emphasise the contrast between the outstanding status of the centre and the inferiority of the periphery. Under the New Order regime, the obvious focus was not only on Java, but on Jakarta in particular, while the periphery became even more peripheral (Vickers 2005: 183, 187).

Constructing marginality during the *Orde Baru*

The dominance of Jakarta, which reached its peak during the New Order period, was characterised through 'the imposition of a unique administrative model by centre-based administrators, a top-down development approach and a policy of economic extraction to benefit the development of the central region, that is Java' (Charras 2005: 88).

The New Order government successively issued several sectoral laws[3] on forestry, mining, oil and natural gas, irrigation and fisheries, which all increased state control over natural resources and facilitated their exploitation by private interests (Lucas and Warren 2000: 222; Thorburn 2004: 37). Customary *adat* rights to land and forests were increasingly limited, and millions of hectares of communal forests, fallow land and forest gardens were given to logging companies or converted for commercial agriculture, as demonstrated by Grumblies (this volume). While industrialisation and development progressed in Java (and some specific locations like Batam), hardly any incentives existed to set up industries in the Outer Islands (Charras 2005: 90) and to develop infrastructure and services beyond their urban areas. Sakai *et al.* (2009: 1) use the impressive view of Indonesia from space at night to illustrate the resulting disparities:

> Java positively glows with an incandescent light, southern and central Sumatra is a radiant oasis, and Bali is an intense spot of heat. The rest of the archipelago is marked by an inky darkness splattered occasionally by the lights of provincial capitals and other isolated points of illumination.

Within the highly centralised administrative structure of the *Orde Baru*, the regions became financially dependent on the centre. Important governmental positions were often held by Javanese, and officials were drawn into a huge network of patronage dominated by Jakarta (Booth 2001 cited in Charras 2005: 91). The process of territorialisation, initiated during colonial times and extended during the *Orde Baru* (Peluso and Vandergeest 2001), did not only increase state control over land, natural resources and labour in the Outer Islands (Li 1999: 13). It further facilitated the centrality of Jakarta through spatial partition:

> Provinces have been created to divide the national territory without any effort to develop linkages between them. Instead, each province was connected individually and exclusively to Jakarta. [...] This led to fragmented space, easier to dominate but preventing any larger regional dynamics.
>
> (Charras 2005: 92)

The authoritarian and often destructive top-down development approach of the *Orde Baru* period was based on the image of Java as Indonesia's 'showcase of development' (Tsing 1993: 23), opposed by a distant and disorderly periphery. The term 'Outer Islands' embodies this dichotomous image and is closely related to the common dichotomy of the lowlands and uplands in Southeast Asia (Li

1999; Scott 2009). The expression 'Outer Islands' can be traced back to the Dutch term *Buitengewesten*, which means 'Outer Areas' (see above) and was further popularised in the 1960s among a wider audience by Clifford Geertz (1963b). He provided the distinction between Indonesia's Outer and Inner Islands with an agro-ecological background by equating the Outer Islands with swidden agriculture and low population densities, as contrasted by labour-intensive wet-rice agriculture and high population densities in the Inner Islands. Under Suharto's reign, this dichotomous image became representative for a political agenda that depicted Java as the political, economic and cultural centre of Indonesia while the surrounding islands were seen as a vast uncivilised periphery. As a consequence, state interventions and development policies in the regions beyond Java, and especially in the Indonesian uplands, have been framed through a discourse of marginality, backwardness and the need for 'development' (Li 1999: 14). This image denied the cultural diversity of the Outer Islands and greatly contributed to the installation of the Javanese culture of the centre as the dominant national culture (Charras 2005: 88).

The promulgation of Law No. 5/1979 on village administration[4] signifies a major step in this process. By standardising village structures according to the Javanese model throughout Indonesia, it destroyed local political institutions and traditional forms of leadership, and integrated villages into the national bureaucratic structure. The transmigration programme, though essentially aimed at relieving the population pressure on Java, Bali, Madura and Lombok and incorporating the regions of the Outer Islands into the Indonesian nation, constituted an additional powerful tool to expand central control and a nationalist vision of development (Hoey 2003: 110). Introduced under Dutch rule, continued under Sukarno and accelerated under Suharto, transmigration programmes have moved millions of people to the Outer Islands in order to spread 'loyal citizens', Javanese culture and wet-rice cultivation to the supposedly uncivilised margins of Indonesia. Ethnic minorities have suffered most from transmigration policies and related processes of 'Indonesianization' (Gietzelt 1989), which in many cases created tensions between migrants and indigenous groups and often fuelled outbreaks of violence (Duncan 2004: 105). The transmigration of active and retired military personnel, allegedly for security reasons, played an important role in frontier regions of Kalimantan, West Papua and East Timor (Fearnside 1997: 556). Recent protests against plans to settle thousands of military members along the Indonesian-Malaysian border in Kalimantan show that transmigration continues to be an important issue for exercising and resisting central control over the Indonesian periphery (Kompas 2014 and Tribun Pontianak 2015).

Religion served as another important means in the construction of marginality on the Outer Islands. After independence the state followed the guiding principle of *Bhinneka Tunggal Ika*, 'Unity in Diversity' – a guideline that also covered the sphere of religion. While belief in One God (*Ketuhanan Yang Maha Esa*) is the first principle of the national philosophy *Pancasila*, neither the latter nor the constitution specify what precisely should be understood as religion (*agama*). By acknowledging only Islam, Protestantism, Catholicism, Hinduism, Buddhism and Confucianism as official religions, presidential decree No. 1/PNPS/1965 on the Prevention of the Misuse/Insulating of a Religion – the so-called Blasphemy Act – was a decisive step toward the curtailing of religious freedom. But it was only after Suharto had come to power that religious affiliation acquired crucial significance. Not adhering to one of the officially recognised religions was now equated with communist affiliation and therefore potentially dangerous. As a consequence, atheism became illegal. The fact that all citizens were obliged to announce their confession via their identity cards resulted in the conversion of millions of Indonesians whose belief was not included in the national understanding of religion (Sidel 2006: 189). In 1969, Suharto converted the Decree on Blasphemy into law, thus 'turning state-sanctioned religions into mutually exclusive categories, putting increasing pressure on heterodox views to conform' (Picard 2011: 14). This also included indigenous groups whose beliefs were excluded from the official definition of *agama* and thus received heavy pressure to convert either to Islam or to Christianity (Henley and Davidson 2007: 10). Indigenous religions were considered mystical beliefs (*aliran kepercayaan*), which in 1978 fell under the authority of the Ministry of Education and Culture, whereas matters of official religions were governed by the Ministry of Religion. In the wake of Suharto's pursuit for development, religion was also associated with the new drive for modernity and development, whereas expressions of indigenous belief systems were reduced to folklore. In traditional rituals focusing on political aspects of *adat*, for example, all elements of *kepercayaan* were profoundly 'aestheticized' as a traditional art form because of their supposed incongruity with religion and modernity (Acciaioli 1985; Rössler 2000). Religion, therefore, had become a strong marker of a new national identity and portrayed 'a dividing line that sets off the mass of peasants and urban dwellers, on the one side, from small traditional communities (weakly integrated into the national economic and political system), on the other' (Atkinson 1983: 688). Thereby indigenous groups were generally described as *orang yang belum beragama*, people who do not yet have a religion – a term that subsumes a general moral imperative for conversion (Rössler 1987: 110f.; Aragon 2003: 33). Religious dynamics have thus been closely intertwined with processes of political and economic change that followed the fall of Suharto's New Order regime.

Decentralisation, democratisation and changing centre–periphery relations

Democratisation and decentralisation have significantly altered the political landscape of Indonesia (Aspinall and Mietzner 2010). Although scholarly opinions concerning the quality of the democratisation process differ considerably, ranging from rather pessimistic (Robison and Hadiz 2004), over moderate (Davidson 2009; Aspinall 2010) to more optimistic perspectives (MacIntyre and Ramage 2008), they all agree that the new system offers more freedom than previous ones did (Aspinall and Mietzner 2010). The recent election of Joko Widodo as Indonesia's seventh president is considered to further promote the development of democracy in Indonesia and has been praised as a 'significant milestone' for the nation (The Australian 2014).

Indonesia's far-reaching decentralisation reforms were carried out rashly in the face of economic and political crisis, when particularly resource-rich regions in the Outer Islands threatened to break away. A central aim of introducing regional autonomy was to provide the regions with more power and a larger economic share. Law 25 of 1999 on fiscal balance set out a new system of fiscal arrangements between the centre and the regions, under which regencies (*kabupaten*) receive a much larger share of the revenues generated within their borders and additionally are allowed to generate their own revenues. Law 22 of 1999 regulated the devolution of political authority. While foreign policy, defence and security, monetary policy, the legal system and religious matters remained in the hands of the central government, authority over all other fields, including such important areas as education, health, labour, public works and environmental and natural resource management was ceded to regional governments. Law 22 of 1999, which replaced Law 5 of 1979 on village administration, granted larger autonomy to village communities (*desa*), a fact which in several cases encouraged the revival of customary forms of *desa* government (see von Benda-Beckmann 2001). In addition, decentralisation successfully calmed down separation tendencies. Yet the sudden and disorderly nature and often weak implementation of the decentralisation process also resulted in obscure task sharing and in the overlapping of authorities between central and regional governments. As a result, the first set of decentralisation laws was replaced in 2004 by Laws 32 and 33, which provide clearer guidelines concerning the roles and responsibilities of the different government levels, and strengthen the position of the provinces while retaining regional autonomy. The implementation of Law 23 of 2014 on local government further empowered provincial governors. But despite these tendencies to strengthen the provincial level, Indonesia continues to be one of the most decentralised states in the world (cf. Ziegenhain, this volume).

An important consequence of decentralisation has been the 'blossoming' of new administrative and budgetary units (McWilliam 2011). While the principal idea had been to create new levels of regency governments (*kabupaten*), large numbers of new districts (*kecamatan*) and villages (*desa*) emerged as well. Although this phenomenon is found all over Indonesia, it is most striking in the Outer Islands. While between 1996 and 2007 the number of regencies increased by 7.8 per cent in Java and Bali, it rose by 72.4 per cent in Sulawesi, by 82 per cent in Kalimantan, and even by 150 per cent in Papua and Maluku (Brata 2008; cf. Jäger and Eilenberg, this volume).

While the far-reaching political transformations created tremendous new opportunities in the periphery, they also resulted in severe conflicts over authority, participation and representation between elites and disadvantaged groups, between the regions and the central government, as well as between local elites. Shortly before the downfall of Suharto and during the first years of decentralisation, communal violence shook West and Central Kalimantan, Poso, Ambon and North Maluku. Although each of these conflicts has its specific history, fierce competition over local leadership and access to new economic opportunities have been crucial drivers behind these outbreaks of violence, as local elites mobilised their supporters along ethnic and religious lines (van Klinken 2007b).

So far the impacts of decentralisation have varied enormously between different regions (Aspinall and Fealy 2003). While some provinces and regencies have remained in the grip of oligarchic cliques, others are run by reformist leaders in relatively transparent and accountable ways (von Luebke 2009). Whereas some regions have been devastated by local power struggles, others are characterised by successful developments and great enthusiasm on the part of the population (van Klinken 2002). Although Indonesia has in general recovered well from the economic crisis that hit the country in 1997 and reached its peak in autumn 1998, large discrepancies remain and further increased between its regions. Besides Jakarta, the centre of both power and money, there are a number of resource-rich regencies that eagerly exploited new economic opportunities. Other regions, notably Bali, profited from the rise in tourism, whereas in other areas marginalisation and poverty continued to increase (Vickers 2005: 190). An example is provided by eastern Indonesia, which has experienced a shift from constituting a major centre in regional and even international trade over several centuries, to a marginalised region within the Indonesian nation (Bräuchler and Erb 2011: 121). In 2010, the poverty rate as measured by the Indonesian Central Statistics Agency (*Badan Pusat Statistik*, BPS) ranged from 4 per cent in Jakarta and 8 per cent in East Kalimantan to 25.3 per cent in Maluku and up to 34.1 per cent in Papua (BPS 2010).

A major effect of decentralisation was that mid-size towns and even small rural communities have increasingly been directly integrated into the global economy. National companies, as well as transnational corporations, increasingly prefer to deal directly with local governments, thereby often bypassing the central government and undesirable tax payments. Increasing budgets of local governments in resource-rich regions, however, do not automatically improve the well-being of the local population (cf. Haug, this volume). Economic development, which presses ahead in the shape of persistent (illegal) logging, mining and large-scale plantation schemes, is meanwhile not only leading to far-reaching transformations of local livelihoods and environmental damage but is also further aggravating conflicts over land and natural resources.

The lack of detailed regulations that characterised the implementation of the first two decentralisation laws created a situation of considerable legal uncertainty. As a consequence, many local actors 'took matters into their own hands' (Warren and McCarthy 2009: 6) and seized the chance to (re)formulate claims on land, forests and other natural resources (Bakker 2009; Bakker and Moniaga 2010). Negotiations between local stakeholders were thereby often solely based on their personal perceptions and interpretations of regional autonomy (Rhee 2000; Sakai 2002b; Boulan-Smith 2002). In this context, power struggles over natural resources and related benefits erupted not only among various local actors but also between the central government and newly empowered regions. Typical examples were the struggle between forest-rich regions and the Ministry of Forestry over rights to issue small-scale logging licences (Resosudarmo 2004), and the discrepancies over control of business interests in the mining sector (Sakai 2003; Prasetyawan 2005, 2006). Furthermore, new alliances have been formed by ambitious leaders on the regional and provincial level to strengthen economic development in their regions (Sakai and Morrell 2006) and to defeat economic domination from Java. An example is provided by the successful collaboration of all six Sulawesi province governors against the export ban of unprocessed or semi-processed rattan (Morrell 2010).

Democratisation further prepared the ground for an increasing Islamisation, but also for the revival of *adat* institutions throughout the archipelago. Beginning with the era of decentralisation, religious affairs became subject to regency control, which led to an increase of religious policies that favour the Muslim majority while discriminating against religious minorities – groups that are mainly found in the Outer Islands (Crouch 2009: 53). Political decisions are thus frequently connected to religious relations that differ from those prevailing in the centre. It is not in Java or Bali, but rather in the Outer Islands 'where many comparable battles between Indonesia's "indigenous" or homeland communities and the migrant or diaspora communities are being fought' and framed as religious conflicts (Aragon 2000: 47f.). Ethnoreligious tensions often display essential core–periphery relations on a micro scale. In addition, the *masyarakat adat* movement in Indonesia, which is commonly labelled a revival of tradition (Davidson and Henley 2007) is, more generally, one of the most surprising developments of the post-1998 period. While affairs of *adat* revival are often closely intertwined with ethnic rivalries, economic competition and political power struggles, they are commonly interpreted, and portrayed by the media, as being religious in character. In addition, it is on the Outer Islands where upland groups, who do not conform to the Indonesian state's ideal of development, are still subject to resettlement programmes and missionary endeavours, in the main because they are not affiliated with one of the six officially recognised religions (Duncan 2007).

Recent research results (Sakai and Morrell 2006; Kimura 2007; Morrell 2010; McWilliam 2011) suggest that new multidirectional ties are emerging between the regions and the centre at all levels of government as well as in commerce, non-governmental organisations, social and religious groups. New networks provide creative local elites with new opportunities to advocate regional interests. Yet it is also argued that relations with Jakarta, although in a more complex way than previously, continue to be of great importance. This particularly concerns the formation of new provinces, as well as disputes between the central government and regional governments over control of natural resources (Morishita 2008: 85). The contributions to this book show how local actors engage in these new and increasingly complex links between regions and centre as well as among the regions themselves. They further shed light on how political, economic and religious rearrangements result in shifting relations among marginal groups and elites within peripheral regions.

The rise of the margins: an analytical perspective

Marginality is a relational concept which captures the asymmetric relationship between a centre and its periphery (Li 1999: 2). However, the position of the two is neither naturally given nor fixed but constantly shaped by 'an ongoing relationship with power' (Tsing 1993: 90). Taking a historical perspective provides a good illustration of the fact that people's current economic, political and cultural environments on Indonesia's Outer Islands need to be understood as resulting from hegemonic schemes that define them as peripheral. Therefore, they are, as is typical for all relationships between margins and centres, 'subject to contestation and reformulation' (Li 1999: 2).

Marginality implies social as well as spatial aspects. Research focusing on the latter has emphasised the territorial characteristics of a location. Marginal regions tend to be characterised by a great distance from the centre, are difficult to reach and lack appropriate infrastructure (Leimgruber 2004; Gurung and Kollmair 2005). Societal approaches, on the other hand, highlight marginality as constructed and focus on the social, political and economic processes by which the peripheral positions of individuals or groups are (re-)produced (cf. Grumblies, this volume). Additionally, the concept of 'remote areas' has recently (re-)gained attention, and it has been argued that 'the idea of the remote can be detached from its geographical moorings and understood not simply as a spatial concept but as a sociological concept of relative association or familiarity' (Harms *et al.* 2014: 362). If remoteness, just as marginality, is increasingly seen as a product of social constructions, the differentiation between 'marginality' and 'remoteness' and the related concept of 'periphery' becomes increasingly blurred. However, the case studies presented in this book encourage us to apply these concepts in a differentiated way in order to comprehend the diverse conditions and experiences experienced by people living in the Outer Islands, while embracing both the societal and the spatial aspects of marginality.

While 'periphery' and 'marginality' sometimes do intersect, this may not necessarily be the case. 'Periphery' implies some kind of spatial distance, such as finds expression in the terms 'Outer Islands' or 'Uplands'. By way of contrast, 'marginality' stands for a context of political-economic and social disenfranchisement. Borders may exemplify these two different aspects well: while on the one hand they are territorially 'peripheral' and located far from the centre, they might, on the other hand, be of great significance and gain much attention (cf. Eilenberg, this volume). Remote 'out-of-the-way places' (Tsing 1993) e.g. dense forests or rugged mountains, which are often characterised by a poor infrastructure, constitute the third category. While they are often, but not necessarily, located at great distances from a centre, people living in such places express feelings of isolation and can be subject to distressing situations that are strongly linked to the physical characteristics of these locations (cf. Haug, this volume).

Although the empirical case studies deal with different regions and focus on different kinds of transformation processes, four major common themes run through this book: (1) the territorial dimension of marginality, (2) institutions and their role in shaping and (re-)creating centres and peripheries, (3) local actors and their agency as well as relationships between actors and (4) the temporal dimension of marginality.

Recent political changes have brought about manifold changes concerning 'marginality' in the Outer Islands. In this respect, the empowerment of many groups that had previously been marginalised by the central government is of utmost significance. However, these processes of 'de-marginalisation' are diversely articulated by different groups, and at the same time, new processes of marginalisation can be observed on a local level (Haug 2014). On the other hand, inhabitants of geographically remote places continue to experience severe drawbacks caused by their physical isolation, as local governments face great difficulties in providing transportation facilities as well as health care and educational infrastructure in such regions.

Institutions play a crucial role in shaping and (re)creating centres and peripheries in post-Suharto Indonesia. Among them, political and administrative institutions occupy a most prominent position in that their modification throughout the process of decentralisation was basically responsible for the broad spectrum of changes discussed in this volume. Economic institutions comprise those which are governing subsistence economies, market arrangements and patterns of trade as well as those that are regulating environmental issues. Importantly, all kinds of institutions must be regarded as being heavily coined by the dynamics of change within the wider centre–periphery context.

Nearly all contributions pay attention to local actors on the Outer Islands and how they – through their perceptions, actions and relationships with other local as well as (inter)national actors – (re)shape the power relations that once constituted their region as marginal. Decentralisation, democratisation and the spirit of *reformasi* have enormously increased the agency of local actors. They increasingly link up with powerful political and economic 'centres' beyond Java and are frequently positioned within networks of multiple centres, where they are much more actively engaged in a broad spectrum of relationships. Therefore, it is significant to emphasise a focus on the motivations and perceptions of these local actors.

Some of the chapters show that centres and peripheries are continuously changing over the course of time. Areas that once constituted political and economic centres have become peripheral in relation to a new centre, while previously peripheral areas may emerge as new centres. Regional autonomy, and especially the blossoming of new regencies and districts, provided many old centres with the chance to regain authority and control. In many places 'old' elites saw regional autonomy as a chance to capture formal power positions and emerge as 'new local elites'. Despite many transformation processes – which always imply change – it is thus necessary to be aware of continuities and to generate a balanced picture of continuity and change. In the realm of politics, for instance, many things seem to have changed – the most obvious example being the creation of new regencies in the Outer Islands. But at the same time, taking a closer look also reveals considerable continuities. Old structures remain, they just become more visible: former power holders are still powerful, though in the framework of new formal positions, and old territorial and social entities continue to exist, though now embedded in new formal structures. With regard to the economic sphere, it is from a macro perspective dominated by continuous growth. Taking a closer look, however, reveals many changes at the local level, such as modified patterns of distribution of wealth between the regions and between different local groups, as well as new and increasing inequalities in different local settings.

This book is structured in three parts. The first part, which provides a thematic and theoretical framework for the case studies presented in the following parts, starts with an overview of the decentralisation process in Indonesia. Patrick Ziegenhain (Chapter 2) draws on the academic debate on the interrelation of decentralisation and democratisation to demonstrate how the political landscape of Indonesia has been altered since 1998. His analysis shows how on the one hand regional autonomy has strengthened the democratisation process through the successful reduction of separatist tendencies, the election of local leaders (*pilkada*) and increased political activism on a grassroots level. On the other hand, projected pro-democratic needs have not been achieved in the way that was anticipated, and outbreaks of violence, elite capture and corruption have negatively affected the overall quality of democracy. Ziegenhain's chapter reveals how difficult it is to generalise the influence of the decentralisation process in Indonesia due to the great heterogeneity of its political outcomes. The author, tending toward a slightly optimistic view, concludes that the impact of decentralisation on the democratisation process must be assessed ambiguously.

Anna-Teresa Grumblies (Chapter 3) creates a theoretical framework of marginality for the subsequent empirical case studies. She traces how the concept of marginality has been developed within social and cultural anthropology and how it has been applied within the Indonesian context. While the margins have been a key focus in anthropological discourse right from its beginning, marginality today is generally perceived of as a social construction that traces unequal power relations between centres and peripheries. Relating marginality theory to the Indonesian context, Grumblies focuses on the role of upland groups in the Outer Islands that are often constituted as marginal per se. She reveals how upland groups have been subjected to marginalisation processes by the state since colonial times, for example through land right regulations that have continuously ignored indigenous claims. Since upland communities under Suharto were portrayed as backward isolated tribes, they functioned as the opposite of the overall goals the centre strived for: development and modernity. Grumblies further shows how indigenous people after the fall of Suharto have engaged in the *masyarakat adat* movement and thereby have developed a powerful tool to oppose hegemonic structures.

The second part of the book explores dynamics in Indonesian border zones and processes of (re-)drawing boundaries. Taking the recently created Riau Islands Province as an example, Nicolas J. Long (Chapter 4) develops a new perspective on centre–periphery relations by considering how these are perceived by the people living in the Outer Islands. Instead of discussing simple 'effects' of administrative reforms on the creation of new centre–periphery relations, he focuses on how Indonesians discern properties of these relations, which they identify as meaningful and desirable for their daily lives. Accordingly, he argues that analyses of decentralisation should not only consider actions and motivations of the elites, but rather reflect on how ordinary citizens respond emotionally to the new reality of reshaped centre–periphery relations. He pays attention to the political imaginations of people who are not necessarily familiar with common, state-driven centre–periphery discourses, but who nevertheless are profoundly invested in them. Listening to their voices, Long demonstrates that ordinary citizens in the Riau Islands have a great desire to relate to the centre in new ways, and are in favour of an inclusion within the nation, rather than aspiring to a condition of autonomy.

Michael Eilenberg (Chapter 5) investigates changing state–periphery relations from the perspective of the highly contested Indonesian–Malaysian borderlands. He examines how ethnic elites have carved out small zones of semi-autonomy along the border in West Kalimantan. Analysing an ongoing claim for border autonomy, Eilenberg illustrates how local elites attempt to create their own regency within the legal but partly vague framework of recent decentralisation reforms, and how they appropriate state rhetoric of development for local purposes as well as for their personal interests. Eilenberg demonstrates how negotiations over the new regency are deeply interwoven with struggles over the control of natural resources, the distribution of economic gains from anticipated investments, and with competing ethnic, national and regional loyalties. The case also shows how new centres at the Indonesian periphery are constituted, in relation not only to Jakarta but also to other regional centres, as the proponents of the new border regency do not only lobby for their plans in Jakarta but also struggle with the mother regency, which is anxious about losing important resources and future prospects through the *pemekaran* process.

Kirsten Jäger (Chapter 6) explores a complex *pemekaran* process in North Maluku. She argues that the redrawing of borders cannot be solely understood and analysed in economic or political terms, as they also provide people with a strong sense of identity and belonging. The newly created administrative units often represent long existing socio-territorial organisations, resembling the pre-colonial Sultanates of Ternate, Tidore, Bacan and Jailolo, which become visible during the (re-)shaping of local centres and peripheries. This process is exemplified by six villages which came to belong to two regencies – Halmahera Barat and Halmahera Utara – at the same time. After having officially become part of Halmahera Utara, the villagers rejected this status and established a separate district belonging to Halmahera Barat. Although this district has not been officially recognised and therefore remains of unclear status, it allows the villagers to belong to the centre with which they identify. Jäger thereby shows not only how old centres re-emerge in the form of new administrative entities, but also the creativity and persistence with which local actors try to establish their own position – by moving away from unwanted peripheries and attempts to create their own centres.

Finally, the third part, investigates the dynamics caused by economic changes on Indonesia's periphery. Laurens Bakker (Chapter 7) takes perceptions and a critique of neoliberalism among 'ordinary citizens' as an analytical angle to explore how changing centre–periphery relations are perceived in the Outer Islands. His encounters with restaurant entrepreneurs in East Kalimantan and West Sumatra, the struggle for special autonomy in East Kalimantan and the practices of a local ethnic militia in the Minahasa (North Sulawesi) reveal that people share a common conceptualisation of what neoliberalism entails, but express differing notions as to where it is to be found. While in the national debate neoliberalism is depicted as a global threat to Indonesian society and Indonesian values, regional respondents see neoliberal threats originating from 'Jakarta'. Bakker argues that this illustrates an increasingly critical attitude with which the regions behold the centre.

Michaela Haug (Chapter 8) analyses recent processes of 'de-marginalisation' in East Kalimantan, where several new political and administrative centres have been created, previously marginalised Dayak groups have been empowered, and large investments have been made in local infrastructure. Taking the regency of Kutai Barat as an example, the chapter investigates to what extent these changes, and above all newly gained wealth, have brought prosperity to the local population. The findings reveal an invigorated regional centre with an ambitious local elite. However, spatial distance and geographical remoteness continue to be major reasons why people feel poor in Kutai Barat. Haug further demonstrates that new processes of marginalisation are taking place within the regency as the creation of a new administrative and economic centre on the Tunjung Plateau has inevitably created new margins. Inequalities between villages and individuals are sharply increasing as financial benefits are not distributed equally, while environmental degradation has been accelerated by the increasing exploitation of natural resources. The new economic wealth of Kutai Barat has brought prosperity to the region, but while some people profit, far too many continue to live in poverty.

The concluding remarks (Chapter 9) summarise the major findings of the empirical case studies and relate them to the analytical key issues as outlined above. Finally, we identify some important questions which may serve as guidelines for future research on Indonesia's margins.

Notes

1 Meanwhile the government complex consists of more than 20 buildings, and more are under construction.
2 Our focus here is the 'big picture' of increasing centralisation in Indonesia. We do not explore early experiments with administrative decentralisation under Dutch colonial rule. Neither do we consider discussions about federalism, which arose in the 1950s (cf. Legge 1961; Booth 2014), or the cautious attempts of decentralisation initiated under President Suharto in the early 1990s. The latter remained confined to administrative reforms and did not include the assignment of tangible political power to lower levels of government (Beier 1995).

3 Basic Forestry Law No. 5/1967 (Undang Undang No. 5/1967 tentang Ketentuan-Ketentuan Pokok Kehutanan); Basic Mining Law No. 11/1967 (Undang Undang No. 11/1967 tentang Ketentuan-Ketentuan Pokok Pertambangan; BI); Law on Oil and Gas No. 8/1971 (Undang Undang No. 8/1971 tentang Perusahaan Pertambangan Minyak dan Gas Bumi Negara); Law on Irrigation No. 11/1974 (Undang Undang No. 11/1974 tentang Pengairan); Law on Fisheries No. 9/1985 (Undang Undang No. 9/1985 tentang Perikanan).
4 Undang Undang tentang pemerintahan desa UU No. 5/1979.

References

Acciaioli, G. (1985) Culture as Art: From Practice to Spectacle in Indonesia, *Canberra Anthropology* 8: 148–172.

Andaya, L.Y. (1993) Cultural State Formation in Eastern Indonesia, in A. Reid (ed.), *Southeast Asia in the Early Modern Era: Trade, Power, and Belief*, Ithaca, NY: Cornell University Press, pp. 23–41.

Andaya, L.Y. (2014) Ethnicity in Pre-colonial and Colonial Southeast Asia, in N.G. Owen (ed.), *Routledge Handbook of Southeast Asian History*, London: Routledge, pp. 267–277.

Anderson, B. (1972) The Idea of Power in Javanese Culture, in C. Holt, B. Anderson and J. Siegel (eds), *Culture and Politics in Indonesia*, Ithaca, NY: Cornell University Press, pp. 1–69.

Anderson, B. (1983) *Imagined Communities: Reflections on the Origin and Spread of Nationalism*. London: Verso.

Aragon, L. (2000) *Fields of the Lord: Animism, Christian Minorities, and State Development in Indonesia*. Hawaii: University of Hawaii Press.

Aragon, L. (2003) Missions and Omissions of the Supernatural: Indigenous Cosmologies and the Legitimisation of 'Religion' in Indonesia, *Anthropological Forum* 13(2): 131–140.

Aspinall, E. (2010) Indonesia: The Irony of Success, *Journal of Democracy* 21(2): 20–34.

Aspinall, E. and Fealy, G. (eds) (2003) *Local Power and Politics in Indonesia: Decentralisation and Democratisation*. Singapore: Institute for Southeast Asian Studies.

Aspinall, E. and Mietzner, M. (eds) (2010) *Problems of Democratisation in Indonesia: Elections, Institutions and Society*. Singapore: Institute of Southeast Asian Studies.

Atkinson, J.M. (1983) Religions in Dialogue: The Construction of an Indonesian Minority Religion, *American Ethnologist* 10(4): 684–696.

Bakker, L. (2009) The Sultan's Map: Arguing One's Land in Pasir, in F. von Benda-Beckmann (ed.), *Spatializing Law: An Anthropological Geography of Law in Society*, Aldershot: Ashgate, pp. 95–114.

Bakker, L. and Moniaga, S. (2010) The Space Between: Land Claims and the Law in Indonesia, *Asian Journal of Social Science* 38: 187–203.

Beier, C. (1995) *Dezentralisierung und Entwicklungsmanagement in Indonesien. Beobachtungen zur politisch-administrativen und zur wissenschaftlichen Kommunikation: Ein systemtheoretischer Versuch*. Saarbrücken: Verlag für Entwicklungspolitik.

Benda-Beckmann, F. von (2001) Legal Pluralism and Social Justice in Economic and Political Development, *IDS Bulletin* 32: 46–56.

Booth, A. (2001) Indonesia: Will Decentralization Lead to Disintegration? Paper presented at the EUROSEAS meeting, London, September 2001.

Booth, A. (2014) Before the 'Big Bang': Decentralization Debates and Practice in Indonesia,

1949–99, in H. Hill (ed.), *Regional Dynamics in a Decentralized Indonesia*, Singapore: Institute of Southeast Asian Studies, pp. 25–44.

Boulan-Smith, C. (2002) When the Elephants Fight the Grass Suffers: Decentralisation and the Mining Industry in Indonesia, *Antropologi Indonesia* 26: 57–64.

BPS (Badan Pusat Statistik) (2010) *Data dan Informasi Kemiskinan Kabupaten/Kota Tahun 2010*. Available online: www.bps.go.id/hasil_publikasi/flip_2011/3205014/index11.php?pub=Data%20dan%20Informasi%20Kemiskinan%20Kabupaten/Kota%20Tahun%202010 (accessed 19 November 2014).

Brata, A.G. (2008) Creating New Regions, Improving Regional Welfare Equality? Paper presented at the Indonesian Regional Science Association Ninth International Conference: 'The Current and Future Issues of Regional Development, Energy and Climate Change', Palembang, 31 July–1 August 2008. Available as MPRA Paper No. 12540, http://mpra.ub.uni-muenchen.de/12540/ (accessed 19 November 2014).

Bräuchler, B. and Erb, M. (2011) Introduction – Eastern Indonesia under Reform: The Global, the National and the Local, *Asian Journal of Social Science* 39: 113–130.

Charras, M. (2005) The Reshaping of the Indonesian Archipelago after 50 Years of Regional Imbalance, in M. Erb, P. Sulistiyanto and C. Faucher (eds), *Regionalism in Post-Suharto Indonesia*, London: RoutledgeCurzon, pp. 87–108.

Claessen, H.J.M. and Skalník, P. (eds) (1978) *The Early State*. The Hague: Mouton.

Cribb, R. (2000) *Historical Atlas of Indonesia*. Richmond, UK: Curzon Press.

Crouch, M. (2009) Religious Regulations in Indonesia: Failing Vulnerable Groups?, *Review of Indonesian and Malaysian Affairs* 43(2): 53–103.

Davidson, J. (2009) Dilemmas of Democratic Consolidation in Indonesia, *The Pacific Review* 22: 293–310.

Davidson, J. and Henley, D. (eds) (2007) *The Revival of Tradition in Indonesian Politics: The Deployment of Adat from Colonialism to Indigenism*. London: Routledge.

Duncan, C. (2004) From Development to Empowerment: Changing Indonesian Government Policies toward Indigenous Minorities, in C. Duncan (ed.), *Civilizing the Margins: Southeast Asian Government Policies for the Development of Minorities*, Ithaca, NY: Cornell University Press, pp. 86–115.

Duncan, C. (2007) Mixed Outcomes: The Impact of Regional Autonomy and Decentralization on Indigenous Ethnic Minorities in Indonesia, *Development and Change* 38(4): 711–733.

Eilenberg, M. (2009) Negotiating Autonomy at the Margins of the State: The Dynamics of Elite Politics in the Borderland of West Kalimantan, Indonesia, *South East Asia Research* 17(2): 201–227.

Erb, M. and Sulistiyanto, P. (eds) (2009) *Deepening Democracy in Indonesia? Direct Elections for Local Leaders (Pilkada)*. Singapore: Institute of Southeast Asian Studies.

Erb, M., Sulistiyanto, P. and Faucher, C. (eds) (2005) *Regionalism in Post-Suharto Indonesia*. London: RoutledgeCurzon.

Fearnside, P.M. (1997) Transmigration in Indonesia: Lessons from Its Environmental and Social Impacts, *Environmental Management* 21(4): 553–570.

Geertz, C. (1963a) The Integrative Revolution: Primordial Sentiments and Civil Politics, in C. Geertz (ed.), *Old Societies and New States: The Quest for Modernity in Asia and Africa*, New York: Free Press of Glencoe, pp. 105–157.

Geertz, C. (1963b) *Agricultural Involution: The Processes of Ecological Change in Indonesia*. Berkeley, CA: University of California Press.

Gellner, E. (1983) *Nations and Nationalism*. Ithaca, NY: Cornell University Press.

Gietzelt, D. (1989) The Indonesianization of West Papua, *Oceania* 59(3): 201–221.

Gurung, G. and Kollmair, M. (2005) *Marginality: Concepts and Their Limitations*. IP6 Working Paper 4, Zürich: Swiss National Centre of Competence in Research (NCCR) North–South.

Harms, E., Hussain, S. and Schneiderman, S. (2014) Remote and Edgy: New Takes on Old Anthropological Themes, *HAU: Journal of Ethnographic Theory* 4(1): 361–381.

Haug, M. (2010) *Poverty and Decentralisation in East Kalimantan: The Impact of Regional Autonomy on Dayak Benuaq Wellbeing*. Freiburg: Centaurus.

Haug, M. (2014) What Makes a Good Life? Emic Concepts of 'Wellbeing' and 'Illbeing' among the Dayak Benuaq in East-Kalimantan, Indonesia, in T. Stodulka and B. Rött-ger-Rössler (eds), *Feelings at the Margins: Dealing with Violence, Stigma and Isolation in Indonesia*, Frankfurt and New York: Campus, pp. 30–52.

Henley, D. and Davidson, J.S. (2007) Introduction. Radical Conservatism: The Protean Politics of Adat, in J.S. Davidson and D. Henley (eds), *The Revival of Tradition in Indonesian Politics: The Deployment of Adat from Colonialism to Indigenism*, London: Routledge, pp. 1–49.

Hill, H. (ed.) (2014) *Regional Dynamics in a Decentralized Indonesia*. Singapore: Institute of Southeast Asian Studies.

Hoey, B.A. (2003) Nationalism in Indonesia: Building Imagined and Intentional Communities through Transmigration, *Ethnology* 42(2): 109–126.

Holtzappel, C. and Ramstedt, M. (eds) (2009) *Decentralization and Regional Autonomy in Indonesia: Implementation and Challenges*. Singapore: Institute of Southeast Asian Studies.

Ismail, M.G. (1994) Trade and State Power: Sambas (West Borneo) in the Early Nineteenth Century, in G. Schutte (ed.), *State and Trade in the Indonesian Archipelago*, Leiden: KITLV Press, pp. 141–149.

Kimura, E. (2007) Marginality and Opportunity in the Periphery: The Emergence of Gorontalo Province in North Sulawesi, *Indonesia* 84: 71–95.

Kimura, E. (2012) *Political Change and Territoriality in Indonesia: Provincial Proliferation*. London: Routledge.

Kingsbury, D. and Aveling, H. (eds) (2003) *Autonomy and Disintegration in Indonesia*. London: Routledge.

Klinken, G. van (2002) Indonesia's New Ethnic Elites, in H. Schulte Nordholt and I. Abdullah (eds), *Indonesia: In Search of Transition*, Yogyakarta, Indonesia: Pustaka Pelajar, pp. 67–105.

Klinken, G. van (2007a) Return of the Sultans. The Revival of Tradition in Indonesian Politics: The Deployment of Adat from Colonialism to Indigenism, in J. Davidson and D. Henley (eds), *The Revival of Tradition in Indonesian Politics: The Deployment of Adat from Colonialism to Indigenism*, London: Routledge, pp. 149–169.

Klinken, G. van (2007b) *Communal Violence and Democratization: Small Town Wars*. London: Routledge.

Klinken, G. van and Berenschot, W. (eds) (2014) *In Search of Middle Indonesia: Middle Classes in Provincial Towns*. Leiden: Brill.

Kompas (2014, 30 November) http://regional.kompas.com/read/2014/11/30/1518034/2015. Ribuan.Tentara.Akan.Ditransmigrasikan.ke.Kalimantan (accessed 25 November 2015).

Legge, J.D. (1961) *Central Authority and Regional Autonomy in Indonesia: A Study in Local Administration, 1950–1960*. Ithaca, NY: Cornell University Press.

Leimgruber, W. (2004) *Between Global and Local: Marginality and Marginal Regions in the Context of Globalization and Deregulation*. Farnham, UK: Ashgate.

Li, T. (1999) Marginality, Power and Production: Analysing Upland Transformations, in

T. Li (ed.), *Transforming the Indonesian Uplands: Marginality, Power, and Production*. Amsterdam: Harwood Academic Publishers, pp. 1–45.

Lindblad, J.T. (1988) *Between Dayak and Dutch: The Economic History of Southeast Kalimantan 1880–1942*. Dordrecht: Foris.

Locher-Scholten, E. (1994) Dutch Expansion in the Indonesian Archipelago around 1900 and the Imperialism Debate, *Journal of Southeast Asian Studies* 25(1): 91–111.

Lucas, A. and Warren, C. (2000) Agrarian Reform in the Era of Reformasi, in C. Manning and P. van Diemen (eds), *Indonesia in Transition: Social Aspects of Reformasi and Crisis*, Singapore: Institute of Southeast Asian Studies, pp. 220–238.

Luebke, Ch. von (2009) The Political Economy of Local Governance: Findings from an Indonesian Field Study, *Bulletin of Indonesian Economic Studies* 45(2): 201–230.

MacIntyre, A. and Ramage, D. (eds) (2008) *Seeing Indonesia as a Normal Country: Implications for Australia*. Barton: Australian Strategic Policy Institute. Available online: www.aspi.org.au/publications/seeing-indonesia-as-a-normal-country-implications-for-australia/Seeing_Indonesia.pdf (accessed 19 November 2014).

McLeod, R. and MacIntyre, A. (eds) (2007) *Indonesia: Democracy and the Promise of Good Governance*. Singapore: Institute of Southeast Asian Studies.

McWilliam, A. (2011) Marginal Governance in the Time of Pemekaran: Case Studies from Sulawesi and West Papua, *Asian Journal of Social Science* 39: 150–170.

Morishita, A. (2008) Contesting Power in Indonesia's Resource-Rich Regions in the Era of Decentralization: New Strategy for Central Control over the Regions, *Indonesia* 86: 81–107.

Morrell, E. (2010) Local Agency and Region Building in Indonesia's Periphery: Shifting the Goalposts for Development, *Asian Journal of Political Science* 18(1): 48–68.

Owen, N.G. (2014) Nationalism and Other Impulses of the Colonial Era, in N.G. Owen (ed.), *Routledge Handbook of Southeast Asian History*, London: Routledge, pp. 55–64.

Peluso, N. and Vandergeest, P. (2001) Genealogies of the Political Forest and Customary Rights in Indonesia, Malaysia, and Thailand, *The Journal of Asian Studies* 60(3): 761–812.

Picard, M. (2011) Introduction: 'Agama', 'Adat', and Pancasila, in M. Picard and R. Madinier (eds), *The Politics of Religion in Indonesia: Syncretism, Orthodoxy, and Religious Contention in Java and Bali*, London: Routledge, pp. 1–20.

Prasetyawan, W. (2005) Government and Multinationals: Conflict over Economic Resources in East Kalimantan, 1998–2003, *Southeast Asian Studies* 43: 161–190.

Prasetyawan, W. (2006) The Unfinished Privatization of Semen Padang: The Structure of the Political Economy in Post-Suharto Indonesia, *Indonesia* 81: 51–70.

Reid, A. (1988) *Southeast Asia in the Age of Commerce, 1450–1680. Volume 1: The Land below the Winds*. New Haven, CT: Yale University Press.

Reid, A. (1993a) Introduction: A Time and a Place, in A. Reid (ed.), *Southeast Asia in the Early Modern Era: Trade, Power, and Belief*. Ithaca, NY: Cornell University Press, pp. 1–19.

Reid, A. (1993b) *Southeast Asia in the Age of Commerce, 1450–1680. Volume 2: Expansion and Crisis*. New Haven, CT: Yale University Press.

Reid, A. (2010) *Imperial Alchemy: Nationalism and Post-colonial Identity in Southeast Asia*. Cambridge: Cambridge University Press.

Resosudarmo, I.A. (2004) Closer to Peoples and Trees: Will Decentralisation Work for the People and the Forests of Indonesia?, *European Journal of Development Research* 16(1): 110–132.

Rhee, S. (2000) De facto Decentralization during a Period of Transition in East Kalimantan, *Asian-Pacific Community Forestry* 13: 34–40.

Robison, R. and Hadiz, V. (eds) (2004) *Reorganising Power in Indonesia: The Politics of Oligarchy in an Age of Markets*. New York and London: RoutledgeCurzon.

Rössler, M. (1987) *Die soziale Realität des Rituals: Kontinuität und Wandel bei den Makassar von Gowa (Süd-Sulawesi/Indonesien)*. Berlin: Reimer.

Rössler, M. (2000) From Divine Descent to Administration: Sacred Heirlooms and Political Change in Highland Goa, *Bijdragen tot de Taal-, Land- en Volkenkunde* 156(3): 539–560.

Sakai, M. (ed.) (2002a) *Beyond Jakarta: Regional Autonomy and Local Societies in Indonesia*. Adelaide: Crawford House.

Sakai, M. (ed.) (2002b) Solusi Sengketa Tanah di Era Reformasi Politik dan Disentralisasi Indonesia, *Antropologi Indonesia* 26: 40–56.

Sakai, M. (2003) Privatisation of the State-owned Padang Cement Company: Regional Identity and Economic Hegemony in Indonesia's New Era of Decentralisation, in E. Aspinall and G. Fealy (eds), *Local Power and Politics in Indonesia: Decentralisation and Democratisation*, Singapore: Institute of Southeast Asian Studies, pp. 148–163.

Sakai, M. (2009) Creating a New Centre in the Periphery of Indonesia: Sumatran Malay Identity Politics, in M. Sakai, G. Banks and J. Walker (eds), *The Politics of the Periphery in Indonesia: Social and Geographical Perspectives*, Singapore: NUS Press, pp. 62–83.

Sakai, M. and Morrell, E. (2006) Reconfiguring Regions and Challenging the State? New Socio-economic Partnerships in the Outer Islands of Indonesia, in *Asia Reconstructed: Proceedings of the 16th Biennial Conference of the ASAA*, Wollongong, NSW, 26–29 June 2006.

Sakai, M., Banks, G. and Walker, J. (eds) (2009) *The Politics of the Periphery in Indonesia: Social and Geographical Perspectives*. Singapore: NUS Press.

Schulte Nordholt, H. and van Klinken, G. (eds) (2007) *Renegotiating Boundaries: Local Politics in post-Suharto Indonesia*. Leiden: KITLV Press.

Schutte, G. (1994) Introduction, in G. Schutte (ed.), *State and Trade in the Indonesian Archipelago*, Leiden: KITLV Press, pp. 1–6.

Scott, J. (2009) *The Art of Not Being Governed: An Anarchist History of Upland Southeast Asia*. New Haven, CT: Yale University Press.

Selling, E. (1981) *The Evolution of Trading States in Southeast Asia before the 17th Century*. Ann Arbor, MI: UMI Dissertation Services (PhD thesis Columbia University).

Sidel, J.S. (2006) *Riots, Pogroms, Jihad: Religious Violence in Indonesia*. Ithaca, NY: Cornell University Press.

The Australian (2014, 23 July) www.theaustralian.com.au/national-affairs/foreign-affairs/tony-abbott-congratulates-indonesian-presidential-election-winner-joko-widodo/story-fn59nm2j-1226998397424 (accessed 19 November 2014).

Thomaz, L. (1993) The Malay Sultanate of Melaka, in A. Reid (ed.), *Southeast Asia in the Early Modern Era: Trade, Power, and Belief*, Ithaca, NY: Cornell University Press, pp. 69–90.

Thorburn, C. (2004) The Plot Thickens: Land Administration and Policy in Post-New Order Indonesia, *Asia Pacific Viewpoint* 45(1): 33–49.

Tribun Pontianak (2015, 18 May) http://pontianak.tribunnews.com/2015/05/18/ratusan-mahasiswa-demo-tolak-program-transmigrasi-di-kalbar (accessed 25 November 2015).

Tsing, A. (1993) *In the Realm of the Diamond Queen: Marginality in an Out-of-the-way Place*. Princeton, NJ: Princeton University Press.

Vel, J. (2008) *Uma Politics: An Ethnography of Democratization in West Sumba, Indonesia, 1986–2006*. Leiden: KITLV Press.

Vickers, A. (2005) *A History of Modern Indonesia*. Cambridge: Cambridge University Press.

Warren, C. and McCarthy, J. (eds) (2009) *Community, Environment and Local Governance in Indonesia: Locating the Commonweal*. London: Routledge.

Watson-Andaya, B. (1993) Cash-Cropping and Upstream-Downstream Tensions: The Case of Jambi in the Seventeenth and Eighteenth Centuries, in A. Reid (ed.), *Southeast Asia in the Early Modern Era: Trade, Power, and Belief*, Ithaca, NY: Cornell University Press, pp. 91–122.

Part I
Basic issues

2 Decentralisation and its impact on the democratisation process

Patrick Ziegenhain

Introduction

The decentralisation process in Indonesia is remarkable in many ways. From a global comparative perspective, Indonesia's way of transferring political and economic power from the central to the local level is very specific and includes unique features.

Indonesia transformed its governance and administrative structures within a remarkably short time span and turned from an extremely centralised state to a notably decentralised one. Under Suharto's New Order (*Orde Baru*), Indonesia was one of the most centralised countries in the world where the central government appointed powerless local leaders, only accountable at a national level, and who did not represent local citizens. Everything changed after the resignation of long-term ruler Suharto in May 1998. Whereas in other countries decentralisation processes were reputed to be cumbersome and incremental, lasting decades – Indonesia opted for a 'big bang' solution. Democratisation and decentralisation were initiated simultaneously and had a large impact on the politics, administration, economy, identities and culture of the vast island state. In particular, within the past 15 years, the previously neglected so-called Outer Islands witnessed a far-reaching transformation of their socio-economic environment. Local elites of the various regions outside Java that were either excluded or co-opted by the Suharto regime became powerful local decision-makers and businessmen. The drastic change in the legal framework empowered them to build up their own centres of power without any support from Jakarta. In a similar way, local institutions such as mayors (*walikota*), regency heads (*bupati*), and local parliaments, DPRD (*Dewan Perwakilan Rakyat Daerah*) became decisive centres for local decision-making in political, economic and cultural terms within the span of just a few years.

Another peculiarity of the Indonesian decentralisation was the power transfer to the third administrative layer (*kabupaten, kota*) and not – as in nearly all other countries of the world – to the province level. The second tier, the provinces, were given only limited powers because of 'historical and re-emergent challenges to the nation-state and separatist threats from some disaffected provinces' (Morrell 2010: 51). With Law No. 23/2014, the Indonesian central government reduced the autonomy of the local governments and strengthened the province governors as Jakarta's representatives in the regions. The governors now guide and oversee the activities in the province's regencies and municipalities. With the introduction of Law No. 23/2014 the central government also gained the right to dismiss local leaders who did not comply with the obligation to report about the budget and local by-laws.

Despite these recent developments, the financial and political autonomy of the sub-national governments is comparatively high such that Indonesia is nowadays one of the most decentralised states in the world.

However, strikingly, despite multiple decentralisation measures and the very high level of regional autonomy, Indonesia is still defined as a unitary state (*Negara Kesatuan Republik Indonesia*, NKRI) in the constitution and all other important legal sources. The Indonesian government avoided calling the decentralisation programme a transfer to a federal state, since the term federalism has negative connotations due to a history of Dutch colonial power, which prevented the creation of a unitary Indonesian state. Instead, the term 'regional autonomy' (*otonomi daerah*) was coined for the decentralisation process. Indonesia lacks one of the most characteristic features of federalism, namely the representation of the sub-national entities at the national level. Here, the powerful regencies and cities (*kabupaten* and *kota*) are not represented at all, whereas elected representatives from the provinces are members of a more or less meaningless Second Chamber, the *Dewan Perwakilan Daerah* (DPD). The 'father' of decentralisation in Indonesia, Ryaas Rasyid, described the measures as a compromise between highly centralist and federal systems and an acceptable middle-way solution (Rasyid 2003: 63f.). From a global perspective, the Indonesian approach is unique in that it is more decentralised than federal democratic states.

The promotion of democracy was one of the main targets of the decentralisation process. President Habibie stated that democracy should be reflected 'through the way in which governance was practiced in the regions' (Habibie 2006: 275). The strengthening of the local level was supposed to give citizens a greater stake in their political systems and, as a consequence, produce a stronger, more vibrant democracy. The Indonesian model of local autonomy should thus 'bring decision-making to a level where communities were more inclined to participate and where they could hold politicians accountable for their actions' (Aspinall and Fealy 2003: 4). In this regard, the Indonesian governments have 'crafted and implemented administrative and political decentralization as a way of consolidating their new democracy at local levels' (Choi 2011: 20).

This chapter aims to draw some preliminary and tentative conclusions in how far the projected pro-democratic targets could be reached in practice. Moreover, it sketches some of the unintended consequences of the decentralisation process, which were rather harmful to the overall quality of the democracy in Indonesia.

The first part of the chapter gives a short overview of the academic debate on the connection between decentralisation and democratisation. It then focuses on Indonesia and identifies positive and negative contributions of *otonomi daerah* to the deepening of democracy before weighing and interpreting the findings in the conclusion. Methodologically, the chapter relies on a thorough literature review and on personal impressions gained during various field trips in several provinces, such as Aceh, North Sumatra, Central Java, East Kalimantan, South Sulawesi and NTB (Nusa Tenggara Barat). Dozens of interviews with local government officials and ordinary citizens were conducted during two evaluation missions for the German Society of Technical Cooperation (GtZ, now GIZ). Most of the interviews with local administrative leaders were problem-focused guided interviews, which started with opinions about the GtZ support for capacity-building and training measures of local administrations, but soon turned into more general evaluations of the advantages and problems of decentralisation. Interviewees were, for instance, mayors (such as Joko Widodo, then-mayor of Surakarta), the leaders of the local planning board (*Kepala Bappeda*, such as H. Ainul Asikin in the city of Mataram, Lombok) or the local secretary (*Sekretaris Daerah*, such as H. Muchlis in the regency of Bima, Sumbawa). Some aspects of this chapter are published in my comparative study on political accountability in Thailand, Indonesia and the Philippines (Ziegenhain 2015).

Decentralisation and democratisation

Decentralisation processes, often in connection with democratisation processes, are phenomena that can be observed in all parts of the world. The third wave of democratisation (Huntington 1991) in the 1980s and 1990s was accompanied by a similar wave of decentralisation measures. Of 75 countries with a population of over five million people, 63 started or continued with decentralisation measures in the 1980s and 1990s (Selee 2004). In Southeast Asia, decentralisation can be seen as a 'post-authoritarian response' (Alicias and Velasco 2007: 4), since real and effective reform measures concerning decentralisation only took place after the end of authoritarian rule.

Decentralisation alone, however, is not necessarily in accordance with democratic principles. After all, authoritarian regimes also try to broaden their legitimacy by deconcentrating state powers in order to control state territory more efficiently. Thus, decentralisation must include the principles of devolution in order to contribute successfully to democratisation processes. Devolution is a specific form of decentralisation that implies that sub-national authorities have legally defined areas of competence, possess autonomy for tax-raising and public expenditures and have discretion or decision-making power for local regulations. Additionally, local leaders must be elected by their constituents and not appointed by the national executive. Devolution is *a priori* anti-authoritarian, since it is by definition the dispersion of central government powers. It helps to counter the possible excessive domination of a national executive branch. Decentralisation and local self-government are thus major institutional safeguards for individual liberty and protection against authoritarianism. Accordingly, decentralisation can lead 'toward vertical power-sharing among multiple layers of government' (Norris 2008: 157).

Besides this aspect, devolution can produce other positive effects on the deepening and the quality of democracies. A major point is that the election of local leaders by the local citizenry makes the local leaders accountable to the interests of the citizens. If they only follow selfish interests and ignore the people's preferences and demands, they might not be re-elected. Therefore, the local leaders – at least in theory – try to avoid illegal practices and self-enrichment, since the local elections provide a mechanism to register satisfaction or dissatisfaction with a representative's performance (Kulipossa 2004: 769).

Another often quoted advantage of decentralisation is the idea that local elections enhance pluralism and political competition – both major preconditions for a liberal democracy – at the local level. Several contenders from different social backgrounds have the opportunity to compete in free and fair elections. Devolution offers previously disadvantaged groups and candidates the opportunity to take part in elections and political decision-making processes afterward.

One of the most intended effects of devolution is the containment of separatism and communal violence. Often, these conflicts are caused by a perception of discrimination of ethnic or religious minorities within a nation state. Local autonomy offers these groups the chance to practise their culture/traditions and manage their affairs without central government interference contributing to crisis prevention and socio-political stability (Mehler 2001: 292f.). The legitimacy of those in power at the local level is enhanced, often facilitating the deepening of existing democracy.

Increased political awareness and participation are also generally quoted as two of the main advantages of decentralisation processes, because ordinary citizens witness democratic procedures directly in their villages and can even run as candidates. Democracy is thus not limited to the distant capital but is closer to the needs of the citizens and directly involves the individual in political decision-making (Rondinelli 1980: 135f.). Having a closer relationship with political systems can lead ordinary citizens to experience a strengthening of a democratic political culture and democratic patterns of attitude.

Decentralisation and Indonesian democracy: a success story?

There are many indicators that the decentralisation process has indeed contributed to the deepening of democracy in Indonesia. The decisive factor was that decentralisation came as a real devolution giving local authorities substantial financial and political discretion. More than 60 per cent of the state budget is spent by local governments (Harvard Kennedy School Indonesia Program 2010: 74). The danger that Indonesia will return to an authoritarian regime ruled by a dictator or a small elite in Jakarta has been diminished enormously by decentralisation. In practice, real devolution (i.e. giving local authorities substantial financial and political discretion) dispersed political and economic power from the centre to the periphery. Any serious attempt to re-centralise power in Jakarta would face stiff resistance from the ruling local elites as well as the ordinary citizens, so that the political costs of eventual far-reaching re-centralisation attempts would be vast.

In terms of democracy, the introduction of the direct election of local executive positions (*pilkada, pilihan kepala daerah*) in 2005 strengthened the accountability of local leaders towards their citizens. Frequent elections, pluralist local councils as well as critical local media and citizens' groups ensure those in power are held responsible for their actions or inactions.

In decentralised Indonesia, local elections determine who will be province governor, regency head or mayor. Although success in these elections often depended on the election campaign expenses of the individual candidates, most of these elections were generally free and fair. In most cases no violence occurred before and after election day. However, frequent disputes occurred on the validity of election results. In many cases, the loser of the local election accused the winner of using 'money politics' and cheating. Many cases had to be settled in court. Nevertheless, so far, 'the *pilkada* have generally taken place without serious crises that might have undermined the whole [democratisation] process' (Sulistiyanto and Erb 2009: 31).

Particularly after the introduction of *pilkada* and the admission of independent candidates, local candidates from various backgrounds came to local power. Former bureaucrats, business people, military officers, religious leaders, academics, community leaders, NGO activists and media personalities competed for the office of *bupati* or *walikota*. Representative contestation led to a broader and more diverse composition of local councils and the bureaucracy (Carnegie 2010: 131).

This marks a major contrast to the authoritarian period, when military leaders were often appointed as local leaders. At the end of the *Orde Baru*, all local leaders had to be from Golkar, and more than 80 per cent of all governors were from the military. Nowadays, Indonesia sees a colourful and heterogeneous local political leadership. Frequent elections have led to an increased circulation of local elites, which since 2005 removed many remnants of the authoritarian order that had formerly been appointed by then-President Suharto. About 40–50 per cent of the incumbent governors, mayors and regency leaders were not re-elected in 2005 and 2006 (Hadiz 2010: 161).

The intensification of competition for local power led to an 'overall trend towards greater [...] inclusiveness in local executive elections' (Buehler 2010: 271). The direct local elections also allowed middle-class citizens to enter the political scene. Wealth did not guarantee success at the local level. Often, the delivery of good public services and policies in the previous term was a decisive voting factor for constituents. Additionally, there are many examples where candidates with the support of some political parties and grassroots support groups were more successful than traditional local elites with a dubious background. Incumbent local leaders who failed to deliver were often not re-elected as a punishment. In Java, as in the Outer Islands, corruption allegations and scandals with incumbents very often resulted in electoral defeat. According to credible estimations, local elections have a 'high turnover rate of about 40 percent, with voters showing that they will not hesitate to oust local government heads whom they view as corrupt or incompetent' (Aspinall 2010: 33). Compared to established Western democracies, this is a very high rate, and underlines the democratic competence of Indonesian voters.

People generally voted in a rational and pragmatic manner and did not follow party lines or ideologies. Personality mattered more than party affiliation or ideology. Increasingly, the quality of previous governance performance was decisive for electoral support. The decentralisation process thus led to 'an unprecedented level of public scrutiny being imposed on Indonesian local governments and legislatures' (Buehler 2010: 283).

A recent example of rational voting behaviour was the election of Joko Widodo, commonly known as Jokowi, as governor of Jakarta in October 2012, who won the elections due to his credibility and previous successes as mayor of Surakarta. Party support from PDI-P played a minor role and local parties generally do not have sufficient wealth or a working party machinery. As in established democracies, Indonesian 'local voters tended to vote for local leaders whom they knew best and who had delivered something back to society' (Sulistiyanto and Erb 2009: 20).

All recent surveys show the high support for democracy in Indonesia (IFES 2010; Pew Research Center 2011: 19). Decentralisation was a major factor in this, maintaining support for the democratic system among the general public, since the social base of political decision-making was broadened enormously. Whereas previously ordinary people had difficulties following political processes in the distant capital Jakarta, they are now able to see how decisions that have a direct impact on their daily lives are made in their city or regency. They now have the chance to participate in and to influence politics.

Decentralisation has also led to a strong increase in political activism at the local level. This has led to a vibrant civil society in many places, which comprises many social and political organisations and that focuses on matters of local interest. A recent study by Antlöv and Wetterberg (2011) revealed that the activities of civil society organisations have to a great extent become augmented and a regular feature of local politics. The political awareness of ordinary people has also increased. Local authorities are now monitored more strictly, not only by the elected local council (DPRD), but also by civil society organisations who act as custodians of good governance. The transparency and accountability of local administrations have risen enormously in recent years, which can be credited to devolution. Additionally, political participation on the local level increased significantly in many places. Public hearings on local budgets, for instance, have been introduced in dozens of regencies and cities, for example, in the regency of Bima in Sumbawa.

The most visible success of the decentralisation process was the drastic reduction of separatist tendencies since the early 2000s. The decision of the national governments to give the local units discretion over their natural and other economic resources reduced the resentments against the national elite in Jakarta. Some regions witnessed an economic boom and now belong to the fastest economically growing areas in the country.

In the past, development in areas such as the Outer Islands had been hindered by the political elites who had exploited resources and kept the profits. To a great extent, conflicts between the centre and periphery over the distribution of wealth gained from the natural resources of the Outer Islands have now decreased.

Additionally, the political devolution of tasks to locally elected governors, mayors and *bupati* gave political space to a multitude of specific local identities and reduced separatist tendencies. Locals who are not satisfied with political, social and economic developments at their local level now blame first their elected local representatives rather than the central government. Thus, in many areas that saw trouble during 1998–2000, such as Poso, the Moluccas and West and South Kalimantan, decentralisation led to a sharp decrease in communal violence. Ethnic conflicts that were caused by local elites in search of power and material gains abated since many of these elites could achieve their goals without having to resort to violence (Aspinall 2010: 28). Instead, they were empowered to take over local government positions which enabled them to rule and to enjoy material benefits for themselves.

Thus, decentralisation has been (among other factors) responsible for a strong reduction of ethnically motivated violence in recent years. The balkanisation of Indonesia, which some authors predicted would occur around the millennium (Hadar 2000), was prevented not least due to increasing political and financial powers for local governments. However, decentralisation cannot be successful 'if the social and economic grievances that lie at the hearts of the conflicts are not addressed' (Heiduk 2009: 311). Poverty and unemployment in many regions outside Java have been reduced in recent years. However, it is not clear if this can be attributed to the efforts of the local governments or rather to the very positive overall macro-economic improvements in Indonesia.

The dark side of decentralisation

Despite all of the above-mentioned and undeniable positive aspects, Indonesia's decentralisation process is definitely not a complete success story in terms of achieving democracy. The relatively fast devolution of political authority to lower state structures such as provinces and particularly regencies unleashed intense competitive dynamics among local political and economic elites (van Klinken 2007: 139). In various parts of Indonesia's periphery, some of the previously ruling local elites tried to keep their privileged access to political and economic power under the new decentralised political conditions. At the same time, forces which had been excluded from this access so far tried to use the new legal and political framework as their chance to expand their political and economic influence. In other words, 'anxiety and uncertainty mixed with gambler's hope for the main chance' (van Klinken 2007: 49).

In the centralised *Orde Baru*, having good connections to those in power in Jakarta was a precondition to gaining a leading local government position such as *bupati* in the periphery. In the *era reformasi*, however, in which local elections determined who became a local leader and who would not, the route to accessing power changed dramatically and led to fierce competition among the various local elites involved. In many cases, these elites mobilised their supporters along ethnic and religious lines. This in turn created tensions between these groups and in some cases led to outbreaks of communal violence.

At Indonesia's periphery, the struggle surrounding the reorganisation of state power was particularly violent since outside Java, the state plays a bigger role in the local economy (van Klinken 2007: 139). Therefore, the grip for political power in Indonesia's periphery was much more connected with perceived economic gains than in Java.

Today, the most apparent feature for Indonesian citizens is the fact that the decentralisation of political decision-making has also led to a decentralisation of corruption. Graft, which had been, under Suharto, mainly restricted to the president, his family and his closest cronies, has become an all too familiar aspect of daily local politics and administration. Since responsibility for significant financial means and discretion over business deals has also been delegated to local decision-makers, the latter became an attractive partner for illegal but financially attractive backroom dealings. Since it became so attractive in terms of power and money, debates and fights to influence the local administration and exploit (natural) resources became a frequent feature of local politics. In times of *otonomi daerah* it made more sense to collude with local politicians and bureaucrats instead of trying to bribe national officials who had lost much of their influence on the ground.

Dozens of mayors and regency leaders (*bupati*) in all parts of the country have been convicted of incorrect public procurement processes, manipulating public contracts or unlawfully spending public money. Almost weekly, the Indonesian public hears about these types of scandals, which – thanks to the national anti-corruption commission KPK (*Komisi Pemberantasan Korupsi*) – led to investigations and finally penalties for local politicians and bureaucrats. However, it can be assumed that these cases are only the tip of the iceberg. Indonesia has a long tradition of corruption in politics and economic dealings. It would be surprising if local elites were an exception, since obviously they are not per se better people and less greedy than national elites.

No wonder that in some regencies and municipalities, in Java as well as in the Outer Islands, decentralisation has been accompanied by the rise of local mafia-style leaders who use their power for criminal activities and the intimidation of political contenders. Often, they are supported by *preman* (gangsters) who provide the muscle power and security-related services for the local power struggle (Hadiz 2010: 133f.). It is therefore justified to state that in some areas local bosses, corruptors and thugs 'have been innovative in capturing the new democratic spaces provided by the dismantling of the Suharto empire and the centralized state' (Antlöv 2003: 72). These dubious and often criminal local elites were able to capture political and economic power and to establish local authoritarian zones.

Similar to the Philippines, there are several regencies that are dominated by local elites, who are powerful and wealthy enough to ensure electoral victory. A case in point is the province of Banten, where the Chosiyah clan soon dominated in various levels of local government. These 'little kings' (*raja kecil*) are 'unaccountable to their citizens [...] and, due to decentralization, no longer constrained in their confiscatory impulses by a strong central government either'

(Pepinsky and Wihardja 2011: 361). These local government leaders often implement policies that benefit themselves at the expense of the community at large and consolidate their power base.

As has been described before, in many local elections Indonesian voters favoured clean and motivated candidates with a good governance track record over corrupt but powerful elites. However, in other cases, traditional factors of power 'such as patronage networks, social prestige and wealth still matter more than ideas and programs in the selection of local leadership' (Choi 2011: 106). Despite the entry of new faces in many local governments, patrimonial relationships and practices still dominate in many regions. In many areas, voters are frustrated since they have no real alternatives to vote for, because potential replacements regularly belong to the same pool of corrupted business and administrative elites (Buehler 2010: 269).

As discussed above, many new social forces were able to enter the local political and economic scene. A different phenomenon, however, was the re-emergence of traditional elites such as local nobles as a consequence of the introduction of local autonomy. In many parts of the country, members of these traditional families, which have been deprived of access to power by Dutch colonial rule or the authoritarian New Order, got enough public support to re-emerge as political decision-makers on the local level.

Sometimes, these local elites were not legitimated by popular suffrage. A case in point is local politics in Yogyakarta. Being a long-established monarchy under a sultan, many citizens in the special province (*daerah istimewa*) of Yogyakarta refused to accept elections as a tool to determine the governor. President Susilo Bambang Yudhoyono, however, voiced his opinion that Yogyakarta cannot have 'a monarchy system that contradicts our constitution or democratic values' (Sihaloho *et al.* 2010). After strong pressure from local citizens and associations, the national parliament eventually passed a law in August 2012 affirming that the sultan of Yogyakarta would automatically be the governor of the province. This case shows that long-established pre-democratic traditions still persist in a formally democratic and decentralised country. If the sultan ran as a candidate in the governor elections of Yogyakarta, he would most likely win overwhelmingly. For a democratic state, however, unelected and inherited lifetime rule is not in accordance with democratic principles.

The given space for local autonomy did not only lead to the re-emergence of the mentioned pre-democratic social attitudes, but also to a revival of traditional religious values that are also not in accordance with core values of democracy, such as the universal equality of men and women and of different religions. Both values are guaranteed in the constitution, but are in many cases not reflected in local regulations or by-laws (*peraturan daerah, perda*), which are openly discriminative against women and religious minorities.

In many districts with a Muslim majority, the *bupati* or *walikota* together with the local parliament DPRD (*Dewan Perwakilan Rakyat Daerah*) passed *perda* that required all citizens to comply with Islamic law (*shari'ah*) in terms of behaviour and dress. Since there is no universal interpretation of the *shari'ah*, the implementation depended on the opinion of the local decision-makers, which differed from place to place.

In some areas, a very conservative interpretation of the *shari'ah* came into effect and influenced many aspects of daily life. This concerned, for example, the dress code for women, requiring them to wear a veil (*jilbab*) in public. In the Bulukumba regency in South Sulawesi, for example, all women (Muslim or not) must wear a *jilbab* to receive the services of the local government. In the same district, Qu'ran reading ability became a criterion to gain access to the local administration (Buehler 2008: 257). In Sawahlunto in West Sumatra, Muslim couples must prove that they can read the Qur'an before receiving a marriage licence (Bush 2008: 178). In some areas, such as Tangerang in Banten, women were prohibited to be outside of their home without male accompany after dark. Male and female interaction was limited in various areas, for example in public transport. The sale and consumption of liquor and other alcoholic beverages were also banned or reduced. The Islamic obligatory alms giving (*zakat*) was transformed by many local governments into a tax and opened up new sources of income for the local government, which was meant to be spent for social purposes.

All the mentioned local regulations contradict the values of a liberal, pluralistic and tolerant democracy which also cares for minority protection. The religious by-laws have thus created many problems with regard not only to the multi-ethnic Indonesian identity and tradition but also to the constitution (Bünte 2009: 118), which states the equality of sexes and religious beliefs. The national motto, *Bhinneka Tunggal Ika* (Unity in Diversity) of the Indonesian state, which reflects the multi-ethnic and multi-religious composition of the archipelago, is not in accordance with the spirit of the above-mentioned local regulations. In 2006, 56 members of the national parliament (*Dewan Perwakilan Rakyat*, DPR) demanded from the president the removal of all local regulations concerning the interpretation and implementation of the *shari'ah* because they were unconstitutional, but Susilo Bambang Yudhoyono (SBY) refused (Legowo and Djadijono 2007: 87). The Ministry of Home Affairs, which has the legal authority to supervise and eventually annul local regulations, has so far taken no action against most discriminative *perda*. As in many other cases, the Indonesian national government under SBY (2004–2014) remained too reluctant to protect religious minorities and to deal with the highly sensitive issue of local *shari'ah* interpretation. It is noteworthy that in some parts of the country, where other religions dominate (i.e. Christianity in Papua, Hinduism in Bali), similar local regulations have been passed to the detriment of the minority religions.

It is a general feature of local politics that the majority ethnic group of a regency or city, termed sons of the region (*putra daerah*), is often favoured against other ethnic minorities. In many cases, decentralisation brought local discrimination in terms of access to jobs and public service, public procurement as well as licences and permits.

Conclusion

The multitude of regencies and their different experiences make it very difficult to generalise about the influence of the decentralisation process on the deepening of democracy in Indonesia. Whereas in some areas the positive contributions prevailed, other regencies and cities appear to be rather negative examples. Instead of a uniform pattern all over the country, decentralisation triggered local dynamics which went in various directions. The impact of decentralisation on the democratisation process is thus ambiguous.

In his article 'Debating Indonesia's Reformasi: Bridging "Parallel Universes"', Japanese political scientist Yuki Fukuoka distinguished between two contrasting scholarly interpretations of the transition process in Indonesia (Fukuoka 2013). On the one hand, there is the so-called liberal camp that underlines the changes compared to the previous authoritarian system, the rising importance of progressive political actors and civil society organisations. This group of scholars is relatively optimistic about Indonesia's political future, seeing the country slowly but surely moving towards greater liberal democracy (Fukuoka 2013: 541). On the other hand, there is the so-called oligarchy camp, which stresses the continuities of the authoritarian past. According to these scholars, such as Hadiz (2010), the patrimonial power structure of the *Orde Baru* has remained largely intact albeit it had to adapt to the new legal and political conditions. Democratisation and decentralisation have thus largely failed since their results have only led to a reorganisation of the old predatory power relations (Fukuoka 2013: 544). Under such conditions, a deepening of democracy is not realistic and the country will be ruled by corrupt oligarchs, or other predatory forces in the near future.

These two very different interpretations of Indonesia's transition process since 1998 are also relevant for the main question of this chapter regarding how far the decentralisation process has contributed to a deepening of democracy in Indonesia.

Decentralisation certainly has had many positive effects on the democratisation process, not least since it 'has allowed the discussion and debate on the idea of "democracy" to flourish' (Sulistiyanto and Erb 2009: 4). Local autonomy in combination with increased participation possibilities as well as the accountability of local governments towards their constituencies provided a stable foundation for the deepening of the democratisation process. According to one of the fathers of Indonesian decentralisation, Ryaas Rasyid, the process was an important precondition for the development of democracy in Indonesia (Rasyid 2003: 64).

The high significance of decentralisation lies in the dissolution of the centralist power monopoly and in causing social and political power diffusion. Regional and local grievances are now addressed to the local government and not, as previously, to the central government. The local level thus has taken the role of a shock absorber. Consequently, the whole political system became more flexible and at the same time more stable.

However, one should be aware that the political and personal objectives of various local and national stakeholders still typically dictate the nature and implementation of decentralisation, rather than democratic ideals (Seymour and Turner 2002: 48). Therefore, decentralisation was not conducive to the deepening of democracy in all areas. Widespread corruption, local mafia bosses, 'little kings' and discriminative local legislation are negative unintended consequences of the decentralisation process. It must be recognised that these anti-democratic tendencies are not singular problems but occur in a considerable amount of local government units.

Given the high number of individual and sometimes contradicting cases, it is very difficult to assess if the positive or negative aspects of decentralisation prevail. An analysis of the current situation must include the shortcomings and negative contributions for the overall quality of democracy in Indonesia, but should not neglect the democratic progress reached in many regions. It should also consider that the decentralisation process, which has brought democracy and self-determination to the local level, began just 15 years ago and is still ongoing.

Taking into account what has been achieved so far, the author concludes that there are more positive than negative contributions of decentralisation towards the Indonesian democratisation process. Despite all of the negative developments in various local areas, the opportunities to reach a consensus and thus for a further development of democracy are given. Much depends on how the national and local government tackle the urgent problems of corruption, abuse of power and minority discrimination. A strengthening of the rule of law, a consequent law implementation including effective sanctions for criminals in office as well as further incentives for good governance could considerably improve the overall picture.

The further development of local and national democracy is also dependent on the attitudes and actions of the ordinary people. In a long-term perspective and with an improved education, health and welfare system they might be able to impact local politics in order to reduce the mentioned undemocratic practices and to choose local representatives that benefit them in a sustainable way.

It is difficult to predict in which direction the development of the simultaneous decentralisation and democratisation processes will go. Both processes do exert a permanent influence on each other. As long as the overall quality of democracy in the country stagnates or decreases, the successes of decentralisation will be limited. At the same time, if the weaknesses of decentralisation continue, Indonesia's democracy is far from being consolidated.

References

Alicias, D. and Velasco, D. (2007) Decentralization and Deepening Democracy, in D. Alicias, M. Djadijono, T.A. Legowo, C. Ramos, J. Rocamora, D. Velasco and J. Wong (eds), *Decentralization Interrupted: Studies from Cambodia, Indonesia, Philippines and Thailand*, Quezon City, Philippines: Institute for Popular Democracy, pp. 3–12.

Antlöv, H. (2003) Not Enough Politics! Power, Participation and the New Democratic Polity in Indonesia, in E. Aspinall and G. Fealy (eds), *Local Power and Politics*, Singapore: Institute for Southeast Asian Studies, pp. 72–86.

Antlöv, H. and Wetterberg, A. (2011) Citizen Engagement, Deliberative Spaces and the Consolidation of a Post-Authoritarian Democracy: The Case of Indonesia. www.icld. se/eng/pdf/ICLD_wp8_printerfriendly.pdf (accessed 21 June 2014).

Aspinall, E. (2010) Indonesia: The Irony of Success, *Journal of Democracy* 21(2): 20–34.

Aspinall, E. and Fealy, G. (2003) Introduction: The New Order and Its Legacy, in E. Aspinall and G. Fealy (eds), *Local Power and Politics in Indonesia: Decentralisation and Democratisation*, Singapore: Institute for Southeast Asian Studies, pp. 1–14.

Buehler, M. (2008) The Rise of Shari'a By-Laws in Indonesian Districts: An Indication for Changing Patterns of Power Accumulation and Political Corruption, *South East Asia Research* 16(2): 255–285.

Buehler, M. (2010) Decentralisation and Local Democracy in Indonesia: The Marginalisation of the Public Sphere, in M. Mietzner and E. Aspinall (eds), *Problems of Democratization in Indonesia: Elections, Institutions and Society*, Singapore: Institute for Southeast Asian Studies, pp. 267–285.

Bünte, M. (2009) Indonesia's Protracted Decentralization: Contested Reforms and Their Unintended Consequences, in M. Bünte and A. Ufen (eds), *Democratization in Post-Suharto Indonesia*, London: Routledge, pp. 102–123.

Bush, R. (2008) Regional Sharia Regulations in Indonesia: Anomaly or Symptom?, in G. Fealy and S. White (eds), *Expressing Islam: Religious Life and Politics in Indonesia*, Singapore: Institute for Southeast Asian Studies, pp. 174–191.

Carnegie, P.J. (2010) *The Road from Authoritarianism to Democratization in Indonesia*. New York: Palgrave Macmillan.

Choi, N. (2011) *Local Politics in Indonesia: Pathways to Power*. London: Routledge.

Fukuoka, Y. (2013) Debating Indonesia's Reformasi: Bridging 'Parallel Universes', *Journal of Contemporary Asia* 44(3): 540–552.

Habibie, B.J. (2006) *Decisive Moments: Indonesia's Long Road to Democracy*. Jakarta: Ilthabi Rekatama.

Hadar, L.T. (2000) *Averting a 'New Kosovo' in Indonesia: Opportunities and Pitfalls for the United States*. Washington, DC: Cato Institute.

Hadiz, V.R. (2010) *Localising Power in Post-Authoritarian Indonesia*. Stanford, CA: Stanford University Press.

Harvard Kennedy School Indonesia Program (2010) From Reformasi to Institutional Transformation: A Strategic Assessment of Indonesia's Prospects for Growth, Equity and Democratic Governance. http://unpan1.un.org/intradoc/groups/public/documents/ UN-DPADM/UNPAN042322.pdf (accessed 10 February 2013).

Heiduk, F. (2009) Two Sides of the Same Coin? Separatism and Democratization in Post-Suharto Indonesia, in M. Bünte and A. Ufen (eds), *Democratization in Post-Suharto Indonesia*, London: Routledge, pp. 295–313.

Huntington, S.P. (1991) *The Third Wave: Democratization in the Late 20th Century*. Norman, OK: University of Oklahoma Press.

IFES (2010) IFES Survey on Indonesian Political Attitudes Reveals Satisfaction with Democracy, Lack of Political Information. www.ifes.org/~/media/Files/Publications/ Press%20Release/2010/Indonesia_election_survey_2010.pdf (accessed 21 June 2014).

Klinken, G. van (2007) *Communal Violence and Democratization: Small Town Wars*. London: Routledge.

Kulipossa, F.P. (2004) Decentralisation and Democracy in Developing Countries: An Overview, *Development in Practice* 14(6): 768–779.

Legowo, T.A. and Djadijono, M. (2007) Decentralization in Indonesia: How Far Can It Go?, in D. Alicias, M. Djadijono, T.A. Legowo, C. Ramos, J. Rocamora, D. Velasco and J. Wong (eds), *Decentralization Interrupted: Studies from Cambodia, Indonesia, Philippines and Thailand*, Quezon City, Philippines: Institute for Popular Democracy, pp. 59–108.

Mehler, A. (2001) Dezentralisierung und Krisenprävention, in W. Thomi, M. Steinich and W. Polte (eds), *Dezentralisierung in Entwicklungsländern. Jüngere Ursachen, Ergebnisse und Perspektiven staatlicher Reformpolitik*, Baden-Baden: Nomos, pp. 287–299.

Morrell, E. (2010) Local Agency and Region Building in Indonesia's Periphery: Shifting the Goalposts for Development, *Asian Journal of Political Science* 18(1): 48–68.

Norris, P. (2008) *Driving Democracy: Do Power-Sharing Institutions Work?*. Cambridge: Cambridge University Press.

Pepinsky, T.B. and Wihardja, M.M. (2011) Decentralization and Economic Performance in Indonesia, *Journal of East Asian Studies* 11(3): 337–371.

Pew Research Center (2011) Obama's Challenge in the Muslim World: Arab Spring Fails to Improve U.S. Image. www.pewglobal.org/files/2011/05/Pew-Global-Attitudes-Arab-Spring-FINAL-May-17-2011.pdf (accessed 21 June 2014).

Rasyid, R. (2003) Regional Autonomy and Local Politics in Indonesia, in E. Aspinall and G. Fealy (eds), *Local Power and Politics in Indonesia: Decentralisation and Democratisation*, Singapore: Institute for Southeast Asian Studies, pp. 63–71.

Rondinelli, D.A. (1980) Government Decentralization in Comparative Perspective: Theory and Practice in Developing Countries, *International Review of Administrative Sciences* 47(2): 133–145.

Selee, A. (2004) Exploring the Link between Decentralization and Democratic Governance, in J.S. Tulchin and A. Selee (eds), *Decentralization and Democratic Governance in Latin America*, Washington, DC: Woodrow Wilson International Center for Scholars, pp. 3–35.

Seymour, R. and Turner, S. (2002) Otonomi Daerah: Indonesia's Decentralisation Experiment, *New Zealand Journal of Asian Studies* 4(2): 33–51.

Sihaloho, M.J., Nanginna, B. and Rachman, A. (2010) Will the Yogyakarta Sultan Be Leader in Name Only with New Law?, *Jakarta Globe*, 4 December. www.thejakartaglobe.com/news/will-the-yogyakarta-sultan-be-leader-in-name-only-with-new-law/410023 (accessed 26 February 2014).

Sulistiyanto, P. and Erb, M. (2009) Indonesia and the Quest for 'Democracy', in P. Sulistiyanto and M. Erb (eds), *Deepening Democracy in Indonesia: Direct Elections for Local Leaders (Pilkada)*, Singapore: Institute for Southeast Asian Studies, pp. 1–37.

Ziegenhain, P. (2015) *Institutional Engineering and Political Accountability in Thailand, Indonesia, and the Philippines*. Singapore: Institute for Southeast Asian Studies.

3 Conceptualising marginality in Indonesia

Anna-Teresa Grumblies

Indonesia's vast landmass offers a wide range of marginalised regions and people. Colonial and postcolonial processes of nation-building have produced various constellations of marginalisation, of inclusion and exclusion, access to rights and resources that resulted in strict centre–periphery dependencies. The downfall of Suharto in 1998 put an end to the hegemony of the country's core, Java, and realigned power to the margins of the nation. The outcome of decentralisation is a complex system that produced new constellations of dependency on Indonesia's Outer Islands (cf. Introduction to this volume). Against this background marginality remains a powerful theoretical tool to explore changing power relations as well as the politics of exclusion and contestation. This chapter discusses the meanings of marginality within anthropological discourse and its use for elaborating deeper on the understanding of periphery and margins in Indonesia. The chapter deals with the concept of marginality in general, showing how it has been defined in anthropology, and how the notions of periphery and marginality have been applied to the Indonesian context. Yet the representation of 'marginality theory', as undefined as the field is, can at best be partial. For a deeper understanding of these notions for Indonesia's Outer Islands, the chapter therefore concentrates on the meanings of marginality with particular focus on the Indonesian uplands, regions that are historically described as marginal spheres per se and thus offer valuable insights for the transformation of power constellations within Indonesia.

Marginality as an anthropological concept

Anthropologists, due to their 'traditional' focus on minorities, genuinely tell stories of marginalisation while other disciplines, for example, psychology or geography, try to assess scales of marginalisation for developing scope models for measuring marginality. Marginality is thus in general a key term in the broader social science literature as well as in the humanities. Before discussing the meanings of marginality more closely, a first glimpse at the concept could take a useful start with etymology. Easily as it seems, the term 'margin' has its roots in Latin, originating from the term *margo*, which means edge or border. Once we see margin as the border or edge, the necessarily concurring question directs the focus towards the corresponding component, the core or centre. Therefore, a margin cannot stand for itself; it is a relational term that has its roots in a dualistic dialectic. The same accounts for the phenomenon itself, i.e. marginality, and the process resulting from it, i.e. marginalisation. Closely related to 'its family resemblances', as Dowdy reminds us, marginality is often referred to in the same way as ' "border", "frontier", "limit", "boundary", "edge", "periphery", "threshold", "space between" ' (Dowdy 2011: 2).[1] For example, in 2014 Harms et al. concentrated on the concept of 'remoteness' in a very similar sense as marginality is discussed in this contribution; as something

> never fixed [...] but a process situated in dynamic fields of power. The condition is always infused with the edgy feeling experienced by people living in a world where the relations of inside and outside, near and far, proximate and remote are always contested.
>
> (Harms *et al.* 2014: 364)[2]

Putting aside the similarity of terms, anthropological writing, in general, has remained astonishingly indistinct concerning the concept (Rösing 2000: 89), although marginality has been a matter of investigation in anthropological studies from the earliest starting point of the subject's history, and is dealt with in a range of ethnographies. However, anthropological literature has so far maintained a strategic distance from a general methodology towards marginality as a concept. Instead, most authors dealing with marginality survey the subject with a particular spotlight on local relations and local ideas. Röttger-Rössler and Stodulka, for example, thus acknowledge a lack of a more general theoretical insight on marginality: 'As an inherently anthropological topic, it is surprising though that marginality has rarely been scrutinised conceptually beyond the particularities of its respective ethnographic setting' (2014: 16). Nevertheless, taking a closer look at the way in which marginality entered anthropological discourse, the concept's genealogy as a theme of anthropological studies shows a profound, although not always explicit conceptualisation of marginality and margins as a tool of analysis within the discipline.

Marginality as a concept in anthropology is mainly based on an approach towards marginality as a social construction. This has been exemplified by anthropologists who take the social constructedness of marginality as a starting point to elaborate on fixed categories such as centre and margin, and subsequently explore how both are constitutive of each other (Hussain 2009: 5). This is the approach the chapter will focus on in the course of this contribution.

Anthropology as a discipline has from its beginnings focused on marginal communities. At a time when evolutionist ideas were on the rise, marginal groups served anthropologists who 'studied the marginal other as a means of catching a glimpse of how they themselves once were' (Hussain 2009: 5f.) to figure out how human development had evolved. When later theories made space for new conceptualisations of culture and cultural diversity, anthropologists continued to study marginal communities which they constructed as 'primitive Other'

(Fabian 1983). Early anthropologists thus created a vast amount of anthropological writings that focused on indigenous communities in a rather naturalist fashion. When in the rise of colonial criticism Talal Asad published his book, *Anthropology and the Colonial Encounter* in 1973, anthropology set the ground for a self-reflective mode of writing. Postcolonial thinkers, such as Said, for example, postulated the construction of the Orient, the margin, as an object of Western hegemony. Spivak paid some critical attention towards marginality as a concept, which for her, as she writes in 1993, is a 'buzzword in cultural critique' (1993: 55). The conceptualisation of margins and the inclusion of those who are marginalised into a centre-based discourse have to be perceived as mere constructions of the centre (Spivak 1988). Drawing upon Foucault's work on sexuality she claims:

> One must not suppose that there exists a certain sphere of 'marginality' that would be the legitimate concern of a free and disinterested scientific inquiry were it not the object of mechanisms of exclusion brought to bear by the economic or ideological requirements of power. If 'marginality' is being constituted as an area of investigation, this is only because relations of power have established it as a possible object.
> (Foucault 1978: 98; textual modification added by and quoted in Spivak 1993: 59)[3]

Within the so-called literary turn (Scholte 1987), anthropology thus focused on a new conceptualisation of margins and other essentialist categories as fundamentally socially constructed. While, among others, Appadurai (1988: 36) pointed towards the anthropological construction of natives, the idea of margins as social constructions can also be found in a number of studies (e.g. Tsing 1993; Li 2000; Hussain 2009), highlighting and intriguing the dynamics nested within the term marginality and its counterpart, centricity. Anna Tsing, who also draws her theoretical considerations from postcolonial thinkers like Fanon, Bhabha and Spivak, states: 'the promise of a postcolonial anthropology that goes beyond the re-analysis of its own problematic past depends upon engagement with the questions and challenges raised by those concerned with cultural heterogeneity, power, and "marginality"' (1993: 14). Deconstructing the legitimate power and authority of centres is thus best engaged from the site of the margin. Anthropologists have thus focused on how people living at the margins have found their own ways to deal with power constellations palpable at the periphery, giving them meaning, challenging them and reconstituting them in their own unique fashion – in the Indonesian context exemplified by the literature on the current indigenous peoples' movement (*Aliansi Masyarakat Adat Nusantara*, AMAN) to which I will return later.

While postcolonial ideas made way for the entrance of marginality into anthropological academia, the notion of centre and periphery also became a topic of intense debate within the field (e.g. Douglas 1966; Ortiz 1969; Tambiah 1977). In 'Centre and Periphery' (1982) British sociologist Edward Shils, inspired by the works of Weber and Parsons, speaks of a centre in which power is bundled, and a periphery, which is characterised by its distance to the centre. For him, every society draws upon a centre, which affects and impacts people who are living within its realm. The relationship to the centre serves as a point of reference and orientation for individuals who are distanced from the society's core (Shils 1982: 93). By this means, the centre is the focal point of a societal symbolic system:

> It is the centre of the order of symbols, of values and beliefs, which govern the society. It is the centre because it is the ultimate and irreducible; and it is felt to be such by many who cannot give explicit articulation to its irreducibility.
>
> (Shils 1982: 93)

In contrast to Shils, who provided a rather simplified and static vision of a centre and its periphery, Robert Dunne points to a plurality of centres and shows that marginality 'is a multidimensional phenomenon in that a given person may be simultaneously integrated with one or more centres while being marginal from one or more other centres' (Dunne 2005: 15). Those communities or people who live at the margins, i.e. who are distant from a centre, can only to a certain extent be portrayed as marginal. Even marginal groups may be included in a variety of other local centres, which differ from the societal centre, or, Dunne adds, 'perhaps even a local centre that is marginal in relation to the societal centre' (2005: 23).

Shils' simplified version of the centre hints at the importance of the notion of the state as an analytical point that needs to be addressed when considering the margins. In this context, the notion of state power is of particular importance. As Steedly (1999) notes, the state has become a 'must' in anthropological theory, especially among anthropologists working on Southeast Asia, and she offers a way to perceive certain ways of marginalisation as being state-related. The categorisation of what lies beneath the state or even outside of its power radius has become more and more inevitable. Culture, Steedly argues, is regarded

> as an attribute of the state – as an object of state policy, an ideological zone for the exercise of state power, or literally a creation of the state – whereas the state itself is comprehended in ways analogous to totalizing or superorganic models of culture.
>
> (1999: 433)

It is in this state-related context that marginality gained prominence in anthropological research:

> The idea of marginality offered an important corrective to the anthropological yearning for a bounded, autonomous place for culture, outside the circuits of global capitalism and state power. It insisted that even the most

isolated locales were shot through with – indeed, one might say constituted by – power and influence emanating from dominant centers located elsewhere.

(Steedly 1999: 443)

For example, groups such as the Meratus Dayak in Borneo or the Lauje in Sulawesi are part of a marginal sphere within the Indonesian state, which is deeply affected by policies and governmental structures, so that 'their lifeways are formed not outside of state agendas but relationally, in and through them' (Li 2001: 44). But, Steedly adds, a potential danger lies in the concluding assumption that everything has to be perceived through a state-centred lens and that therefore minorities excluded from state power are essentially marginalised (1999: 443), a phenomenon that becomes highly meaningful for the Indonesian context.

Nested deeply in the notions of centre, periphery and the state is the notion of power – who has full and who has only limited power at their disposal? It is important to note here that power and authority are not reduced to state apparatus alone. Ferguson shows that it is not always the state that is exclusively exercising power and that the relationship between centre and power is not always easily traceable:

The place from which power is exercised is often a hidden place. When we try to pin it down, the centre always appears to be somewhere else. Yet we know that this phantom centre, elusive as it is, exerts a real, undeniable power over the whole social framework of our culture, and over the ways we think about it.

(Ferguson 1990: 9)

This phantom centre, it must be noted, is part of an interdependent complexity between centre and margin, in which power is never exclusive. In his book *Places on the Margin* Rob Shields (1991) develops the concept of cultural marginality and asserts that marginal places, and I believe he would also include marginal groups, are part of a cultural ranking system, where spaces are ranked in relation to each other. A categorisation between high and low spaces is similar and relational to the constitution of margin and centre. Attributes discarding a space, place or group as marginal are settled in the field of categorising social relations, objects, beliefs and practices that are designated as parts of 'low' culture. Referring to Edward Said's (1995) ideas on Orientalism – categorising the margins as located 'at the edge of civilization' – Shields points to the 'positional superiority' (Said) on which the 'symbolic exclusion' (Shields) is dependent: 'one which puts the High in a whole series of possible relationships with the Low without ever losing the upper hand' (Shields 1991: 5). Borrowing further from Stallybrass and White (1986), Shields asserts that the High is in constant need of the Low and that the High in some part includes the Low. It is through a centre-based discourse that the difference or social 'Other' of the margins is composed in the first place. Simultaneously it constitutes the centre's superiority (Shields 1991: 5). The central issue addressed here is the binary relationship between margins and centres that are deeply entangled by social, political and economic ties. While being in the margin, being marginalised, experiencing marginalisation implies a certain symbolic exclusion from the centre. Margins, however, are 'signifiers of everything centers deny or repress; margins as "the Other", become the condition of possibility of all social and cultural entities' (Shields 1991: 276). The centre needs a counterpart, a mirror displaying, portraying, representing and reconstituting its own character as a centre – a process that becomes very clear in the relationship between the Indonesian state and its margins in specific historical constellations. Thus, the notion of margin implies 'an analytical placement that makes evident both the constraining, oppressive quality of cultural exclusion and the creative potential of rearticulating, enlivening, and rearranging the very social categories that peripheralize a group's existence' (Tsing 1994: 279). It is this potential of marginality, which makes it such an attractive heuristic tool for anthropological discourse. Power relations between centre and margins are therefore best understood from a position at the periphery, paying attention to the perspective of those who are marginal and who 'actively engage their marginality by protesting, reinterpreting and embellishing their exclusion' (Tsing 1993: 5).

It becomes clear that a theorisation of marginality is always in need of a critical approach in order to avoid an oversimplifying application of a mere dualistic notion of centre–periphery relations. It is further necessary to pay attention to centre–periphery relations in Indonesia also from the perspective of the margins, which have been deeply shaped by colonialism and the creation of the modern nation.

Marginality in the Indonesian context

Beginning in the period of colonial rule, the island of Java has constituted the state's imagined centre, tying together the archipelago's tremendous diversity, with the regions surrounding it constructed as Indonesia's periphery, which makes up around 93 per cent of the whole land area (Charras 2005: 91). More than 50 years of centralised government have produced characteristic features and experiences that today are significant for the whole of Outer Indonesia and especially for upland communities that were generally perceived of as isolated and marginalised from the Indonesian mainstream (cf. Duncan 2004: 91). Applying marginality theory to the Indonesian context thus requires a reflection of historical as well as political circumstances, especially for marginal communities in the Outer Islands, in order to reveal how the centre and supposed margins in Indonesia are deeply interwoven and thus are subject to transformation processes.

Tania Li's edited volume, *Transforming the Indonesian Uplands* (1999) was the first book to focus explicitly on marginality in Indonesia, exemplified by the context of the Indonesian uplands. Li's works have become, next to Anna

Tsing's, research lines that guide scholars interested in marginality questions in general, or in questions of the relation between the state and indigenous peoples. In her introduction to the 1999 volume, Li specifically focuses on the aspect of marginality among upland groups. The Indonesian uplands, she asserts, 'have been constituted as a marginal domain through a long continuing history of political, economic and social engagement with the lowlands' (1999a: xvii). In this sense, following Shields' idea of a binary connection between centre and margins (see above), the relational character of the term 'marginal experiences' becomes palpable. As Li points out, it is the social construction of marginality that deserves special attention in the analysis of the Indonesian uplands as a marginal area. In this context uplands and lowlands need to be analysed and perceived of within a single analytical frame, because both are part of one integrated system and, therefore, require equivalent analytical attention (Li 1999b: 1f.). Marginality as a social construction is always the result of unequal power relations and thus implies 'a hegemonic project, subject to contestation and reformulation. [...] [T]he cultural, economic and political projects of people living and working in the uplands are constituted in relation to various hegemonic agendas but never are they simple reflections of them' (Li 1999b: 2).

   Therefore, a conceptualisation of the Indonesian uplands as marginal must lead to the logical and coercive conclusion that the categorical units of uplands and lowlands constitute and mediate each other. It, therefore, is hardly surprising that marginality as a concept has played an important role for studies dealing with Indonesia from an anthropological perspective, especially concerning the Indonesian uplands.

Early constellations

In precolonial times, as Li reminds us, Indonesia's interior regions were for a long time not marginal but were known and feared for their 'alleged spiritual powers' (1999b: 3). But with the spread of Islam throughout the archipelago, triggered through intense maritime trade relations around the fifteenth to seventeenth centuries, power was increasingly allocated to coastal Muslim settlements. A great number of political centres such as Aceh, Melaka, Brunei or Makassar rose to significant power and size while interior regions lost significance (Andaya 1993). As a result, a gap emerged between those who became Muslims or chose to live close to Muslim communities along the Indonesian coasts, and those who lived in the upland regions of the islands, underlining a 'marked social distinction between "people of the littoral kingdoms and the barbarian population of the tribal interior"' (Li 1999b: 4, citing Henley 1989: 8). While upland and lowland communities depended on mutual trade,[4] most coastal communities were able to assert some form of political authority over upland neighbours due to their strategic position at the mouth of a river, or their access to the sea.[5] While the upland regions generally served as a point of escape from authoritarian rule, they were also perceived of as 'inferior and [were] treated in a derogatory way' (Hauser-Schäublin 2013: 13). Nevertheless, upland neighbours also offered an opportunity of wealth in the form of forest products that were (and remain) valuable for national and international markets and trade, and thus were a precious source of income for coastal authorities. In political terms a number of states, centres and margins existed, while neither a general periphery nor an overall centre had been formed in precolonial times.

With the rise of colonial activity in Indonesia, upland communities soon felt the impact of colonial land commodification that started to play an important role for colonial production for the international market. As will be shown below, until today the legal situation of land rights has remained highly contested and land has therefore emerged as the most contentious subject in debates between indigenous communities and the government (Hauser-Schäublin 2013: 7). When land became the most important resource for the colonial project in the nineteenth century, the state put its full focus on the territorialisation of the archipelago and its inhabitants (Li 1999b). The Agrarian Act of 1870 put all land that was not privately owned under direct colonial control, with the so-called *domeinverklaring* principle (Cleary 1996: 41). Albeit legal, acceptance of customary land rights was manifested in the act, in fact, it meant that all land that was perceived by the authorities as uncultivated became a source for colonial production, thus making forest use and swidden agriculture, a form of cultivation that includes land lying fallow, an illegal practice (Li 1999b: 13). Many upland communities thereby lost the right to cultivate land that had traditionally been under indigenous land tenure. Kahn (1999) shows that between 1870 and the 1920s more than 110,000 hectares of Minangkabau land in West Sumatra, declared as waste land suddenly became official state land that was available mostly for European companies for tenure periods of at most 75 years (Kahn 1999: 93) – the initial goal of the 1870 Agrarian Act.

By this means, the second half of the nineteenth century brought significant transformations for the Indonesian uplands that also included a new perception of Indonesia's cultural diversity. Hitherto, 'the Dutch knew next to nothing about the adat law of the Javanese and other Indonesians whom they had been ruling for such a long time' (Fasseur 2007: 51). But with the establishment of the Leiden School of *adat* law studies, differences among the archipelago's societies came to be explained in terms of culture. Dutch officials, scholars as well as some local elites 'began to understand social interaction in the colony, and even in the empire as a whole, as instances of intercultural interaction' (Kahn 1999: 101). Kahn's analysis of the cultural constitution of Indonesian diversity contributes significantly to an understanding of a stereotypical imagination of the Indonesian uplands as being 'more traditional'. According to Kahn, inequality among Indonesia's people is nowadays interpreted mainly as the product of cultural difference, and not as resulting from unequal access to power or resources (1999: 83). The discovery of *adat* and *adat* law as a categorical unit further induced the Dutch colonial government to rule indirectly and via local leaders over regions where no colonial authorities were present (Arizona and Cahyadi 2013: 46). After the implementation of the so-called Ethical Policy in 1901, upland communities in the Outer Islands, habitually living in dispersed settlements in the hilltops, were often forced to resettle to centralised lowland villages where they were compelled to practise wet-rice cultivation. The new agricultural development plan thereby also aimed at increasing governance and control over upland communities (Schrauwers 2000: 71).

These precolonial constellations and colonial interventions had significant effects for territorial claims on Indonesian peripheries, and especially among upland groups, which are still traceable in current legal arrangements today.

Constituting margins during the New Order

After the colonial era, unjust treatment of swidden cultivators and minorities, especially in the uplands, continued. Under Dutch colonial rule Batavia (Jakarta) had evolved as a centre of trade, while former political centres lost importance because they were now located at new geographic and commercial peripheries (Röttger-Rössler and Stodulka 2014: 12). The island of Java also played a central role in the fight for independence before and after the Japanese occupation. Under Sukarno, who became the first Indonesian president in 1945, national unity was for the first time manifested in the preamble of the 1945 constitution, the *Pancasila*. While national unity was, for example, further promoted through the introduction of Bahasa Indonesia (BI) as the national language, other national initiatives had severe effects for indigenous communities and thus increased the Outer Islands' political marginality. Following the Basic Agrarian Act of 1870, Sukarno 'established a single, unitary land law that represented a "classic" form of agrarian reform legislation for the times' (Peluso *et al.* 2008: 381) – the Basic Agrarian Law of 1960. Once again land in Indonesia, provided that it was not in private ownership, received the status of state property. Territorial claims of indigenous communities were recognised in the law as *hak ulayat*, but only if they were 'exercised in such a way as to accord with national and state interests based on national unity, and so as not to contradict laws and other regulations which are of a higher order' (Article 3).[6] By this formulation customary land rights were subordinated to national goals while the overall sovereignty to land remained with the state (Acciaioli 2007: 312). All *adat* land that was not under permanent cultivation was, therefore 'virtually "up for the taking", without compensation' (Wallace 2008: 203).

When Suharto came to power, he intensified the centralistic government with the promise of fast economic growth for the nation. With the formulation of laws such as the Basic Mining Act and the Basic Forestry Act of 1967, Suharto tremendously increased government control over the nations' natural resources. Previously, the central Department of Forestry in Jakarta had only exercised minor authority, which since the 1960 Basic Agrarian Law paid, in some sense, respect to customary land rights.[7] Under Suharto, however, the Department of Forestry in Jakarta was ascribed all power over the nations' forests encompassing more than 75 per cent of the overall territory (Gunawan 2004: 72). Unlike the Basic Agrarian Law, the new Forestry Law excluded existing *adat* laws through Article 17: 'The enjoyment of *adat* rights, whether individual or communal, to exploit forest resources directly or indirectly [...] may not be allowed to disturb the attainment of the purposes of this law' (Ross 2001: 168, cited in Gunawan 2004: 72).

Suharto's top-down agenda of *pembangunan* (development) as well as the practice of Outer Indonesia's economic extraction for the sake of the centre's progress thus deepened the gap between the Inner and Outer Islands. Jakarta, the 'colonizer of [the] outer regions' (Charras 2005: 88), imposed a unifying administrative apparatus on the whole nation. Through the government's centralisation impetus, Outer Indonesia, at least since the 1960s, represented the idea of the state's marginalised periphery, or, as Charras states: 'Outer Indonesia was left without any prospects' (2005: 88). Along the lines of Shils' postulation of a central place in society where power is bundled (see above), Java represented the absolute centre. Under Suharto, Java had become the place of reference and orientation for Indonesian society where everything and everyone had, according to national ideology, to be framed by their relationship to it (Shils 1982: 93). Javanese culture thus was supposed to serve as the overall 'Leitkultur', denying the archipelago's cultural diversity – a practice which seriously affected local power structures (cf. Introduction to this volume). However, it is important to note that although Java had evolved as the political centre, local communities had been an integrated part of several other centres that were meaningful to them, for example, regional governments, economic networks, religious associations or cultural formations.

Most local and customary leaders experienced a serious demise of their authority in favour of centre-based administrative regulations. Local initiatives were hard to invoke since every project needed to be redirected through the centre. The cultural diversity that had gained attention during the colonial period was now regarded as something derogatory, and indigenous communities were no longer perceived as a symbol of diversity but were instead unified under an 'overriding common cultural pattern – that is by their alleged "primitive" nature' (Colchester 1986: 91). The government strived for modernity and development, and invented a new strategy to make sure that the nation followed by identifying possible obstructive factors in this process: 'a "by-product" of this dynamic development was the creation of categories of marginal peoples: people [...] who refused or were refused the experience of modernity' (Kuipers 1998: 15).

Indigenous communities received a new entitlement in this period – *suku terasing*, a term invented by the government in 1976, meaning isolated tribe. In 1987, it was replaced by *masyarakat terasing* (isolated community) (Duncan 2004). As stated above, a centre is generally in constant need of its periphery since it is the margin's fundamental difference that forms the centre's pre-eminence in the first place. Both are therefore deeply entangled with each other not only by economic and political but also symbolic means. The margins, according to Shields (1991), portray the opposite of the centre, i.e. all those aspects that the centre tries to repress. During the New Order, the marginality of upland groups was in this regard interpreted as backwardness. Opposed to Suharto's objective of development and modernity, the marginality of upland groups was therefore marked by socio-cultural aspects that included, for example, swidden agriculture, in contrast to state promoted wet-rice cultivation, a nomadic or semi-nomadic mode of subsistence that opposed the national idea of permanent settlement units, or the lack of an officially recognised religion but adherence to indigenous belief systems. Indigenous communities during the New Order period would thus 'represent the antithesis of nationalist goals and aspirations' (Atkinson 1983: 689).

Against this background the New Order government invented a whole new state programme, the *Pembinaan Kesejahteraan Masyarakat Terasing* (PKSMT), which was administered by Indonesia's Department of Social Affairs (DEPSOS) and targeted especially 'remote' or 'isolated' people (*masyarakat terpencil* or *masyarakat terasing*) (Haba 1998: 2). One initiative of the PKSMT can be found in resettlement programmes, which became an important tool to move upland groups, in the name of development, into lowland areas where they would be able to profit from access to the state apparatus. The roots of this initiative can be found in identical colonial strategies, which in 1950 were simply revitalised through DEPSOS (Haba 1998). During the New Order regime these resettlement initiatives were a common procedure in Indonesia and aimed at transforming supposedly isolated and primitive uplanders into modern citizens of the Indonesian nation state by assembling them in centralised, administrative villages, following the national idea of *pembangunan* (Li 1999c: 302).

This 'discovery' of marginal people by the Indonesian state in the New Order period thus underlines the aforementioned process of exclusion by a single centre (Shields 1991), the Indonesian, Java-oriented state, that, in search of a counterpart to its own modernity, represented indigenous people as a negative reflection of its own progress.

Post-New Order Indonesia – margins as a site of opportunity

After the downfall of Suharto in 1998, a new era of government made way for the process of general decentralisation within the Indonesian state. With the enactment of regional autonomy, Law 22/1999 transferred a great amount of political power to local authorities. While those aspects which were considered strategic, such as foreign affairs, remained under central control, natural resources and conservation, among others, became regional responsibility (Resosudarmo 2004: 107).[8] The legal situation, however, remained unclear since Forestry Law 41/1999, in general, continued the line of the former Basic Forestry Law and kept a centralist approach towards forest regulation, leading to 'considerable conflict among the various levels and branches of government, and resulting in various incongruencies such as the granting of overlapping forest concessions and development of conflicting forest practice laws' (McDermott *et al.* 2010: 171). This ambiguous legal framework supports what Dunne (2005, see above) has postulated as the plurality of margins and centres. While customary land rights are subject to national law, with the invention of regional autonomy they had also become subject to regional law, leading to a confusing and complex situation of land rights. Forest regulation thus remained and remains weak, and still ignores upland communities and their customary rights. The effects of unjust land regulations are particularly relevant for those people living in Indonesia's forest areas such as the Wana of Central Sulawesi, who under the New Order government were regarded as a backward indigenous group and an obstacle for the overall drive for modernity. However, the governments succeeding Suharto still lacked serious efforts to back indigenous peoples' rights.

Because the legal situation for their land has remained unclear, the Wana have recently become involved in the politics of the so-called *masyarakat adat* movement. The constant danger of land loss and enforced resettlement has led several Wana to establish new networks with a number of NGOs. The acquisition of the status of *masyarakat adat* brought with it a new attitude towards their position as a marginalised people, leading to what might be called empowerment through marginality (Grumblies 2013).

The *masyarakat adat*[9] movement was born out of grassroots organisations like WALHI, Friends of the Earth Indonesia (*Wahana Lingkungan Hidup Indonesia*), which in the 1980s started to deal with the legal standing of indigenous people in the country. In 1999, these early initiatives culminated in the first congress and founding of the biggest *masyarakat adat* organisation of Indonesia called AMAN (*Aliansi Masyarakat Adat Nusantara*), the Indigenous Peoples' Alliance of the Archipelago. With AMAN, formerly muted indigenous communities had now developed a powerful voice in the struggle for recognition and just treatment. Now the potential of Indonesia's margins as productive fields of agency, or in bell hooks' words, a 'site of radical possibility, a space of resistance' (1990: 341) became visible. After having been defined for decades as estranged, isolated and backward people, the new appellation as a *masyarakat adat* marked a new era of self-determination for these communities. They are defined, according to AMAN, as

> communities that live on the basis of their hereditary ancestral origins in a specific customary territory, that possess sovereignty over their land and natural riches, whose socio-cultural life is ordered by customary law, and whose customary institutions manage the continuity of their social life.
>
> (AMAN n.d., quoted in Acciaioli 2007: 299)

The term *masyarakat adat* is deeply infused with claims to indigenous rights and recognition of communities that have suffered various forms of marginalisation; it is thus a political term that offers multi-faceted meanings, hopes, expectations and claims for communities that declare themselves as *masyarakat adat*, diverse as they are. The process of decentralisation and democratisation after Suharto's downfall thus inaugurated a new era for formerly marginalised peoples and 'offered the opportunity to the indigenous peoples (*masyarakat adat*) and to the government to recover the injustices and dispossessions which these people had suffered' (Hauser-Schäublin 2013: 7). By means of marginality, this process tremendously reconfigured the idea of power and notion of opportunity. With the rise of AMAN indigenous communities had formulated another form of symbolic centre that opposed the national as well as local centres by challenging hegemonic structures and rules as well as derogatory practices. At the same time, the embracement of a status as an indigenous community had become a tool of empowerment.

Deeply connected to the *masyarakat adat* movement is a new trend in forest and land rights regulations that focuses more on customary land rights. On 16 May 2013, the Indonesian Constitutional Court announced in Decision No. 35/ PUU-X that customary forests are no longer declared as state forests. This case was based on a petition by AMAN and two indigenous communities filed in March 2012 (Arizona and Cahyadi 2013: 53). It basically objected to the Forestry Law of 1999, which ignored customary rights of local communities to land and forest in favour of issuing concessions over natural resources to commercial enterprises. With the state's decision, approval by customary land holders thus became mandatory, and AMAN celebrated the decision as the return of rights to around 40 million indigenous communities in Indonesia (Butt 2014: 59). The new legislation was perceived as a serious breakthrough in the fight for indigenous rights within the country, but to this day, the results remain unclear.[10]

Upland marginalisation processes in Indonesia meanwhile continue, not only in terms of land rights but also for example in terms of the indigenous struggle for an official recognition of local belief systems. Religious affiliation already played an important role during the New Order (cf. Introduction to this volume), but still today several upland groups do not adhere to an officially acknowledged scriptural religion. This also holds for the Wana of Central Sulawesi who are generally perceived of as people who do not yet have a religion, *orang belum beragama*.[11] Apart from the issue of official recognition, for Wana, adherence to their own belief system is furthermore deeply connected to their own understanding of their marginal standing, as it differs profoundly from national and other ascriptions and has its roots in a cosmological explanation.

Wana explain their current marginality with the loss of a golden era that constituted Wana in the past as a powerful community possessing magical knowledge, wealth and power. According to oral tradition, the golden era ended when a special group of Wana's powerful allies, the *taw baraka*, went to another place at the end of the world. Wana were left in a state of misery and poverty that lasts until today. However, they expect that one day the *taw baraka* will come back as long as the Wana remain in their current marginal position. The return of the *taw baraka* will usher in a new golden era for Wana people (e.g. Atkinson 1989: 44; Grumblies 2013). Wana thus obtain a self-ascribed marginalised standing within the Indonesian society, which is deeply intertwined with cosmological narratives and a millenarian movement. They have constructed their very own cosmological centre that serves as a central point of reference and reveals an indigenous understanding and justification of their marginal position.

This perspective underlines the diversity of positions that are meaningful for the construction of marginality and highlights the importance of the perspective of those who are deemed marginal for understanding the relation between centre and periphery that is referred to in the first part of this chapter. Wana, just like other communities and individuals, are always embedded in a number of centres and margins. Thereby Wana also refer to a national centre to explain their political and economic marginal status, a centre that is in some ways analogous to Indonesian state power and becomes especially meaningful in terms of land rights, as is shown above. With the *masyarakat adat* movement, Wana have found yet another opportunity to reformulate their marginality and to oppose state-centred initiatives. Wana cultural construction of their marginality thereby underlines the insecurity of categories and centres. As Tsing has stated, margins are 'zones of unpredictability at the edges of discursive stability, where contradictory discourses overlap, or where discrepant kinds of meaning-making converge' (Tsing 1994: 279). It is precisely their unsteady character that makes margins a highly potential analytical field of study.

Conclusion

As shown in the beginning of this chapter, marginality has become a standard relational term in anthropological discourse to guide debates on social and economic inequalities. Marginality is always subject to power relations. Margins are not simply geographical locations, natural facts or locations, which are easily traceable, nor are they 'sites of deviance of social norms' (Tsing 1994: 279). Taking an analytic perspective from the margin offers a valuable comprehension of the goals, mechanisms and functions of the centre and its multiple modes of power operating to constitute itself and its edges (Tsing 1994: 279). Land rights, for example, can serve as a starting point for identifying structural disadvantages for people living in the periphery. In this context, land struggles also display analytical markers of marginalisation processes and further depict the role of agency connected to it.

The works of scholars like Shields and Tsing have revolutionised the idea of marginality, revealing the potential that marginal spheres have for resisting and counteracting hierarchical centre–periphery relations. In Indonesia marginality, exemplified in this chapter by the changing role of upland groups within the state, is deeply connected to state ambitions and perceptions of cultural difference. The era of decentralisation has resulted in developments that have taken on the potential of the margins as sites of opportunities, in critiquing the centre and questioning dualist notions of centre and periphery. People's socio-religious, economic and political environments on Indonesia's Outer Islands are comprised by and related to hegemonic schemes, which constitute them as peripheral. The Wana, for example, have developed their own specific perspective on constellations of centres and margins. This perspective reveals that the margins have never been solely reliant on a supposed centre, but always managed to find their own ways independent of nationalist agendas, thereby continuously reformulating centre–periphery relations. Considering marginality as an essential concept for Indonesia's periphery, it is thus the politics of state power on the one hand, and the performance and cultural construction of marginality on the other, that significantly shape hierarchical relations between margins and centres.

Notes

1 Dowdy further points to the fact that many fields

> employ 'margins' and 'centres' as conceptual metrics to grasp the hierarchical entailments of socio-historical flux. Moreover, much of this literature unites normative and descriptive methods, thereby giving 'margins' a rhetorical charge it often lacks in ordinary discourse.
>
> (Dowdy 2011: 2)

2 By this means the spatial dimension of marginality, which is commonly described as geographical or physical marginality, becomes relevant. The distance to infrastructure or economic centres is always a relational concept. Unequal allocation of economic goods and income relations are factors that determine marginality, while local environments as well as cultural settings further add to the spatial condition of marginality. Yet spatial marginality is never a question of sheer geographical location. Detailed studies, for example, have analysed urban marginality, which in terms of space is directly located within the centre's core (e.g. Mehretu *et al.* 2000; Hopper 2003).

3 Original quote by Foucault:

> One must not suppose that there exists a certain sphere of sexuality that would be the legitimate concern of a free and disinterested scientific inquiry were it not the object of mechanisms of prohibition brought to bear by the economic or ideological requirements of power. If sexuality was constituted as an area of investigation, this was only because relations of power had established it as a possible object.
>
> (Foucault 1978: 98)

4 Such relations are also referred to as relations between *hulu* (BI), meaning upstream, and *hilir* (BI), meaning downstream (Andaya 1993).

5 However, there were also occasional upland–lowland relations that presented a different picture, as Andaya reminds us. In some cases upstream communities were authoritative powers because the lowland states were suffering heavily under malaria in the coastal swamplands, or were often subjects of coastal attacks (Andaya 1993: 92).

6 Translation by Hooker (1975: 291f.), cited in Acciaioli (2007: 311).

7 Furthermore, provincial governments had been equipped with the right to hand out forest concessions up to 10,000 hectares and to manage their region's natural resources independently.

8 The situation became further complicated with government regulation 6/1999, which gave districts the authority to hand out small-scale timber licences for areas of at most 100 hectares, but only in areas where no large-scale concessions had previously been issued (Resosudarmo 2004: 112).

9 For a discussion of the development of the category *masyarakat adat* see Acciaioli (2007), Moniaga (2007) and von Benda-Beckmann and von Benda-Beckmann (2011); for a legal analysis of the term see Arizona and Cahyadi (2013).

10 Butt (2014) draws a rather pessimistic picture: Indonesia's court cannot induce its regulations to national parliament but rather can review statutes against the constitution. Most cases that affect indigenous communities are challenging 'statutes granting the state legal authority to issue concessions. However, that authority is usually exercised by way of subordinate regulations – most commonly ministerial decrees or local government bylaws' (Butt 2014: 71). A second reason can be found in the fact that the court so far has not paid attention to the 'practical difficulties facing traditional communities to achieve formal "recognition" of their status as such' (Butt 2014: 72). The *Jakarta Post* noted that

> [u]nder Environment and Forestry Ministerial Regulation No. 12/2015, which was issued in March, the percentage of areas dedicated for local people increased to at

least 20 percent. While technical details of the regulation are still being formulated, the association is worried that the government would require its members to reduce the size of their existing industrial forest area to fulfill the 20 percent quota for use by local communities.

(Amin 2015)

11 In a nation that gives first priority to the Belief in One God, as formulated in *Pancasila*, non-recognition of indigenous faith becomes especially meaningful. Citizens have had to state their religious affiliation on their identity cards since the New Order, forcing indigenous groups either to register under an official religion or to leave the column blank. It was only recently that the state announced that also 'followers of indigenous faiths would have to cite their religious preferences on ID cards' (Aritonang 2015), a first step towards official recognition.

References

Acciaioli, G. (2007) From Customary Law to Indigenous Sovereignty: Reconceptualizing Masyarakat Adat in Contemporary Indonesia, in J.S. Davidson and D. Henley (eds), *The Revival of Tradition in Indonesian Politics: The Deployment of Adat from Colonialism to Indigenism*, London and New York: Routledge, pp. 295–318.

AMAN (n.d.) *Menyatukan Gerak Langkah Menuju Kedaulatan Masyarakat Adat: Buku Panduan Umum bagi Pengurus, Anggota dan Pendukung*. Jakarta: Sekretariat Nasional Aliansi Masyarakat Adat Nusantara.

Amin, K. (2015) New Ruling Upsets Forestry Firms, *The Jakarta Post*, 8 July 2015.

Andaya, B.W. (1993) Cash Cropping and Upstream-Downstream Tensions: The Case of Jambi in the Seventeenth and Eighteenth Centuries, in A.J. Reid (ed.), *Southeast Asia in the Early Modern Era: Trade, Power, and Belief*, Ithaca, NY: Cornell University Press, pp. 91–122.

Appadurai, A. (1988) Putting Hierarchy in Its Place, *Cultural Anthropology* 3(1): 36–49.

Aritonang, M. (2015) Indigenous Faiths Allowed on ID Card, *The Jakarta Post*, 20 May 2015.

Arizona, Y. and Cahyadi, E. (2013) The Revival of Indigenous Peoples: Contestations over a Special Legislation on Masyarakat Adat, in B. Hauser-Schäublin (ed.), *Adat and Indigeneity in Indonesia: Culture and Entitlements between Heteronomy and Self-Ascription*, Göttingen: Universitätsverlag, pp. 43–62.

Asad, T. (1973) *Anthropology and the Colonial Encounter*. London: Ithaca.

Atkinson, J. (1983) Religions in Dialogue: The Construction of an Indonesian Minority Religion, *American Ethnologist* 10(4): 684–696.

Atkinson, J. (1989) *The Art and Politics of Wana Shamanship*. Berkeley, CA: University of California Press.

Benda-Beckmann, F. von and K. von Benda-Beckmann (2011) Myths and Stereotypes about Adat Law: A Reassessment of Van Vollenhoven in the Light of Current Struggles over Adat Law in Indonesia, *Bijdragen tot de Taal-, Land- en Volkenkunde* 167(2/3): 167–195.

Butt, S. (2014) Traditional Land Rights before the Indonesian Constitutional Court, *Law, Environment & Development Journal* 10(1): 57–73.

Charras, M. (2005) The Reshaping of the Indonesian Archipelago after 50 Years of Regional Imbalance, in M. Erb, P. Sulistiyanto and C. Faucher (eds), *Regionalism in Post-Suharto Indonesia*, London and New York: Routledge, pp. 87–108.

Cleary, M.E.P (1996) *Tradition and Reform: Land Tenure and Rural Development in South-East Asia*. Kuala Lumpur and New York: Oxford University Press.

Colchester, M. (1986) Unity and Diversity: Indonesia's Policy towards Tribal Peoples, *The Ecologist* 16(2/3): 89–98.

Douglas, M. (1966) *Purity and Danger: An Analysis of Concepts of Pollution and Taboo*. London: Routledge.

Dowdy, S.M. (2011) Adorning the Margins, *Margins: A Journal of Literature and Culture* 1(1): 1–46.

Duncan, C. (2004) From Development to Empowerment: Changing Indonesian Government Policies toward Indigenous Minorities, in C. Duncan (ed.), *Civilizing the Margins: Southeast Asian Government Policies for the Development of Minorities*, New York: Cornell University Press, pp. 86–115.

Dunne, R.J. (2005) Marginality: A Conceptual Extension, in R.M. Dennis (ed.), *Marginality, Power and Social Structure: Issues in Race, Class, and Gender Analysis*, Amsterdam: Elsevier, pp. 11–28.

Fabian, J. (1983) *Time and the Other: How Anthropology Makes Its Object*. New York: Columbia University Press.

Fasseur, C. (2007) Colonial Dilemma: Van Vollenhoven and the Struggle between Adat Law and Western Law in Indonesia, in J.S. Davidson and D. Henley (eds), *The Revival of Tradition in Indonesian Politics: The Deployment of Adat from Colonialism to Indigenism*, London and New York: Routledge, pp. 50–67.

Ferguson, R. (ed.) (1990) *Out There: Marginalization and Contemporary Cultures*. Cambridge, MA: MIT Press.

Foucault, M. (1978) *The History of Sexuality. Volume 1: An Introduction*. New York: Pantheon.

Grumblies, A.-T. (2013) Being Wana, Becoming an 'Indigenous People': Experimenting with Indigeneity in Central Sulawesi, in B. Hauser-Schäublin (ed.), *Adat and Indigeneity in Indonesia: Culture and Entitlements between Heteronomy and Self-Ascription*, Göttingen: Universitätsverlag, pp. 81–98.

Gunawan, I.K. (2004) *The Politics of the Indonesian Rainforest: A Rise of Forest Conflicts in East Kalimantan during Indonesia's Early Stage of Democratisation*. Göttingen: Cuvillier.

Haba, J. (1998) *Resettlement and Sociocultural Change among the Isolated Peoples in Central Sulawesi, Indonesia: A Study of Three Resettlement Sites*, PhD Thesis, University of Western Australia.

Harms, E., Hussain, S., Newell, S., Piot, C., Schein, L., Shneiderman, S., Turner, T.S. and Zhang, J. (2014) Remote and Edgy: New Takes on Old Anthropological Themes, *HAU: Journal of Ethnographic Theory* 4: 361–381.

Hauser-Schäublin, B. (2013) Introduction: The Power of Indigeneity. Reparation, Readjustments and Repositioning, in B. Hauser-Schäublin (ed.), *Adat and Indigeneity in Indonesia: Culture and Entitlements between Heteronomy and Self-Ascription*, Göttingen: Universitätsverlag, pp. 5–15.

Henley, D. (1989) *The Idea of Celebes in History*. Working paper, Centre of Southeast Asian Studies. Clayton: Monash University.

Hooker, M.B. (1975) *Legal Pluralism: An Introduction to Colonial and Neo-Colonial Laws*. Oxford: Clarendon Press.

hooks, b. (1990) Marginality as a Site of Resistance, in R. Ferguson (ed.), *Out There: Marginalization and Contemporary Cultures*, Cambridge, MA: MIT Press, pp. 341–343.

Hopper, K. (2003) *Reckoning with Homelessness*. Ithaca, NY: Cornell University Press.

Hussain, S. (2009) *A History of Marginality: Nature and Culture in the Western Himalayas*, PhD Thesis, Yale University.

Kahn, J.S. (1999) Culturalising the Indonesian Uplands, in T.M. Li (ed.), *Transforming the Indonesian Uplands: Marginality, Power and Production*, Amsterdam: Harwood, pp. 81–106.

Kuipers, J.C. (1998) *Language, Identity, and Marginality in Indonesia: The Changing Nature of Ritual Speech on the Island of Sumba*. Cambridge: Cambridge University Press.

Li, T.M. (1999a) Introduction, in T.M. Li (ed.), *Transforming the Indonesian Uplands: Marginality, Power and Production*, Amsterdam: Harwood, pp. xiii–xxiv.

Li, T.M. (1999b) Marginality, Power and Production: Analysing Upland Transformations, in T.M. Li (ed.), *Transforming the Indonesian Uplands: Marginality, Power and Production*, Amsterdam: Harwood, pp. 1–45.

Li, T.M. (1999c) Compromising Power: Development, Culture, and Rule in Indonesia, *Cultural Anthropology* 14(3): 295–322.

Li, T.M. (2000) Articulating Indigenous Identity in Indonesia: Resource Politics and the Tribal Slot, *Comparative Studies in Society and History* 42(1): 149–179.

Li, T.M. (2001) Relational Histories and the Production of Difference on Sulawesi's Upland Frontier, *Journal of Asian Studies* 60(1): 41–66.

McDermott, C.L., Cashore, B. and Kanowski, P. (2010) *Global Environmental Forest Policies: An International Comparison*. London: Earthscan.

Mehretu, A., Pigozzi, B. and Sommer, L.M. (2000) Concepts in Social and Spatial Marginality, *Human Geography* 82(2): 89–101.

Moniaga, S. (2007) From Bumiputera to Masyarakat Adat: A Long and Confusing Journey, in J.S. Davidson and D. Henley (eds), *The Revival of Tradition in Indonesian Politics: The Deployment of Adat from Colonialism to Indigenism*, London and New York: Routledge, pp. 275–294.

Ortiz, A. (1969) *The Tewa World: Space, Time, Being, and Becoming in a Pueblo Society*. Chicago, IL: University of Chicago Press.

Peluso, N., Afiff, S. and Rachman, N.F. (2008) Claiming the Grounds for Reform: Agrarian and Environmental Movements in Indonesia, *Journal of Agrarian Change* 8(2–3): 377–407.

Resosudarmo, I. (2004) Closer to Peoples and Trees: Will Decentralisation Work for the People and the Forests of Indonesia?, *European Journal of Development Research* 16(1): 110–132.

Rösing, I. (2000) Creative Self-Marginalisation, *India International Centre Quarterly* 27(2): 89–104.

Ross, M.L. (2001) *Timber Booms and Institutional Breakdown in Southeast Asia: Political Economy of Institutions and Decisions*. Cambridge and New York: Cambridge University Press.

Röttger-Rössler, B. and Stodulka, T. (2014) Introduction: The Emotional Make-up of Marginality and Stigma, in T. Stodulka and B. Röttger-Rössler (eds), *Feelings at the Margins: Dealing with Violence, Stigma and Isolation in Indonesia*, Frankfurt and New York: Campus, pp. 11–29.

Said, E.W. (1995) *Orientalism: Western Conceptions of the Orient*. Reprint. London: Penguin.

Scholte, B. (1987) The Literary Turn in Contemporary Anthropology, *Critique of Anthropology* 7(1): 33–47.

Schrauwers, A. (2000) *Colonial 'Reformation' in the Highlands of Central Sulawesi, Indonesia, 1892–1995*, Toronto: University of Toronto Press.

Shields, R. (1991) *Places on the Margin: Alternative Geographies of Modernity*. London and New York: Routledge.

Shils, E. (1982) Center and Periphery, in E. Shils (ed.), *The Constitution of Society*, Chicago, IL: University of Chicago Press, pp. 93–109.

Spivak, G.C. (1988) Can the Subaltern Speak?, in C. Nelson (ed.), *Marxism and the Interpretation of Culture*, Basingstoke: Macmillan, pp. 271–313.

Spivak, G.C. (1993) *Outside in the Teaching Machine*. London: Routledge.

Stallybrass, P. and White, A. (1986) *The Politics and Poetics of Transgression*. Ithaca, NY: Cornell University Press.

Steedly, M. (1999) The State of Culture Theory in the Anthropology of Southeast Asia, *Annual Review of Anthropology* 28(1): 431–454.

Tambiah, S. (1977) The Galactic Polity: The Structure of Traditional Kingdoms in Southeast Asia, *Annals of the New York Academy of Science* 293: 69–97.

Tsing, A.L. (1993) *In the Realm of the Diamond Queen: Marginality in an Out-of-the-Way Place*. Princeton, NJ: Princeton University Press.

Tsing, A.L. (1994) From the Margins, *Cultural Anthropology* 9(3): 279–297.

Wallace, J. (2008) Indonesian Land Law and Administration, in T. Lindsey (ed.), *Indonesia: Law and Society*, 2nd edition, Sydney: Federation Press, pp. 191–223.

Part II
Borders, identities and belonging

4   The edge of glory

Theorising centre–periphery relations in and from Indonesia's Riau Islands

Nicholas J. Long

The Riau Archipelago is a place where people love to talk about centres and peripheries. When I told Pak Iman, a politics lecturer at a local university, that I was writing a paper on the topic, he almost fell off his chair. 'It's the most interesting thing you've ever worked on!' he exclaimed, 'That's a paper I definitely want to read'. He went on to outline many issues that my paper could potentially address. The new regional autonomy laws had made centre–periphery relations a 'hot topic', with intense debate surrounding the administrative ambiguities they had precipitated. Who, for example, had the authority to issue a contract for bauxite mining in the newly created Riau Islands Province (popularly and here-after known as Kepri): the local district heads, the governor or the central ministries in Jakarta? A local district head had recently redrawn the boundaries of a protected forest to facilitate resource extraction – but was this really within his jurisdiction? These were the kinds of issues, Pak Iman felt, where research was desperately required.

Vina, a local historian, was hoping I would write an account grounded in the longue durée. The Riau Islands had, she noted, once been a major centre in and of themselves: in the seventeenth century the island of Bintan had hosted one of the liveliest trading posts in Southeast Asia, while the sultan's and viceroy's palaces on Lingga and Bintan had been the epicentres of one of the Malay world's most important indigenous polities. Yet, after the territory encompassed by this sultanate was bifurcated by the 1824 Treaty of London, the Riau Islands had become a marginal backwater within the Dutch East Indies, their strategic significance rapidly eclipsed by the rise of Singapore. Things had changed further during the twentieth century, as the archipelago witnessed waves of migration from all across Indonesia: its low levels of conflict, numerous job opportunities (in factories, mining and small-scale entrepreneurship), and wide-spread circulation of strong Singaporean and Malaysian currency all attracting Indonesians in search of a new beginning. Others still hoped to use Kepri as a stepping-stone to migrant work overseas, but ended up getting stuck. As a consequence of these demographic shifts (described in more detail in Long 2013: 30–43), the islands boasted an impressively multicultural population. However, this in itself led many Riau Malays – who conceptualised themselves as the 'indigenous people' of the region – to feel they had become peripheral. The 2010 census estimated Malays to make up less than 30 per cent of the province's population – just 14.4 per cent in the city of Batam (Minnesota Population Center 2011) – and many will not even have been 'indigenous' Riau Malays, but migrants from Borneo, Bangka-Belitung or the Sumatran mainland. For Vina, then, the possibilities afforded by regional autonomy – most especially the formation of a new province, created 'in the name of the Malay people' – were important precisely because they allowed Kepri and its Malays to be 'at the centre' of something once again. This, she thought, would be a good story to tell in my paper. I could even note how a handful of Riau Islanders were going even further and arguing that Kepri should detach from Indonesia altogether, forming a new Republic of Riau, or reconnecting with the Singaporean and/or South Malaysian territories over which it had once presided (see Faucher 2005).

If Pak Iman or Vina ever read this chapter, they may be disappointed. The issues they flag are interesting, certainly, but they are stories that have already been told elsewhere.[1] More significantly, they are quite problematic stories to reiterate yet again. Vina's narrative risks overstating the extent to which the history of the Malay world shapes contemporary political imaginations, and thereby silencing the migrant majority whose claims to place are grounded in principles of citizenship, rather than autochthony (Long 2013). Pak Iman's research agenda reflects genuine problems that are much discussed among Kepri's educated elite: academics, civil servants, journalists and activists. However, the vast majority of Riau Islanders are far too preoccupied with the mundane business of everyday life to give such matters much thought, and so an investigation into those issues would do little to capture what either decentralisation or the simple fact of living in the Outer Islands means to *them*. Even when people offer up narratives like Vina's or Pak Iman's, these may not be the only (or even the most important) ways in which they think and feel about their position in Indonesia's geographic margins – they may simply be the most familiar and most readily articulated narratives available. This would not be surprising: both narratives ultimately have their roots in an epistemology of centre–periphery relations that derives from the institutions and knowledge practices of the modern state, and so reflect stories that informants with backgrounds in the civil service or political activism have been trained to know how to tell. Problems arise, however, when a similar bias is replicated within academic approaches to centre–periphery relations – and as this chapter will demonstrate, that very much remains the case. The result is a situation in which Indonesianists are well-positioned to appreciate the impacts of decentralisation upon statecraft and political movements, but have achieved only a partial grasp of how Indonesia's recent transformations have affected 'the construction of marginality' (see Introduction to this volume) in its broadest sense.

I therefore want to use this chapter to expand the conversation, by giving centre-stage to the political imaginations of people who did not often talk about centre–periphery relations but who nevertheless revealed themselves to be profoundly invested in them. These investments came to the fore in intense, affectively charged moments, the study of which reveals that decentralisation can be as much about the desire for connection as it can be about autonomy; that life in a borderland can engender distinctive responsibilities towards a centre; and that the bodily and psychic legacies of past marginality continue to stand out as problems in the decentralised present. Taken as a whole, the material indicates that we should avoid any hasty conclusions about the 'effects' of decentralisation, as if administrative reforms in and of themselves are capable of creating new 'centre–periphery relations'. My argument instead is that decentralisation has created new conditions of possibility under which Indonesians can attempt to realise the imaginaries of 'centre–periphery relations' that are meaningful and desirable to them – and that the affects and ethics that underpin local ideas about how Indonesia's periphery should relate to its centre should therefore take centre-stage in analysis. Although the chapter concentrates exclusively on the Riau Island case, this broader theoretical argument would apply to any of the regions discussed in this volume.

Metanarratives of marginality: a critical review

To date, much writing on centre–periphery relations in Indonesia has been inflected by theoretical models associated with structural Marxism, especially Wallerstein's (2004) 'world-systems theory', which draws a sharp analytic distinction between regions that can be designated as 'the core' – those that hold the greatest amount of economic power – and the 'peripheries', which supply resources, commodities and manpower to that core (Pitzl 2004: 38). The core–periphery relation is thus conceptualised as an inherently antagonistic one marked by domination and exploitation. Indeed, some scholars who built on Wallerstein's framework (e.g. Hechter 1975) included in their models descriptions not only of expropriation, but of accompanying cultural denigration and political marginalisation of the 'periphery' by the central 'core' or 'metropole' as well.

This analytic vocabulary of periphery and centre/core/metropole has given rise to several patterns in academic approaches to 'centre–periphery relations' in Indonesia. Some scholars, most notably those affiliated with the discipline of economic geography, have been concerned with mapping the changing configurations of 'centre' and 'periphery' as economic relations in Southeast Asia have become increasingly transnational under a regime of globalised 'late capitalism'. This question is particularly complex in the Riau Archipelago given the creation of an international 'Growth Triangle' scheme between Indonesia, Malaysia and Singapore, in which the Riau Islands serve as a cross-border 'hinterland' for Singapore. Factories set up on the islands combine Singaporean management expertise with cheap Indonesian land and labour, offering an attractive package to clients, while Singapore has access to some of Bintan's plentiful natural resources, most notably its scenic northern coastline (now developed into an 'international resort area') and its water. Scholars were quick to identify this as a 'cross-border hinterlandisation' of Singapore's economy (Bunnell *et al.* 2012: 466) – a sign that the Riau Islands had become a periphery to Singapore's centre, even as this process was being carefully managed by the central Indonesian government in Jakarta (Phelps 2004: 217).

Such analyses have certainly led to the development of increasingly subtle and complex renderings of the means by which the jurisdiction of international political and financial 'centres' is exercised in a globalised world (e.g. Goldblum and Wong 2000; Ong 2000) – a development that makes a significant contribution to our understanding of political economy. Yet the *character* of the centre–periphery relation within such work remains sketched in an analytically conservative way, as indeed it must if the endeavour of charting emergent new configurations of centre–periphery relations is to make any sense. As a consequence, however, the question of precisely how Riau Islanders and Singaporeans might imagine their mutual encounters is left aside, despite the crucial role that such perceptions play in shaping both lived experience in the region and the concrete outcomes of cross-border collaborations (Long 2013: 201–204).

A second body of literature has paid more attention to the mutability of relations between Indonesia's centre and its peripheral regions, an issue of increasing significance once the post-Suharto regional autonomy laws offered up new opportunities for these relations to be recalibrated. However, the *level* at which such recalibration is investigated is typically a relatively formal, abstracted conception of the 'balance of power'. Such an approach continues to assume an underlying antagonism between centre and periphery, as consistent with the structural Marxist model. The periphery has been conceptualised as resentful of the way its resources were being expropriated by its centre, of the heavy-handed imposition of centrally appointed bureaucrats to manage regional affairs and of the cultural hegemony that typically accompanied this (Diprose 2009: 108–111; Kimura 2010: 426). From this point of view, decentralisation – as well as the flourishing of regional-level democracy that it was believed to inculcate – serves as a means of ensuring the longevity of the Indonesian nation state. By relieving long-standing tensions through a rebalancing of power, and giving the periphery relative autonomy, decentralisation was seen as 'reconciling' the regions with 'a centre that had systematically undermined their local identities since the 1950s' (Aspinall 2010: 22).

This assessment remains the most dominant metanarrative of centre–periphery relations within contemporary Indonesian Studies. It is not without its merits, and illuminates many of the social and political struggles that took place in the early years of *Reformasi*, both within and outside the Riau Islands. The separatist movement *Riau Merdeka*, for example, premised its legitimacy on correcting the injustice that had led oil-rich Riau to be the second poorest province in Sumatra, despite generating an estimated 20 per cent of Indonesia's total wealth (Long 2013: 47). Analysing a parallel separatist movement among Malay-Bugis aristocrats in the Riau Islands,[2] Vivienne Wee (2002: 500) notes that the movement was underpinned by a resentment of the cultural hegemonies visited upon the region by Jakarta, coupled with a 'logic of power' in which the periphery paid formal lip service to the official narratives promulgated by the centre, while preserving in informal spaces of everyday life a second narrative, inspired by memories of the precolonial sultanate, that could form the basis of an alternative sovereignty movement. Even away from the spheres of formally organised separatism, informants would sometimes tell me of how their province had placed too much faith in the central administration provided by Jakarta and would benefit from having a greater degree of autonomy over its own affairs. I encountered such sentiments most frequently among members of the civil service, who would have encountered constraints being placed upon their own agency by regulations coming from the centre. The dominant metanarrative of decentralisation is thus far from irrelevant to the Riau Islands case, but it is only one – highly situated – imaginary of what was involved in lobbying to become a new province. For many Riau Islanders, a somewhat different set of issues was at stake.

As noted by Booth (2011), Quinn (2003) and Kimura (2007, 2010), many of the political movements set in motion by the decentralisation process were directed not at Jakarta but rather at attempting to secure autonomy from *regional* centres. Examples include the creation of new provinces in Gorontalo, West Sulawesi and Banten, and the calls for greater autonomy in Madura, Luwu and Toraja. In Kimura's (2007: 72) view, such movements can best be understood as responses to a condition of 'marginality in the periphery', in which a population feels held back by the actions of their regional government and thus at a disadvantage in terms of infrastructure, economic opportunities, services and skills, compared to other members of the same district, regency or province. In some cases the regional centre might be considered guilty of discriminatory practice towards those under its jurisdiction on the basis of their ethnicity and/or religion – a condition experienced by the Gorontalese with reference to the administration offered from Manado, in North Sulawesi (Kimura 2007: 74–85). A sense of 'marginality in the periphery' could also emerge from a centre's perceived or actual failures to invest in a province's remote outer regions. Both such themes were evident in the Riau Islands, where there was widespread dissatisfaction with the region's administration from the Mainland Sumatran city of Pekanbaru, which my informants told me was dominated by mainland Sumatran ethnic groups and had preferentially invested in mainland development projects rather than the archipelagic Malay heartlands, leaving the islands – which had once been a vibrant and wealthy region of Indonesia – little more than a stagnant backwater. Thus, although some actors in the islands (such as the Malay-Bugis aristocrats mentioned above) hoped that the archipelago might become as free from Indonesian rule as possible,[3] the majority simply wanted to be free of interference from Pekanbaru. It was to this effect that a campaign to create a new province was initiated. As a result, we should be cautious about seeing the enthusiastic embrace of decentralisation laws within the region as being a negative judgement of Jakarta as national centre. Not only does the creation of a new province require the active co-operation of political actors within the central government (Kimura 2010: 442), it can also reflect a desire within the marginal periphery to get a greater degree of unmediated access to the national centre, which in many regards represents a powerful and desirable resource (Wollenberg *et al.* 2009: 7).[4]

In short, decentralisation may not have been about pulling away from the centre so much as about engaging it more directly, and on more equal terms. Although this involved a tug away from the stymieing control of Pekanbaru, it would be a mistake to interpret the push to decentralise as an attempt to achieve a relatively high degree of self-determination vis-à-vis the rest of Indonesia (cf. cases such as Aceh and Papua). My informants often saw it as a move towards a form of peripherality that was neither 'marginal' in terms of the social and economic wellbeing of its inhabitants, nor 'marginal' in the eyes of those who mattered – other Indonesian citizens, outsiders and indeed the government at the centre.

It could thus be perfectly logically consistent for Riau Islanders to celebrate regional autonomy and its achievements (infrastructural improvements were most widely cited on this front), and yet also hold a sense of responsibility towards, or a need to make claims upon, a 'centre' – typically Jakarta, but sometimes Singapore. Such feelings were made particularly evident in discourses surrounding one of the most negative consequences of regional autonomy: the rise of self-serving local elites, often described as 'little kings' (*raja kecil*), who exploited their capacity to grant business tenders, and who issued contracts for bauxite mining that destroyed the natural beauty and heritage of the province, as well as endangering the livelihoods of regional fishing communities. These feelings of frustration were widespread, and typically resulted in impassioned calls for the central government to intervene over tables in coffee parlours and late night domino games. Sometimes journalists, outraged by the latest announcement of a bauxite extraction project, would go up to regents directly and demand to see their letter of authorisation from the centre – a phantasmic enactment of the centralised authorities that were in fact not exercising the level of surveillance and discipline of the periphery that islanders wished they would. The regent's response – typically described as 'falling silent' or 'fleeing the scene' – would then be relayed in tones of bitter pride to the journalists' friends and colleagues, who would shake their heads and lament to each other, 'That's Indonesia!' As all this took place, however, Riau Islanders were never hoping for a return to the old days of 'centralisation'. Rather, the right to make such claims on the central government was itself a valuable part of what decentralisation had involved for them.

The affective life of a periphery

As the examples just sketched make clear, the failure of the centre to comply with islanders' expectations generated strong emotions. Such affective dimensions of centre–periphery relations has received little attention in the literature, and yet I found it to be one of the most productive ways of understanding the deep-seated investments that Indonesians who, on the surface, had very little to say about matters of national politics might nevertheless have towards the central government and to their own status as inhabitants of the Outer Islands within the nation state. One of the reasons these emotional responses proved such a profitable source of insight was that they prompted people to move beyond the conventional ways of thinking and talking about centre–periphery relations, and instead to articulate their feelings about, and emotional investments in, particular configurations of the political. In this section, I discuss two such cases and reveal how each of them portrays a normative vision of life under decentralisation that does not revolve around detachment and autonomy, but rather a repositioned form of deep engagement with both national and transnational 'centres'.

Sri's story

A Javanese woman in her late forties who had settled in the Riau Islands after a period living overseas, Sri sustained her household through a variety of freelance businesses, including some work accompanying high-status dignitaries from Singapore to appointments around the islands. She told me of the time she had been asked to drive a group of Singaporean officials to a seminar that they had sponsored, which aimed to teach Kepri's civil servants about the latest innovations in healthcare policy. Since their office had paid for the whole event, including the hire of a luxury hotel and a free meal for all participants, the Singaporeans were shocked to discover that most of the Kepri civil servants who attended had asked them whether it would be possible to receive any 'pocket money' (*uang saku*) to compensate them for their time. Such payments are a common feature of seminars in the Riau Islands, but the requests took the Singaporean visitors by complete surprise. When they got back to Sri's car, they animatedly recounted the events of the previous morning.

One dignitary described how he had rebuked an Indonesian who had asked him for money. 'No!' he had replied, 'The Singaporean government does not pay fees.' His colleagues had tutted in horror. 'You know', another man had concluded, 'I don't know what is wrong with these Indonesians!'

All the time, Sri had felt her face darkening, a wave of intense shame (*malu*) sweeping over her. How could these officials have asked for pocket money when they were turning up to a free event that had been staged to help them?! Didn't they realise they were bringing their whole country into disrepute? A Singaporean caught her eye in the rear mirror. 'You can understand English, can't you Sri?' he had asked her, 'You listen to this'.

At the time, Sri had found the experience excruciating. The way in which her client had spoken of 'these Indonesians' was so dismissive, so generalising. And yet, who could blame him?! The officials he had met had behaved in terrible ways. It was then that she began to realise just how important it was that people in Kepri make a good impression. As a border province it was Kepri that overseas visitors would arrive in first; it was their experience of the Riau Islands that would shape their images of the whole nation, of the country that she loved. She came to realise that the province was the 'gateway' (*pintu*) of Indonesia; it had to be up to national standard.

The rhetoric of Kepri as a national 'gateway' was, by the time of my conversation with Sri, very widespread – especially with reference to the idea that the region was a 'gateway' for international tourists. But the corollary to this, keenly felt by Sri and many others to whom I spoke, was that it was vital that this gateway be impressive. As they understood the situation, visitors like the Singaporeans were not viewing the problematic behaviour of Kepri's officials as a reflection of the continuing marginality of Indonesia's Outer Islands periphery. Far from it – visitors would see it as a reflection of the characteristics of Indonesia as a nation, with features and dispositions that were believed to stretch throughout the nation with only negligible variations in evenness. Such fears were not unwarranted, as an equivocation of the Riau Archipelago with the nation is a common discursive manoeuvre in Singaporean commentary on the islands. Riau Island officials who show low discipline and poor human resource quality often become ciphers for 'Indonesians' writ large, as in the case that Sri recounted. Meanwhile, a particularly mean-spirited article by Tan Wee Cheng, an adjunct professor working at the NUS Business School, reveals how the very feel of Tanjung Pinang – a town he describes as looking 'dirty, messy and simply evil' (Tan 2004: 2) synecdochally evokes an image of Indonesia as a nation:

> 'Mister! Mister, listen to me!' the Indonesian touts swarmed over us the moment we walked out of the jetty complex. Offering anything from 'beachside' hotel accommodation in inland locations to deep fried fish chips [*sic*], these touts were a sudden reminder that we were no longer in First World Singapore but in a vast country with fifty times the population yet one-eighth the GDP per capita.
>
> (Tan 2004: 1)

The modernity, development, discipline and high human resource quality that Riau Islanders imagined characterised life in the centre (i.e. Java) was thus not just something that they felt they were owed by the national government, but also something which it was their duty to cultivate. It would be in their own personal interests, as well as upholding – even improving – the image of their nation. This normative position was not derived from first principles or abstract reflection – it emerged viscerally, grounded in their apprehension of the gaze of their visitors and the profound shame and discomfort at the messages they saw their province to be communicating. As Sri's case illustrates clearly, the emotions that were evoked by synecdochal equivocations between the Riau Islands and Indonesia not only are evidence of latent attachment to the centre and to the nation, but served to imbue particular configurations of what it meant *to be a periphery* with personal meaning (Chodorow 1999) and normative force. Far from being a backwater clamouring to have their voices heard, it was precisely their status as an 'Outer Islands' province on the geographic periphery of the state that allowed Riau Islanders to imagine their region as integral to the reputation and international standing of the nation.

Gunawan's story

Such aspirations were particularly strong when it came to 'human resource quality', interest in which has been burgeoning nationwide as the Indonesian government seeks to ensure that its human resources are 'globally competitive', so as to secure a prestigious ranking in much-scrutinised international ranking exercises such as the UNDP's Human Development Index, attract foreign direct investment and cultivate an autochthonous entrepreneurial class. Riau Islanders, like Indonesians from all provinces, were entranced by the prospect of being 'world-class', and by the cosmopolitan possibilities that such high levels of human resource quality might offer them. But the issue also spoke to deeper concerns. Opponents to provincial secession had regularly cited the poor quality of the region's human resources as a reason to block the creation of an autonomous province; many in the archipelago thus felt compelled to prove to the rest of Indonesia that separation from Pekanbaru had allowed the islands' human resources to flourish. As a result, considerable interest was taken in interprovincial competitions – ranging from school-level contests such as maths and science Olympiads to the regular Miss Indonesia and Qur'anic recitation contests (MTQ). In all of these, representatives from Kepri could compete against participants from across Indonesia in a bid to be crowned national champion and even earn the right to represent Indonesia on the international stage. Riau Islanders spoke avidly of how much they wanted to show their countrymen that they were of 'international standard', and many dreamed of the idea that they – even though they were from a backwater periphery – might be able to represent Indonesia to the world.

Such undertakings, however, were far from straightforward. One of the major challenges facing the province's population was their sense that the region continues to be deeply scarred by the legacy of having been Pekanbaru's periphery for over 40 years. A pervasive perception that the region had long been 'held back' by its former centre meant that even after the creation of the new province had led to formal powers between Pekanbaru and Tanjung Pinang (the capital of Kepri) being rendered equivalent, there was still a widespread sense of inferiority among Riau Islanders when comparing themselves to the population of Mainland Riau and other regions of Indonesia. This was especially evident in contexts associated with 'human resource quality', where Riau Islanders saw their current quality as fundamentally compromised by the legacies of neglect that they and their region had received in prior decades. Teams representing Kepri in interprovincial contests desperately wanted to beat Mainland Riau, their former 'coloniser', but were simultaneously terrified by the prospect of meeting teams from regions seen as advanced – including Pekanbaru, but also Bali, South Sulawesi and all the provinces in Java – because of their conviction that such teams would visit upon them a defeat of humiliating proportions (Long 2013: 188–192). Indeed, their levels of anxiety were often so strong that they suffered sleepless nights before competition play-offs, with the result that their fears of defeat became self-fulfilling prophecies.

When I met with Pak Gunawan, a Sundanese man in his early forties who was now the head of a prestigious vocational school in Batam, these were issues with which he was extremely familiar. Gunawan was an educator almost obsessed with the category of achievement – *prestasi* in Indonesian. He explained to me that the whole point of *prestasi* was that it was something that one 'would do absolutely anything to get': it had to 'be reached for as hard as possible', and this meant that an educational institution such as his own had to devise 'all sorts of strategies' for obtaining it. The school management was thus oriented towards scrutinising the particular strengths of individual students and then pushing those as far as possible, 'so that [their strengths] could then be competed at (*dilombakan*) and [the students] can become champions (*dapat juara*)'. Yet despite this outlook, and a formidable track record of success, Gunawan's pupils still suffered from crippling fear of failure.

Teachers at the school all agreed: even mentioning the prospect of encountering Jakarta at a national level competition would be enough to 'make students' chests heave in terror' at what they might have to come up against. This frustrated Gunawan, for whom it made no sense that his students should feel such fear when 'among other provinces, Kepri is known as a province to beat'. Various members of staff proceeded to reel off a catalogue of cases in which this fear had led to self-defeating behaviour on the parts of their pupils, describing students who had performed very well in the provincial contests and in training sessions but who then imploded in the national finals.

I asked Gunawan what he thought might account for this self-defeating behaviour. He offered several possible explanations, all of which were linked to what might be described as a 'mindset of marginality'. In some cases, he thought, the long-distance air travel involved in attending national finals could be a contributing factor. 'Sometimes kids from here don't have much experience of the world', he elaborated:

> We had a kid last year who wanted to go to the finals of the LKS [*Lomba Kompetensi Siswa*; Students' Competency Competition], but he was scared to even get in the plane. He'd never flown before. So before he'd even arrived at the contest, his heart was no longer calm.

Other cases were more explicitly linked to a vocabulary of centre–periphery relations.

> [The students] still feel they're from a *hinterland* region, to the extent they maybe think they're behind other regions, they're a long way from the centre, they arrive and see Jakarta and how big its buildings are, and they start to get scared.

It is important at this point to emphasise that the issue Gunawan has identified is not one of objective differentials in technical competency: pupils from the Riau Islands have already managed to achieve a number of impressive successes in the vocational competitions, and Gunawan's assessment that the province is regarded as 'one to beat' is not inaccurate. Although there may be fewer highly skilled pupils in the Riau Islands competing for the opportunity to represent their province, those who are successful – especially those who have had the benefit of studying in a well-resourced and highly selective school such as Gunawan's – are at no substantial disadvantage compared to their metropolitan peers. What is at stake in the anxiety faced by Gunawan's pupils is thus not a condition of contemporary structural marginality – as a more political economic view of centre–periphery relations might have it – but rather a specific *social imaginary* of how the Riau Islands' human resource quality compares to that evident in Jakarta – a legacy of the marginality that the area did indeed once experience, the memory and narrative of which continues to cast a shadow over its early decentralised days.[5]

'So now I have a new strategy', Gunawan continued.

> We need to have a concept for training our kids as well as possible, to build their resilience (*mental*) and make them more daring (*lebih berani*). They're scared of Jakarta. Okay. I'll take them to Singapore. To Malaysia as well. But above all to Singapore. We'll wander around, see the sights. If there's time, maybe we'll do a comparative study (*studi banding*), but what matters is that we see the sights.
>
> The school got passports for them all, so they could see what Singapore is like – a fantastic city, that is so close, that they're able to experience and enjoy whenever they like.[6] That's what becomes their focus. They will be Kids Who Often Go To Singapore. Kids who often go to a place that's *better* than Jakarta. Then, when they arrive in Jakarta, they'll no longer be afraid. They've already seen somewhere that's truly outstanding – really opulent and tidy. Then they see Jakarta: 'Oh, this is nothing special', they'll say, 'I'm already used to Singapore.' That's my strategy to get the kids to enjoy the atmosphere here in Batam and to build their strength of will.

Although only one dimension of Gunawan's strategy for achieving outstanding results in national competitions (which extended to intensive training regimes and subliminal motivation by professional hypnotherapists), the trips to Singapore are particularly interesting in the context of this chapter, given Gunawan's emphasis on overcoming a 'hinterland' mentality through the manipulation of affect. In his diagnosis, the metropolitan trappings of the Jakarta landscape elicit feelings of shock that are interpreted according to an imaginary of centre–periphery relations that has long enjoyed public circulation – one which sees the centre as developed and advanced, and the periphery as necessarily inferior. Students' negative notions of the provincial self harden in response to these affective cues, in ways that threaten their performance. Interestingly, his response to this is not to challenge the structure of his students' interpretations, for example by reassuring them that they can be credible competitors to national level teams. Instead, he seeks to change the very affects that are elicited by encounters with Jakarta's urban landscape. Trips to Singapore tap into the same affective register of awe that students' arrival in Jakarta would, but with the emphasis on this being a fun trip where the purpose is, above all, to 'see the sights', this awe is turned into not terror but wonder. Through the visits, pupils are encouraged to see themselves as part of Singapore's periphery, rather than Jakarta's. Trips to Jakarta can then take place in full confidence, both because students have become habituated to and comfortable within a centre that is thought to shine even brighter than the national capital, and also because they have come to realise that they are 'so close' to Singapore that their own position in Batam is hardly one of the marginality or extreme peripherality they might otherwise have assumed.

How significant these trips really are for the pupils at Gunawan's school is debatable. Members of the highly successful mechatronics team accorded them only cursory significance, praising the dedication of their teachers, the high volume of training they had received and the excellent facilities in the school as the most important factors that underpinned their success. On the other hand, the trips were never designed to propel an achieving mindset, but rather to prevent a counterproductive form of fear from being experienced, and are thus interventions that the students themselves may not be best placed to evaluate. What is clear, however, is that at the level of emergent institutional theories of achievement psychology, students' imaginaries of how Kepri, as a particular kind of periphery, relates to the centres of Singapore and Jakarta, has been seen as central to the outcomes students achieve, while also amenable to intervention. Moreover, this intervention is not made in structural terms, but in ways that are bodily, experiential and affective.

Conclusion

Studies of decentralisation and centre–periphery relations in Indonesia all too often focus on questions of resource flow or the 'balance of power' as if these were the terminal points of a social analysis. Clearly they are significant: decentralisation has led to very tangible changes in infrastructure and institutional practice, setting conditions of possibility for all the events discussed in this chapter. For example, while Gunawan felt that decentralisation had actually played 'very little part' in improving the human resource quality on Batam (he attributed the high quality to the self-propulsive values that circulated in a city of economic migrants), it was clear that his own school had benefitted considerably from being identified as a flagship institution by the provincial government.

However, what I have hoped to demonstrate is that such structural changes are important only insofar as they lead to new conditions of possibility in which inhabitants of the Outer Islands might be able to pursue the forms of life that are most desirable to them. The question of what mode of life is desired and why thus stands out as a pressing matter for ethnographic investigation, rather than something that should be assumed on the basis of a theoretical model. In the Riau Islands, citizens' desires frequently involve relating to the centre in new ways so as to be a new kind of (non-marginal) periphery, rather than aspiring to become a centre, or longing for a condition of autonomy. Anxieties about marginality and the legacies of past neglect combine with an appreciation of the duties and opportunities that the region might bear as a geographic periphery: but in all cases what seems to be at issue is an intense desire for national parity, underpinned by a desire for full inclusion within the nation – and increasingly, desire for full membership of 'the global'. The recalibration of centre–periphery relations is consequently an affectively and ethically charged concern.

This strong level of personal investment in the political, I suggest, is precisely why my enquiries into centre–periphery relations tended to yield emotionally charged accounts of outrage, shame or distress – and why Gunawan felt that forging affective bonds between his students and the metropolitan centre of Singapore could prove such an effective means of remedying the self-handicapping tendencies that were holding back his own desires for his school. Given the emphasis that the literature on decentralisation continues to place on the actions and motivations of self-interested elites – as if their supporters are simply held in thrall to their ambitions by similarly self-interested practices of clientelism – it is theoretically sobering to reflect on the intense passions that normative questions of centre–periphery relations continue to elicit, as well as to recognise that it was precisely the desire to connect more directly with a beloved national centre that led many Riau Islanders to embrace the prospect of provincial autonomy in the first place.

Acknowledgements

Research for this chapter was supported by a British Academy Postdoctoral Fellowship and ESRC award RES-000-22-4632 in support of a joint project with Professor Susan Bayly on 'The Social Life of Achievement in Indonesia and Vietnam'.

Notes

1 Vina's narrative finds echoes in the works of Carole Faucher (2005, 2007) and Vivienne Wee (2002), while Pak Iman's concerns have been widely recognised as affecting Indonesia's resource extraction industries on a nation-wide scale (see e.g. Casson and Obidzinski 2002; Spiegel 2012).
2 Aristocrats descended from the viceroys of the Riau-Lingga sultanate self-define as 'pure Malays', while nevertheless tracing their patrilineal descent to Bugis seafarers who arrived in the Riau Islands during the eighteenth century. For further discussion of this complex 'Malay-Bugis' identity, see Long (2013: 70–97).
3 These aristocrats had a direct incentive to advocate such a position since they envisaged themselves as being, by birthright, the future leaders of the prospective Republic of Riau.
4 Note also that earlier anthropological accounts of the 'exemplary centre' stressed the desirability of access to a 'potent centre'. Proximity to such a source offered opportunities for cultivating one's own potency (Errington 1983), as well as the comforting, and yet also dangerously distracting, prospect of being 'enveloped in a superior authority's care' (Keeler 1987: 202). Relations with the centre were thus ambivalent, prompting a complex ethics of detachment and engagement. Contrast this with more recent attempts

to use 'cultural' models of potency as a gloss for structural descriptions of centre–periphery relations. Phelps (2004), for instance, uses Anderson's (1972) famous image of a cone of light to emphasise the darkness (and thus marginality) of the periphery – an interpretation that remains in thrall to structural models, and radically underplays the complex tensions and ambivalences that characterised the culturalist model.

5 In some other cases, these two concerns exist in tandem (Long 2013: 190–191).

6 Notwithstanding the immigration restrictions on visitors from Indonesia (Ford and Lyons 2006: 262–263).

References

Anderson, B.R.O. (1972) The Idea of Power in Javanese Culture, in C. Holt (ed.), *Culture and Politics in Indonesia*, Ithaca, NY: Cornell University Press, pp. 1–70.

Aspinall, E. (2010) The Irony of Success, *Journal of Democracy* 21(2): 20–34.

Booth, A. (2011) Splitting, Splitting and Splitting Again: A Brief History of the Development of Regional Government in Indonesia since Independence, *Bijdragen tot de taal-, land-, en volkenkunde* 167(1): 31–59.

Bunnell, T., Grundy-Warr, C., Sidaway, J.D. and Sparke, M. (2012) Geographies of Power in the Indonesia–Malaysia–Singapore Growth Triangle, in B. Derudder, M. Hoyler, P.J. Taylor and F. Witlox (eds), *International Handbook of Globalization and World Cities*, Cheltenham, UK: Edward Elgar, pp. 465–475.

Casson, A. and Obidzinski, K. (2002) From New Order to Regional Autonomy: Shifting Dynamics Of 'Illegal' Logging in Kalimantan, Indonesia, *World Development* 30(12): 2133–2151.

Chodorow, N.J. (1999) *The Power of Feelings: Personal Meaning in Psychoanalysis, Gender, and Culture*. New Haven, CT: Yale University Press.

Diprose, R. (2009) Decentralization, Horizontal Inequalities and Conflict Management in Indonesia, *Ethnopolitics* 8(1): 107–134.

Errington, S. (1983) Embodied *sumange'* in Luwu, *The Journal of Asian Studies* 42(3): 545–570.

Faucher, C. (2005) Regional Autonomy, Malayness and Power Hierarchy in the Riau Archipelago, in M. Erb, P. Sulistiyanto and C. Faucher (eds), *Regionalism in Post-Suharto Indonesia*, London and New York: RoutledgeCurzon, pp. 132–148.

Faucher, C. (2007) Contesting Boundaries in the Riau Archipelago, in H. Schulte Nordholt and G. van Klinken (eds), *Renegotiating Boundaries: Local Politics in Post-Suharto Indonesia*, Leiden: KITLV Press, pp. 443–457.

Ford, M. and Lyons, L. (2006) The Borders Within: Mobility and Enclosure in the Riau Islands, *Asia Pacific Viewpoint* 47(2): 257–271.

Goldblum, C. and Wong, T.-C. (2000) Growth, Crisis and Spatial Change: A Study of Haphazard Urbanisation in Jakarta, Indonesia, *Land Use Policy* 17: 29–37.

Hechter, M. (1975) *Internal Colonialism: The Celtic Fringe in British National Development, 1536–1966*. London and New York: Routledge.

Keeler, W. (1987) *Javanese Shadow Plays, Javanese Selves*. Princeton, NJ: Princeton University Press.

Kimura, E. (2007) Marginality and Opportunity in the Periphery: The Emergence of Gorontalo Province in North Sulawesi, *Indonesia* 84: 71–95.

Kimura, E. (2010) Proliferating Provinces: Territorial Politics in Post-Suharto Indonesia, *South East Asia Research* 18(3): 415–449.

Long, N.J. (2013) *Being Malay in Indonesia: Histories, Hopes and Citizenship in the Riau Archipelago*. Singapore: NUS Press.

Minnesota Population Center (2011) *Integrated Public Use Microdata Series, International: Version 6.1.* Minneapolis, MN: University of Minnesota. Underlying data provided by Badan Pusat Statistik, Indonesia.

Ong, A. (2000) Graduated Sovereignty in Southeast Asia, *Theory, Culture and Society* 17(4): 55–75.

Phelps, N.A. (2004) Archetype for an Archipelago? Batam as Anti-Model and Model of Industrialization in Reformasi Indonesia, *Progress in Development Studies* 4(3): 206–229.

Pitzl, G.R. (2004) *Encyclopedia of Human Geography.* Westport, CT: Greenwood Press.

Quinn, G. (2003) Coming Apart and Staying Together at the Centre: Debates over Provincial Status in Java and Madura, in E. Aspinall and G. Fealy (eds), *Local Power and Politics in Indonesia: Decentralisation and Democratisation*, Singapore: Institute for Southeast Asian Studies, pp. 164–178.

Spiegel, S.J. (2012) Governance Institutions, Resource Rights Regimes, and the Informal Mining Sector: Regulatory Complexities in Indonesia, *World Development* 40(1): 189–205.

Tan, W.C. (2004) Cakes and Gods across Historic Waterways, *Quarterly Literary Review Singapore* 3(4). Available online: www.qlrs.com/essay.asp?id=364 (accessed 1 May 2014).

Wallerstein, I. (2004) *World-Systems Analysis: An Introduction.* Durham, NC: Duke University Press.

Wee, V. (2002) Ethno-nationalism in Process: Ethnicity, Atavism and Indigenism in Riau, Indonesia, *The Pacific Review* 15(4): 497–516.

Wollenberg, E., Moeliono, M. and Limberg, G. (2009) Between State and Society: Decentralization in Indonesia, in M. Moeliono, E. Wollenberg and G. Limberg (eds), *The Decentralization of Forest Governance Politics: Economics and the Fight for Control of Forests in Indonesian Borneo*, London and Sterling, VA: Earthscan, pp. 3–24.

5 Nested sovereignties

Autonomy and authority in the Indonesian borderlands

Michael Eilenberg

Introduction[1]

This chapter examines how, since the onset of decentralisation in 1999, ethnic border elites have struggled to create small zones of semi-autonomy at the territorial fringes of the Indonesian state. The chapter discusses how these creative practices simultaneously transform, challenge and accommodate the idea of the 'sovereign state' by juggling the power relations between the centre and periphery. Borderland zones are often seen as the *raison d'être* of state sovereignty. However, states are frequently unable to make their claims stick when the borderlands lack infrastructure, are covered in forest and are sparsely populated. Hence, the consolidation of territorial sovereignty, i.e. 'the recognition of the claim by a state to exercise supreme authority over a clearly defined territory' (the Westphalian ideal) (Zaum 2007: 3), is high on government agendas. In its role as a key symbol of state sovereignty, the borderland is often a place where central state authorities are most eager to govern and exercise power. However, the borderland is also a place where state sovereignty is most likely to be challenged, questioned and manipulated because of various transnational economic links that transcend state borders and contradict imaginations of the state as guardians of national sovereignty (van Schendel and de Maaker 2014). The classical definition of sovereignty, which presupposes a strong 'unitary' state imposing unlimited control on a clearly defined territory, is widely questioned by scholars who have taken up the challenge of conceptualising the state as fragmented rather than an *a priori*, homogenous whole. Here *de facto* state sovereignty is less clear-cut than its classical definitions entail and the existence of overlapping, nested and competing sovereignties within and across borders are increasingly recognised (Hansen and Stepputat 2005, 2006; Lund 2011; Peluso and Lund 2011).

By analysing an ongoing claim for border autonomy in the border province of West Kalimantan, I illustrate how local border elites within the legal (but fuzzy) framework of administrative decentralisation reforms attempt to create their own administrative border regency. The case illuminates how the 'state' is understood creatively and how national loyalties are claimed at the state fringes by appropriating the state rhetoric of development and good citizenship. It is argued that, because of their contested nature, the Indonesian borderlands provide an exceptionally important site for investigating these paradoxes of state sovereignty, the changing dynamics of state–periphery relations and the kind of governance that Indonesia has experienced since decentralisation.

Since the early 1990s, the border population of the Kapuas Hulu regency (*kabupaten*), a remote and underdeveloped corner of the Indonesian province of West Kalimantan, has pushed for border development and increased local autonomy. Previously, during the New Order regime, ethnic border elites began formulating ideas about how to deal with the chronic underdevelopment of the border area. However, until the fall of President Suharto, this movement remained rather inactive, as efforts to increase local autonomy were not given much leeway under the highly authoritarian New Order regime. The rhetoric of this emerging movement was, therefore, mostly centred on practical questions of development, while issues of increased autonomy were largely downplayed (Kuyah 1992). However, after the fall of President Suharto in 1998, this movement gained momentum and re-emerged as a local response or counter-movement against the increase in outside involvement in what are perceived as local matters. By creating their own regency, the border elite expects to boost local autonomy and strengthen their control of local, natural resources and border trade. They anticipate that controlling border access will become an important political and economic resource in the near future, as enhanced commercial exchange is expected to develop between the two bordering regions of West Kalimantan (Indonesia) and Sarawak (Malaysia).

Post New Order, Law No. 22/1999 on regional autonomy, suddenly made it possible to split existing regencies into smaller ones: a process known as *pemekaran*, or 'blossoming' (McWilliam 2011).[2] The new decentralisation laws led to a general rush to create new regencies in Kalimantan and all over Indonesia (Fitrani *et al.* 2005; Vel 2007). For example, in West Kalimantan in 1999, the large border regency of Sambas was split into the Sambas and Bengkayang regencies and, in East Kalimantan, the resource-rich border regency of Bulungan was split into Bulungan, Malinau and Nunukan regencies. Later, in 2012, that regency, together with the Tana Tidung and Tarakan regencies, was transformed into the new province of North Kalimantan (Wollenberg *et al.* 2006; Tanasaldy 2007; Jakarta Globe 2012).

Portrayed as a bottom-up process in which common people can gain a larger degree of empowerment and transparency in local government matters, regional proliferation became immensely popular in Indonesia. The number of regencies rose dramatically from 298 in 1999 to 526 in 2011 (Firman 2013). Law No. 22/1999, which was hastily drawn up in the early days of decentralisation, has since been revised and superseded by more restrictive laws (Law No. 32/2004 and No. 78/2007) which, among other things, raised the minimum number of districts to be included in a new regency from three to five. This tightening was an attempt to slow down the process of the splitting of regencies. The economic incentives of large financial transfers from the central government to support new regencies and lucrative positions in the new administration have, undoubtedly, been an important motivator for local elites. The decentralisation laws stipulate that new regencies will receive subsidies in the form of both general allocation funds and special allocation funds from the central government. More often than not, the driving force behind *pemekaran* is the urge to gain authority over various resources rather than the establishment of more accountable local governments (Roth 2007; McWilliam 2011).

The Kapuas Hulu borderland

The Kapuas Hulu regency consists of 29,842 km^2 (20.33 per cent of West Kalimantan) divided into no less than 23 districts with a total population of only 209,860. It lies in the northernmost corner of the province, more than 700 km from the provincial capital, Pontianak, on the coast (Kabupaten Kapuas Hulu 2006). To the north, the regency shares an international border with Sarawak, Malaysia; to the east, it borders the Indonesian provinces of Central Kalimantan and East Kalimantan.

This chapter focuses specifically on the border movement that, in 2000, grew out of the five districts of Batang Lupar, Embaloh Hulu, Badau, Empanang and Puring Kencana. The five districts (covering approximately 6,296 km^2 or 22 per cent of the Kapuas Hulu regency) make up the largest stretch of territory along the international border with Sarawak within the 'mother' regency. In 2007, the population was estimated to have reached approximately 37,000 in the five border districts (PPKPU 2007).

The leading members of the border movement are primarily ethnic Iban, who are all part of a small but prominent ethnic elite group of customary leaders, village headmen, members of the regency assembly and regency government officials.[3] The Iban make up the largest section of the population in the five districts while the two other ethnic groups, the Maloh and Malay, make up a small minority.[4] The Maloh and Malay support the movement, but because of their minority status, they are less influential, which creates a fair amount of inter-ethnic distrust. Sections of the Maloh and Malay communities see the border movement as primarily an Iban project with the purpose of capturing political power and natural resources in the proposed new regency.[5] However, such inter-ethnic distrust is partly unspoken in order for the movement to appear strong and united. Ethnic unity is constantly being promoted by the movement members on both sides of the ethnic divide, and, by focusing on their shared 'borderland identity', ethnicity is being downplayed as less relevant (Eilenberg and Wadley 2009). Despite this inter-ethnic rivalry, the various groups realise that, for the movement to succeed, the five districts must at least officially appear as one 'border community'. Therefore, such concerns remain veiled, even as tension continues to build along accentuated ethnic lines. Yet, despite these attempts to ignore ethnicity, the issue is an important one. For example, during local meetings, some Iban participants made jokes about the movement being called the 'Free Iban Movement', or GIM (*Gerakan Iban Merdeka*), seeing it primarily as a movement for Iban revitalisation. The reference here is to the 'Free Aceh

Movement', or GAM (*Gerakan Aceh Merdeka*), in North Sumatra. Among some members, such jokes express the dreams of promoting Iban *adat* (traditional) authority and reclaiming control of what they perceive as their traditional territory, which is now claimed by other ethnic groups. Later, during the same meeting, Iban members changed the acronym GIM to GBM (*Gerakan Bersama Maju*) or 'Jointly We Prosper Movement', and, as such, downplayed the issue of ethnicity. In other parts of Indonesia, *pemekaran* is often carried out along ethnic lines, which, in many cases, has resulted in violent conflicts (Duncan 2007; Aspinall 2011).

The border movement is using the experience of the split of other border regencies in the province, especially the subdivision of the Sambas regency into the Bengkayang and Sambas regencies in 1999.[6] One of the leading members of the border regency movement is a highly educated Iban (originally from the Kapuas Hulu border area) who now upholds an influential government position as head of a regency-level office in the Bengkayang regency. Having a front row seat in which to observe the success of these new regencies and the complicated political processes, which *pemekaran* demands, he, together with a small group of other well-off men, initiated the border movement. The movement further feeds into a larger alliance of border communities known as the 'Forum for Border Community Care', positioned in the provincial capital, Pontianak. This forum was created in 2004 with the purpose of lobbying for and promoting the overall development of the border regions of West Kalimantan; its members are from all the ethnic groups living along the entire length of the border.[7] The forum has mainly been used by the border movement as a meeting place for consolidating new alliances, especially with provincial government officials and politicians. All the founding members of the movement originate from the border area, but they live and work in or near the provincial capital and only seldom visit the border area.

North border regency

In early March 2007, after numerous meetings and discussions, representatives and supporters from the five districts (approximately 400 people) met with the regency head at an official gathering in the regency office in Putussibau. A group known as the 'Committee for the Establishment of the North Border Regency' (*Panitia Pembentukan Kabupaten Perbatasan Utara*, PPKPU), which was the main organisation pursuing the formation of the new regency, boldly proclaimed the new regency name to be 'The North Border Regency' (*Kabupaten Perbatasan Utara*). At the same time, they presented a final report of several hundred pages containing the legally stipulated requirements for a new regency and the signatures of all of the local (elite) supporters (Equator News 2007a). This report, which emphasised the considerable potential of the border area and its current underdevelopment, was the outcome of an unofficial feasibility study carried out by the committee in cooperation with a Jakarta-based NGO (PPKPU 2007).

In the period between 2004 and 2007, the movement had carried out an extensive lobbying campaign. In February 2006, it sent out its first formal letter of aspiration to the regency head, presenting the plan for a new regency. To give the letter an extra touch of formality, the name of the proposed regency was stamped on the letterhead in large black type. Then, in late 2007, the committee attempted to precipitate the *pemekaran* process (Equator News 2007b). With the disappointments of failed efforts of the past in mind, the border movement has been eager to push on. Early in the presidency of Mega-wati (2001–2004), the same border elite had applied to the central government to be recognised as a Special Authority Region (*otorita daerah khusus*) and, thereby, receive favourable conditions such as free border trade and a higher degree of political autonomy (in line with the status of Batam). According to leading movement members, a letter of decree that would have granted special authority to the border area was being prepared. Then, in 2004, a new pres-ident was elected, and the decree was supposedly postponed. A few days before President Megawati left office in October 2004, she signed the revised decentralisation legislation (Law No. 32/2004), which replaced the former law from 1999. This new law states the requirements for creating a Special Admin-istrative Zone (*kawasan khusus*) in an area within a regency or province of special importance for national interest. This autonomous zone would enjoy the status of a free trade zone (Law No. 32/2004, Chapter II, part 2, article 9). During the Megawati presidency, the government prepared a development strategy for the Kalimantan border region, and, according to the members of the movement, the change in the central administration turned out to be a significant setback for the lobbying efforts of the border movement at the time (Bappenas 2003). In a 2007 statement outlining the urgency of the current campaign, a border committee member said,

> We need to push forward now and keep going. We cannot wait for official approval from the regency office. Government regulations, as they look today, may be different tomorrow so we need to act while there is still an opportunity.[8]

The huge popularity of *pemekaran* throughout Indonesia has put immense strain on the central government's resources and budget, while outcomes in the form of improved services for the majority of people have, so far, been meagre. Mean-while, corruption and nepotism have reportedly increased; a development that the central government is largely blaming on self-interested regional elites (Bap-penas and UNDP 2008). Such accusations have since fostered widespread protest from provincial and regency assembly members who accuse the central government of being arrogant and not committed to the development of the outer regions and the re-allocation of promised economic benefits from the centre to its margins.

Appropriating state rhetoric of security and sovereignty

The first step in the *pemekaran* process as stipulated in the government laws and regulations is a demonstration of the viability of a proposed new regency and justification of the need for its creation. As indicated by the name, 'The North Border Regency', the PPKPU committee clearly specified the common ground and key resources of the five districts involved. Despite its vast natural resources, the border area, after more than 60 years of Indonesian independence, is still categorised as a region of extreme poverty with insufficient infrastructure, health services and education facilities (KNPDT 2007). As proclaimed by participants during an August 2006 borderland 'awareness-raising' meeting that was held to discuss the advantages of splitting the regency:

> It has now been 63 years since we became an independent nation, but our roads are still yellow [dirt] and at night, our lamps are still dark. Is this the result of independence? [A chorus of voices from the crowd replied], 'We still live in misery and poverty. Development has left us behind'.
>
> (PPKPU 2007 – my translation)

The main argument put forward for splitting the Kapuas Hulu regency was its sheer size and lack of capacity to develop its outer districts. Members of the border committee stressed that the 'mother' regency of Kapuas Hulu was too large, and the past and current regency administrations had not succeeded in developing the border area compared to other areas in the regency. As a result, they said, the border people were forced to act by themselves if any changes were to take place:

> Until now the border communities have just been a tool of central government in extracting natural resources, that is why the community wants their own autonomy, to take control by themselves, and at least have their own regency.[9]

Applying the central government rhetoric of security, sovereignty and development and emphasising the role of border inhabitants as loyal citizens, were other conscious strategies among the movement members for attaining government good will for their cause. The members proclaimed that the creation of a new border regency was a local effort to maintain a unitary state of the Republic of Indonesia (*Negara Kesatuan Republik Indonesia*); as enhanced political and economic autonomy would prevent acts of separatism among the border communities. Furthermore, the border regency would become the new, bright, outward face of Indonesia towards Malaysia and, most importantly, would improve national defence and guarantee security (Equator News 2006). For centuries, the border communities have been seen as a national security threat because of their strong cross-border ties (Eilenberg and Wadley 2009; Eilenberg 2012a). Since the onset of decentralisation, the shifting reform governments have increased their focus on the nation's borderlands as regions in dire need of development and strong state presence (Bappenas 2004, 2008). Post New Order, numerous news reports touching upon the issue of national loyalty among the West Kalimantan borderland population have appeared in the national press, expressed in headlines such as, 'Communities Living along the Kalimantan-Sarawak Border are Still Isolated within Their Own Country' (Kompas 2000). Such a depiction highlights isolation, underdevelopment and cross-border ethnicity as the main reasons for cross-border solidarity and subsequent lack of national consciousness. As expressed in the headlines of the main provincial newspaper, 'The Border Citizens Still Rely on Malaysia' (Pontianak Post 2005). The numerous news headlines depicting the nation's borderlands as lawless and out of state control triggered a national debate on the inability of the central government in upholding the territorial security and sovereignty of the nation. This debate and the chronic underdevelopment of the borderlands in 2010 resulted in the creation of a 'National Agency for Border Development' that included members of the Indonesian military, relevant ministries and governors of the affected border regions (Jakarta Post 2010b; Perpres 2010). The main role of the border agency was to coordinate development initiatives in the borderlands and boost military presence (Jakarta Post 2010a).[10]

Throughout the *pemekaran* process, movement members were quick to disavow involvement in past public so-called 'illegal' activities in the border area and to claim that such activities were the act of desperate people and were solely in response to a long-standing economic disparity along the border. For example, from 2000 to 2005, the five districts were the scene of large-scale timber smuggling across the border to Malaysia that attracted immense national and international attention (Wadley and Eilenberg 2005; Eilenberg 2012b). According to the movement members, the only way to prevent any further illegal activities and enhance national loyalty was to involve border communities in developing the area through engagement in local-level politics and economic affairs. As stated by a regency assembly member on the motives behind a new regency:

> We do not want the central government to think 'danger'; and what are the politics of the border people in creating a regency. We are Indonesian. We continue to love Indonesia. However, what we want is a change and advancement of the border area. That is our argument and motivation behind a new Border Regency.[11]

Regional autonomy or secession

Movement members may have officially proclaimed their strong national loyalty in local news media, but, during the heated debates in closed local meetings, becoming part of Malaysia was often mentioned as a final option. The Iban border population generally accepted their status as Indonesian citizens, and everybody knew that secession was impossible. However, the threat clearly indicated the preparedness of the committee to play the 'border card' in political negotiations with the regency and central governments. Fear of local separatism has often been expressed by government and news media as a possible future outcome of such special borderland circumstances (Kompas 2001). As an excited supporter of regency splitting announced:

> We will just join Malaysia. We will organise training over there and rebel. We will still try the nice way first but if official procedures turn out to be unworkable, well, what can we do? We will get help from smart people in Malaysia.[12]

During the Dutch colonial period in Indonesia, Raja Brooke, the Sarawak ruler at the time, offered the Iban border population the opportunity to secede to Sarawak, although such offers never resulted in concrete action.[13] However, the border communities were, throughout (and prior to) the Dutch colonial presence in the border area, seen as unreliable and rebellious citizens (Eilenberg 2014a).[14] One major contributing factor to these skirmishes between colonial administrators and the border population was a long history of movement, particularly for trade and warfare that did not recognise arbitrary state borders. The border population strategically took advantage of the artificial line dividing the Dutch and British territories. Dutch attempts to subdue these recalcitrant subjects and extend the colonial administrative discipline to the unruly border areas have resulted in a pronounced local suspicion towards state authority among the majority of the border population (Wadley 2004).

The long historic cross-border relations and ongoing, mostly rhetorical support from small segments of the Iban population in Sarawak boost local confidence among the border population. As one committee member commented during a local meeting, 'We can make things very difficult for them (regency and provincial officials)', referring to former acts of vigilantism and close ethnic ties to similar ethnic groups in Sarawak. The border populations are notorious for acting on their own when they feel that the government system is unjust and not operating in accordance with the special circumstances of life along the border (Eilenberg 2011). Despite these statements, the committee members always stressed that everything they did would have to conform to the law and that they should not attempt to win independence like Aceh. No attempt should be made to disturb the stability of the border. However, on the question of what would possibly happen if the border communities were not given increased autonomy and their own regency, a customary leader answered:

> If the border area is not allowed to emerge as a new regency by the central or local government, I am afraid that many of the communities would lose their faith in the unity of the nation and want to separate themselves or break away to Malaysia. If you ask the community, 99 per cent would prefer to be under the political control of Malaysia, and that would put the unity of the nation in danger. Well, older people like us try to protect the unity of

the Indonesian nation by suggesting the creation of a new regency instead of separatism.[15]

In 2012, the committee decided to change the name of the proposed new regency from the more contested and politicised 'North Border Regency' to 'Banua Landjak Regency'. This was done in order to send a message of national loyalty to the central government and indicate their deep attachment to the region. 'Banua Landjak' could be translated to 'My homeland/fatherland' (Sinar Harapan 2013). History plays an important role in ethnic consolidation in the border area, and past events are generally recalled with great pride. Iban connections to the ancestral past are kept alive through an intricate system of tracing one's ancestry (*tusut*). Most Iban in the border area are able to remember and trace their descent for as many as five generations.

Border access and resource control

On 20 April 2006, approximately 100 people representing the five districts met with members of the regency assembly in the regency capital, Putussibau. The representatives were greeted positively, and the assembly subsequently issued a letter of decree supporting the formation of a new regency in the border area (KepDPRD 2006). Before issuing this decree, a handful of regency assembly members originating from the border area had carried out intensive lobbying within the assembly.

In addition, the regency head of Kapuas Hulu initially appeared to be supportive of the idea of a new regency, attending meetings and personally donating funds to the border committee (Akcaya 2007). Nevertheless, he also seemed to be deliberately stalling the process. Like the regency heads of other resource-rich regencies, he has, since the outset of decentralisation, consolidated his power and support through income from natural resources. Informal interviews with regency government officials in Putussibau produce a picture of a general, although not publicly expressed, worry within the regency office that the mother regency risks losing major income from strategic resources, such as timber, minerals and the future lucrative border trade, if it is split. In the budget for the period 2008–2009, the regency Department of Plantations and Forestry in Kapuas Hulu planned to use no less than 41.3 billion rupiah to develop the forestry and plantation sector in the border area (Perhut Kapuas Hulu 2007). The law further requires the mother regency to economically support the new regency for the first few years before the new regency receives its own fiscal transfers from the central government. The creation of the 'North Border Regency' could further isolate the mother regency, which is already the most remote regency in the province. If the new regency is created, the mother regency will be geographically and (possibly) economically isolated in the most northern corner of the province. The sheer distance to the provincial capital, more than 700 km, makes border access highly important for the local economy; Sarawak economic centres across the border are much closer than the provincial capital (Wadley 2000).

According to a border committee member, the main reason for the regency head to stall the regency splitting was to maintain control of the resource-rich border region:

> Now we are actually able to fulfil the requirements for creating a new regency put forward by central government, but the mother regency seems to be hesitant about letting us go. It keeps holding on to our tail. There is too much potential so they cannot let go and let the new regency emerge. I think if Putussibau lets the border area become a regency, Putussibau will die.[16]

Transnational networks add to the complexity of this case. During the many local meetings about the new border regency, the committee members invited several Malaysian 'investors' from across the border. It was envisaged that a possible new regency should co-operate closely with private business partners within the palm oil and rubber industry across the border in Sarawak and develop large plantations along the border under the control of local ethnic communities. Many of these 'investors' were closely connected with committee members through kinship ties and were deeply involved in the logging boom that ended in 2005 (Wadley and Eilenberg 2005). Economic support from wealthy Malaysians could end up being a key factor in realising the establishment of the new regency. Even more importantly, cross-border resources may make the new regency more autonomous and, thus, less dependent on central government politics and financial support. As indicated by a local executive,

> if we already had a new regency here, many smart people from Malaysia would come and invest their money in plantations and so on. There are plenty of them waiting across the border. But for now, they do not want to come, as they do not trust the government.[17]

Several members of the border movement announced that they would not allow any outside companies to enter local forestlands without prior agreements with local communities. As stipulated by a customary leader in a 2007 interview: 'Many companies want to enter the area and open oil palm plantations, but we have not yet given our consent. We will wait until we have gained official authority over the area.'[18] These comments are symptomatic of the widespread mistrust of government authorities and of the conviction that they (the border communities) would be better off handling things themselves. However, these local cross-border negotiations were partly side-tracked by the regency government (with support from central government and military) in 2006–2007 when the regency allocated large tracts of land within the five border districts for plantation development to the Sinar Mas Group, Indonesia's largest palm oil producer (Suara Bekakak 2006).[19] Internally, within the border movement, this move by the regency government to develop the border region was seen as an attempt to fortify regency authority over the rebellious districts by claiming ownership over land and resources.[20] Despite large-scale protests by local customary leaders, Sinar Mas, with support from the regency government, quickly began converting large tracts of land into palm oil plantations maintained by imported migrant workers from outside the province (Kompas 2011).

At the time of writing (August 2015), the border movement was still awaiting a formal approval to their request for a new regency and the outcomes seemed as uncertain as ever. A positive outcome was highly dependent on rapid political changes taking place locally and nationally and on the readiness of higher-level authorities to take action. The future of the *pemekaran* process very much depended on the good will of key politicians in Jakarta and of local government administrative heads, like the regency head and governor, who have their own, often divergent, agendas for the border area. Since 2005, the regency head of Kapuas Hulu, together with four other regency heads, has been involved in yet another *pemekaran* process. These five regency heads wish to split from the current province of West Kalimantan and create a new province, Kapuas Raya. It is too early to forecast what consequences this plan may have for the future of the border regency, but all available regency resources seemed directed towards carrying out this grand plan for a new province (Kalimantan Review 2008; Jakarta Post 2013). Further, during an interview in late 2007, the head of the provincial legislative assembly (DPRD) in the provincial capital, Pontianak, expressed strong doubts as to whether a new border regency would have any chance of being approved at the central level. According to him, one of the major hurdles was the low population density. With only about 30,000 inhabitants, the proposed border regency would be too sparsely populated to survive on its own. He estimated that it might take another five to ten years before the border population could be ready to manage its own regency.

In the heated debate about the viability of many new regencies in recent years, some national and regional commentators have suggested that the central government should prioritise the establishment of new regencies and provinces in regions with special needs such as underdeveloped and sensitive state border areas. This, they argue, would be in line with one of the original ideas behind decentralisation, namely that of facilitating and ensuring national unity (Equator News 2007b; Jakarta Post 2007a; Kompas 2007). However, despite the creation of a new border agency, the central government has been hesitant and vague regarding the possibility of new regencies in the border regions. The central government's plans for the borderlands will not necessarily involve an increase in local autonomy, but more likely would foster the reclaiming of central authority over these resource-rich peripheral regions (Eilenberg 2014b). From 2009 to 2012, a moratorium was imposed on regional expansion through *pemekaran*, although, several times, local pressure conceded by the House of Representatives has insisted on continuing to open new administrative regions (Aspinall 2013). For example, in October 2013, the Regional Representatives Council (DPRD) in West Kalimantan expressed its strong support for the creation of the new border regency; however, such support does not necessarily reflect the views of the central government in Jakarta (Sinar Harapan 2013). The central government has continuously expressed reservations about the rapidity with which authority and funds are being transferred to the regencies. They argue that the results are mixed and often lead to communal conflict and rampant rent-seeking among political elites, while the benefits for ordinary citizens are less obvious (Bappenas and UNDP 2008; Jakarta Post 2007b, 2012; Tempo 2013).

Conclusions

The *pemekaran* case demonstrates the complexity of relations between local elites and the various levels of government bureaucracy. It constitutes a concrete example of how border elites, over time, have attempted to negotiate authority over resources along the border. Furthermore, the chapter argues that such negotiations are carried out through the appropriation of the state rhetoric of development for local purposes and (personal) interests. At the same time, cross-border connections and trade are used to resist government authority, thus challenging its territorial sovereignty and power.

Although it is still uncertain whether the border movement will succeed in creating a new autonomous regency, the border elite will continue to exploit opportunities presented by decentralisation and the duality of life along the border in order to negotiate authority and attempt to strengthen their position. The alliances formed or renewed during the *pemekaran* process will, despite the process' uncertain outcome, feed into local elite networks of influence. The struggle over access to resources will be waged between such border elite movements, regency officials and central government agencies in the borderland in the years to come. The *pemekaran* phenomenon suggests a complex relationship between state institutions and local control that helps shed light on the often ambivalent relationship between border populations in Kapuas Hulu and their state, as well as the more general processes of state formation taking place along the edges of the Indonesian nation state. It highlights the nested and fragmented character of sovereign power in these regions that is comprised of multiple and overlapping semi-autonomous cores of power, and further shows how competing loyalties (ethnic, national, regional, cross-border) are negotiated on a daily basis. Honest attempts are being made by certain resourceful segments of the border population to attract the attention of highly placed politicians to the chronic underdevelopment experienced by the majority of the inhabitants of the immediate border area. However, despite such good intentions, behind the scenes a mounting struggle for border access and resource control is exposing old sentiments and alliances often consolidated along ethnic lines.

Notes

1 Large sections of this chapter draw upon data previously presented in (Eilenberg 2012a).
2 *Pemekaran* not only refers to the splitting of regencies but also to other levels of administrative fragmentation like the creation of new provinces, districts, villages and hamlets (Kimura 2007).

3 The movement further includes a small handful of Jakarta-based supporters from the University of Indonesia and civil servants from central state ministries like the Ministry of Agriculture and the Ministry of National Education.
4 Compared to the Maloh and Malay, the Iban have strong cross-border ethnic ties with the Iban in Sarawak where the people make up the largest single ethnic group.
5 The Iban, and especially the Maloh, have a long history of inter-ethnic confrontation and conflict over access to land and resources dating back to the colonial period (King 1976).
6 Law No. 10/1999.
7 *Forum Peduli Masyarakat Perbatasan Kalimantan Barat* (FPMP).
8 Personal interview, Badau, 20 March 2007.
9 Personal interview, Lanjak, 1 March 2007.
10 Another more urgent reason for the central government in creating the border agency was to gain control of and access to natural resources and 'unexploited' land for plantation development in the borderlands (Eilenberg 2014b).
11 Personal interview, Putussibau, 13 March 2007.
12 Personal interview, Lanjak, 21 March 2007.
13 See Letter to Nederlands-Indië Governor-General Jacob from Charles Brooke, 25 September 1882, Mailrapport No. 1066, Ministerie van Koloniën, Nationaal Archief, Den Haag, Netherlands.
14 The Iban population have a long and contested history of conflict and confrontation with pre-colonial and colonial states in the region today known as Kapuas Hulu. Prior to the Dutch colonial intrusions the region was under the authority of several small Malay kingdoms to whom the various Dayak groups paid tribute. However the rebellious Iban living in the hilly borderlands refused to pay tribute and were known as the 'free Dayaks' that were under nobody's authority (Eilenberg 2014a).
15 Personal interview, Embaloh Hulu, 13 June 2007.
16 Personal interview, Badau, 19 March 2007.
17 Personal interview, Lanjak, 1 August 2007.
18 Personal interview, Lanjak, 28 March 2007.
19 Among the border population, only very few have formal legal titles on their land and, therefore, are vulnerable to encroachment from plantation companies backed by state power and regulations (Borneo Tribune 2008). Most lands form local categories under various forms of customary land ownership, which through centuries, have been passed from generation to generation through intricate systems of rights (Wadley 1997).
20 Personal interview, Pontianak, 3 March 2011.

References

Akcaya (2007, 9 March) Bupati dukung pemekaran Kabupaten Perbatasan Utara Kapuas Hulu, *Akcaya Kalimantan Barat.*
Aspinall, E. (2011) Democratization and Ethnic Politics in Indonesia: Nine Theses, *Journal of East Asian Studies* 11(2): 289–319.
Aspinall, E. (2013) A Nation in Fragments, *Critical Asian Studies* 45(1): 27–54.
Bappenas (2003) *Strategi dan Model Pengembangan Wilayah Perbatasan Kalimantan.* Jakarta: Kementerian Perencanaan Pembangunan Nasional, Badan Perencanaan Pembangunan Nasional.
Bappenas (2004) *Kawasan Perbatasan: Kebijakan dan Strategi Nasional Pengelolaan Kawasan Perbatasan antarnegara di Indonesia.* Jakarta: Kementerian Perencanaan Pembangunan Nasional, Badan Perencanaan Pembangunan Nasional.
Bappenas (2008) *Bahan Diskusi: Rencana Pembangunan Jangka Menengah Pengembangan*

Kawasan Perbatasan Tahun 2010–2014. Jakarta: Kementerian Perencanaan Pembangunan Nasional, Badan Perencanaan Pembangunan Nasional.

Bappenas and UNDP (2008) *Evaluation of the Proliferation of Administrative Regions in Indonesia, 2001–2007*. Jakarta: Bappenas.

Borneo Tribune (2008, 25 September) Tanah di Perbatasan belum bersertifikat, *Borneo Tribune*.

Duncan, C.R. (2007) Mixed Outcomes: The Impact of Regional Autonomy and Decentralization on Indigenous Ethnic Minorities in Indonesia, *Development and Change* 38(4): 711–733.

Eilenberg, M. (2011) Flouting the Law: Vigilante Justice and Regional Autonomy on the Indonesian Border, *Austrian Journal of South East Asian Studies* 4(2): 237–253.

Eilenberg, M. (2012a) *At the Edges of States: Dynamics of State Formation in the Indonesian Borderlands*. Leiden: KITLV Press.

Eilenberg, M. (2012b) The Confession of a Timber Baron: Patterns of Patronage on the Indonesian-Malaysian Border, *Identities: Global Studies in Culture and Power* 9(2): 149–167.

Eilenberg, M. (2014a) Evading Colonial Authority. Rebels and Outlaws in the Borderlands of Dutch West Borneo 1850s–1920s, *Journal of Borderlands Studies* 29(1): 11–25.

Eilenberg, M. (2014b) Frontier Constellations: Agrarian Expansion and Sovereignty on the Indonesian–Malaysian Border, *The Journal of Peasant Studies* 41(2): 157–182.

Eilenberg, M. and Wadley, R.L. (2009) Borderland Livelihood Strategies: The Socioeconomic Significance of Ethnicity in Cross-border Labour Migration, West Kalimantan, Indonesia, *Asia Pacific Viewpoint* 50(1): 58–73.

Equator News (2006, 28 July) Kabupaten Perbatasan, Upaya pertahankan NKRI, *Equator News*.

Equator News (2007a, 10 March) Masyarakat sepakati Nama Kabupaten Perbatasan Utara, *Equator News*.

Equator News (2007b, 13 November) Pemekaran Kabupaten Upaya menyerap Aspirasi Masyarakat, *Equator News*.

Firman, T. (2013) Territorial Splits (Pemekaran Daerah) in Decentralising Indonesia, 2000–2012: Local Development Drivers or Hindrance?, *Space and Polity* 17(2): 180–196.

Fitrani, F., Hofman, B. and Kaiser, K. (2005) Unity in Diversity? The Creation of New Local Governments in a Decentralising Indonesia, *Bulletin of Indonesian Economic Studies* 41(1): 57–79.

Hansen, T.B. and Stepputat, F. (eds) (2005) *Sovereign Bodies: Citizens, Migrants, and States in the Postcolonial World*. Princeton, NJ: Princeton University Press.

Hansen, T.B. and Stepputat, F. (eds) (2006) Sovereignty Revisited, *Annual Review of Anthropology* 35(1): 295–315.

Jakarta Globe (2012, 22 October) House Agrees on Creation of Indonesia's 34th Province: 'North Kalimantan', *Jakarta Globe*.

Jakarta Post (2007a, 28 August) The Limit of Creating New Regions in Indonesia, *Jakarta Post*.

Jakarta Post (2007b, 24 August) SBY Slams Self-interested New Regions, *Jakarta Post*.

Jakarta Post (2010a, 31 January) New Military Command in Kalimantan to Guard Border Areas, *Jakarta Post*.

Jakarta Post (2010b, 28 March) RI's New Border Management, *Jakarta Post*.

Jakarta Post (2012, 20 April) How Many Provinces Does Indonesia Need?, *Jakarta Post*.

94   *M. Eilenberg*

Jakarta Post (2013, 14 November) Plan to Establish Kapuas Raya Province Draws Mixed Reactions, *Jakarta Post.*

Kabupaten Kapuas Hulu (2006) *Data Pokok – Kabupaten Kapuas Hulu.* Putussibau: Kantor Penelitian, Pengembangan dan Informatika.

Kalimantan Review (2008, 7 March) Pembentukan Provinsi Kapuas Raya, *Kalimantan Review.*

KepDPRD (2006) Persetujuan Pembentukan Kabupaten Sentarum dan Kabupaten di Wilayah Perbatasan Kabupaten Kapuas Hulu. Putussibau: Keputusan Dewan Perwakilan Rakyat Daerah Kabupaten Kapuas Hulu, No. 8.

Kimura, E. (2007) Marginality and Opportunity in the Periphery: The Emergence of Gorontalo Province in North Sulawesi, *Indonesia* 84: 71–95.

King, V.T. (1976) Some Aspects of Iban-Maloh Contact in West Kalimantan, *Indonesia* 21: 85–114.

KNPDT (2007) *Rencana Aksi Nasional Pembangunan Daerah Tertinggal Tahun 2007–2009.* Jakarta: Kementerian Negara Pembangunan Daerah Tertinggal.

Kompas (2000, 7 August) Masyarakat Perbatasan Kalimantan-Sarawak terasing di Negerinya sendiri, *Kompas.*

Kompas (2001, 8 October) Masyarakat Perbatasan RI-Malaysia terasing di Negeri sendiri, *Kompas.*

Kompas (2007, 11 September) Pemekaran Wilayah Perbatasan jadi Prioritas, *Kompas.*

Kompas (2011, 19 October) 200.000 Ha Sawit Malaysia di Perbatasan Indonesia, *Kompas.*

Kuyah, F. (1992) Pengaruh Pembangunan terhadap Peningkatan Masyarakat Perbatasan Kabupaten Kapuas Hulu: Lokaraya Hukum dan Pembangunan Masyarakat Perbatasan Kabupaten Kapuas Hulu, Lanjak 5–7 December 1992.

Lund, C. (2011) Fragmented Sovereignty: Land Reform and Dispossession in Laos, *Journal of Peasant Studies* 38(4): 885–905.

McWilliam, A. (2011) Marginal Governance in the Time of Pemekaran: Case Studies from Sulawesi and West Papua, *Asian Journal of Social Science* 39(2): 150–170.

Peluso, N.L. and Lund, C. (2011) New Frontiers of Land Control: Introduction, *The Journal of Peasant Studies* 38(4): 667–681.

Perhut Kapuas Hulu (2007) Rencana Anggaran Biaya Kegiatan Pengelolaan Perbatasan RI-Malaysia di Kabupaten Kapuas Hulu, Tahun 2008–2009. Putussibau: Dinas Perkebunan dan Kehutanan, Kabupaten Kapuas Hulu.

Perpres (2010) Badan Nasional Pengelola Perbatasan. Jakarta: Peraturan Presiden Republik Indonesia, No. 12.

Pontianak Post (2005, 24 May) Warga Perbatasan masih harapkan Malaysia, *Pontianak Post.*

PPKPU (2007) Gambaran Umum Kelayakan Pemekaran Pembentukan Kabupaten Perbatasan Utara di Kapuas Hulu, Kalimantan Barat. Pontianak/Jakarta: Panitia Pembentukan Kabupaten Perbatasan Utara (PPKPU) dengan Lembaga Kajian Pemerintahan Daerah dan Pembangunan Indonesia (LKPDPI).

Roth, D. (2007) Many Governors, No Province: The Struggle for a Province in the Luwu-Tana Toraja Area in South Sulawesi, in H. Schulte Nordholt and G. van Klinken (eds), *Renegotiating Boundaries: Local Politics in Post-Suharto Indonesia*, Leiden: KITLV Press, pp. 121–147.

Schendel, W. van and de Maaker, E. (2014) Asian Borderlands: Introducing Their Permeability, Strategic Uses and Meanings, *Journal of Borderlands Studies* 29(1): 3–9.

Sinar Harapan (2013, 30 October) Disetujui Pembentukan Kabupaten Banua Landjak, *Sinar Harapan.*

Suara Bekakak (2006, No.XV/Th.6. July–September) Kawasan Perbatasan bukan untuk Sawit, Masyarakat berdaulat atas Pengelolaan Sumber Daya, *Suara bekakak: Berita triwulan Taman Nasional Danau Sentarum.*

Tanasaldy, T. (2007) Ethnic Identity Politics in West Kalimantan, in H. Schulte Nordholt and G. van Klinken (eds), *Renegotiating Boundaries: Local Politics in Post-Suharto Indonesia,* Leiden: KITLV Press, pp. 349–371.

Tempo (2013, 11 September) Govt Declines Formation of New Regions, *Tempo.*

Vel, J. (2007) Campaigning for a New District in West Sumba, in H. Schulte Nordholt and G. van Klinken (eds), *Renegotiating Boundaries: Local Politics in Post-Suharto Indonesia,* Leiden: KITLV Press, pp. 91–119.

Wadley, R.L. (1997) Variation and Changing Tradition in Iban Land Tenure, *Borneo Research Bulletin* 28: 98–108.

Wadley, R.L. (2000) Transnational Circular Labour Migration in Northwestern Borneo, *Revue Européenne des Migrations Internationales* 16(1): 127–149.

Wadley, R.L. (2004) Punitive Expeditions and Divine Revenge: Oral and Colonial Histories of Rebellion and Pacification in Western Borneo, 1886–1902, *Ethnohistory* 51(3): 609–636.

Wadley, R.L. and Eilenberg, M. (2005) Autonomy, Identity, and 'Illegal' Logging in the Borderland of West Kalimantan, Indonesia, *Asia Pacific Journal of Anthropology* 6(1): 19–34.

Wollenberg, E., Moeliono, M., Limberg, G., Iwan, R., Rhee, S. and Sudana, M. (2006) Between State and Society: Local Governance of Forests in Malinau, Indonesia, *Forest Policy and Economics* 8(4): 421–433.

Zaum, D. (2007) *The Souvereignty Paradox: The Norm and Politics of International Statebuilding.* New York: Oxford University Press.

6 Redrawing borders and reshaping marginality in North Maluku

Kirsten Jäger

Introduction

After Suharto's resignation in 1998, new legislation led Indonesia into the reform era (*era reformasi*) and towards a more decentralised nation state. Laws No. 22/1999 and No. 25/1999[1] were intended to increase the autonomy of the provinces (*propinsi*) and especially of the regencies (*kabupaten*), so that regional affairs could be dealt with more effectively and the finances for these objectives be made available. This resulted in a newly ignited competition for natural and financial resources as well as for political influence. This competition was accompanied by violent outbursts all over Indonesia and a re-division of administrative units (*pemekaran*, literally: blossoming) mainly in the so-called Outer Islands. These processes are typically articulated in terms of promoting a more efficient public service and a more representative government. Furthermore, they are often accompanied by the wish to acquire money from the central government and gain access to political offices and the control over natural resources (Schulte Nordholt and van Klinken 2007; Booth 2011).

New centres of power have emerged, as regional governments have acquired more political influence and 'traditional'[2] (*adat*) power holders have been revitalised in many regions of the Indonesian Republic (Bubandt 2004; Bräuchler 2007; Davidson and Henley 2007; Hauser-Schäublin 2013). These newly empowered actors may also associate themselves with commercial enterprises operating on transnational levels in order to benefit monetarily.

This chapter examines the *pemekaran* processes in Halmahera, North Maluku. It explores how new centres emerge and people gain new agency to establish relations to these centres. The chapter also shows how marginality is reshaped in the course of the decentralised state. These processes are exemplified by six villages (*desa*)[3] from the district (*kecamatan*) Jailolo in the province of North Maluku which came to belong to both the regency of West Halmahera (Halmahera Barat) and to the regency of North Halmahera (Halmahera Utara) after *pemekaran* took place.[4]

In addition to financial motivations and the wish for political influence, which can also be observed in the *pemekaran* process in North Maluku, the redrawing of borders was not based solely on economic or political terms. Most territorial units were divided along lines that existed long before the Republic of Indonesia had been established and provided people with a strong sense of identity and belonging (Fox 2011).

In order to understand the interaction between these strategic interests on the one hand, and a sense of belonging on the other hand, I draw on Stuart Hall's theory on articulation (Hall 1986). First, I aim to identify the continuous concepts of the socio-territorial organisation in North Maluku, which may become more visible during the fragmentation of administrative units. My second aim is to explore the (re-)shaping of relations between renewed centres of power and the margins that may emerge due to the *pemekaran* processes.

Socio-territorial organisation in North Maluku

Over one million people reside in North Maluku, which has a land area of 31,982 km². The majority of inhabitants are Muslim and almost a quarter of the population is Christian. Hindus and Buddhists constitute a small minority. Twenty-two different languages are spoken in North Maluku, 12 belonging to the Non-Austronesian Papua Phylum and ten to the Austronesian language family. Halmahera is the largest island in the province of North Maluku. Around 625,000 people inhabit this island, the large majority of them are Muslim, and approximately 20 per cent of the residents are Christian. Christian communities reside mostly in the northern and western part of Halmahera. Politically, the island is segmented into five regencies (BPS Propinsi Maluku Utara 2013). Anthropological and historical research demonstrates that the societies of Halmahera share basic ideas about their cosmological system, in which all social relations are embedded (Platenkamp 2013: 206–232). An ideological concept shared by most inhabitants of North and West Halmahera stipulates that North Maluku as a whole was part of a political and cosmological construction named *Moloku Kie Raha*, a unit of 'four mountains' composed of the Sultanates of Ternate, Tidore, Bacan and Jailolo. According to the myths, their rulers were brothers born to an immigrant father from Arabia and a mother originating in the heavenly sphere of *Kayangan*. The sons divided the land between them, resulting in constant competition for power (van Fraassen 1987; Andaya 1993). Jailolo's and Bacan's political influence faded in the sixteenth century due to internal warfare between the sultanates and the impact of the colonial presence. Ternate and Tidore expanded their territories and their concepts of social order as far as Sulawesi and Papua respectively.

The socio-territorial groups of Halmahera had their own form of organisation before the sultanates exerted their influence on that area. These social units consist of 'Houses', classificatory descent groups that trace their origin to one ancestor. These descent groups are defined as classificatory because it seems more important to connect oneself with the social unit through marriage or adoption and live in the same territory than descend from a common ancestor (Visser 1989: 100). In the course of their rise to power, the sultanates gave these social units in Halmahera an additional meaning as a tribute-paying unit. The social unit was called *soa* in Ternate, which can be translated as 'space', or 'space-in-between'. The terms for these social units in Halmahera, like the *hoana* in Tobelo and the *soan* in Tobaru and Loloda, derives from the lexeme *soa* (van Fraassen 1987/I: 140). These socio-territorial units should be understood as a double-sided category. First, as a social group that inhabits a distinct territory and traces its origin to one ancestor. This group establishes relations to this ancestor, the land, the animals and the plants and is thus strongly connected to the territory (van Fraassen 1987/I: 140–142; Bubandt 1991: 18).

Second, it can be understood as a unit which pays tribute (*upeti*) to the sultanate. In this understanding, the *soa* is defined by social status and the function it performs within the sultanate's domain (Bubandt 1991: 30–31). The sultanates constituted the socio-cosmological and political centre, incorporating their subjects into a broader socio-political framework. Therefore, the heterogeneous population was united under the 'umbrella' of the four sultanates (Andaya 1993).

Despite large-scale changes in the region due to constant territorial disputes between the sultanates, the period of the colonial regime, nation-building and the recent processes of *pemekaran*, the history of creating administrative units in North Maluku reveals that these socio-territorial units preserved much of their significance.

After a long history of indirect rule and cooperation between the Dutch colonial powers and the sultanates, the latter's influence was restricted in the early twentieth century, and they continued to lose political significance with the rise of nationalism throughout Indonesia. The claims to land titles made by the sultanates were legally declared invalid by the Basic Agrarian Law issued in 1960 (UU 5/1960). Following this law, the land of the sultans was redistributed, as land not owned by individuals was declared the property of the state (van Klinken 2007: 150). In spite of their diminishing political influence, the borders of the units of administration in North Maluku were still those of the sultanate's historical territories (BPS Propinsi Maluku Utara 2013). Dutch colonial officials mapping administrative units in Maluku largely complied with the existing *soa*-units as determined by the sultanates. These historical borders still constituted the terrain after Indonesian independence and even after the implementation of the new laws on regional and *desa* government (UU 5/1974 and UU 5/1979), which established a uniform administrative structure throughout Indonesia.

Articulating a common social identity in North Maluku

I draw on Stuart Hall's concept of articulation to understand social identity constructions in North Maluku. For Hall

> [a]n articulation is [...] the form of the connection that *can* make a unity of two different elements, under certain conditions. It is a linkage which is not necessary, determined, absolute and essential for all time. [...] Thus, a theory of articulation is both a way of understanding how ideological elements come, under certain conditions, to cohere together with a discourse,

and a way of asking how they do or do not become articulated, at specific conjunctures, to certain political subjects.

(1986: 53)

I use Hall's concept of articulation to avoid two pitfalls. First, to avoid the binary opposition of authentic and inauthentic, or invented and genuine. Second, ideological elements in this sense are never essential and timeless. They are always intermingled with socio-political and historical circumstances on the one hand. One the other hand, ideological elements are never a mere function engineered by the elites (Li 2000: 152).

According to Hall, the constructions of social identities are the contingent products of agency and the cultural and political work of articulation. They are '[…] subject to the continuous "play" of history, culture and power' (Hall 1990: 225). In which way these identities are articulated depends on the conditions for its articulation within the historical and present discourses (Li 2000: 169). Thus, identities are '[…] multiple constructed across different, often intersecting and antagonistic, discourses, practices and positions. They are subject to a radical historicization, and are constantly in the process of change and transformation' (Hall 1996: 3).

Even if the republican administrative units mostly resembled the socio-territorial units in North Maluku, people usually did not articulate their common identity in terms of the sultanate openly during the nation-building process of the Republic of Indonesia. The Indonesian fight for independence in 1920 until the 1940s was against colonial powers as well as against old aristocratic elites, which were perceived as the colonialists' allies. Accordingly, it was inappropriate for the sultanates to articulate claims to territory and power in terms of aristocratic concepts. Under Suharto, who was president between 1966 and 1998, aristocratic families may have gained prestigious and economically attractive governmental positions, but their sphere of power was exclusively articulated within republican terms (Magenda 1989/I: 10). Anthropologists who conducted their fieldwork in North Maluku in the late 1970s and early 1980s therefore concluded that the sultanates were finally dissolved (van Fraassen 1987/I: 65; Baker 1988: 115).

Pemekaran in North Maluku 1999–2001

Before North Maluku became a province, the area was a regency of the province Maluku, with its capital Ambon. In October 1999, North Maluku was assigned the status of province comprising two regencies, Central Halmahera (Halmahera Tengah) and North Maluku (Maluku Utara[5]), and a municipality (*kotamadya*) Ternate.

Malifut: a new district

In May 1999, prior to the declaration of the province North Maluku, Makianese migrants were able to obtain an official status for their district, known as Malifut.

In 1975 they had been evacuated from the island of Makian and brought to the Kao district due to anticipated volcanic outbursts on the island. Many of these migrants resided in Halmahera in the same socio-territorial constellation, using the same village (*desa*) names as they did in Makian (Lucardie 1983: 333; PP 42/1999(1a)). In their understanding, they retained their social identity of being Makianese (*orang Makian*) as long as they identified themselves as originating from that island; otherwise, they would lose their right to bear that name. These origin relations were expressed in the names of the *desa* and were manifest in preserving the Makian language even after their emigration to other parts of the archipelago. The creation of their own district was therefore essential for the maintenance of their distinct identity as Makianese. Moreover, they perceived themselves as official (local) transmigrants who had been assigned their own territory by the government after the involuntary resettlement in the Kao district (Lucardie 1983: 336–341).

Malifut was a long-term project of many Makianese migrants. Creating Malifut as a district was thought of as '[…] only a first step towards achieving a long-held goal for many connected with Malifut – establishing the town as the capital of a [regency]' (Wilson 2008: 58). Besides some ministers from the Ministry of the Interior, the former regency head (*bupati*) of Maluku Utara, a Makianese, along with other regional politicians, the majority of them of Makianese descent too, were involved in this process.

In order to fulfil the requirements for establishing a new district, six *desa* from the neighbouring district Jailolo[6] and five from the district Kao[7] were meant to merge with the 16 *desa* of Makian residents (PP 42/1999).

Dispute over the pemekaran process

The people of the Kao and Jailolo districts, however, refused to merge with the migrants from Makian and to be incorporated into the entity named Makian Daratan Malifut (Mainland Makian in Malifut). Kao is the name of the district and of the ethnic group (*suku*) who mainly inhabits that territory. The majority of this group are Christian, some Kao are Muslim. People who consider themselves as ethnic Kao live mainly in the aforementioned five villages from the Kao district. The Kao community stated their ethnic unity would be separated as the border of the new district cut through their territory (Duncan 2005: 63). Furthermore, they perceived the migrants as guests on their ancestral land.[8]

The inhabitants of the six *desa* from the Jailolo district are quite heterogeneous. Most inhabitants are from North and West Halmahera, some migrated from Ternate since the sixteenth century. Some people from Sangir, North Sulawesi, migrated in the 1970s to the area as well. The residents of four *desa* (Gamsungi, Tetewang, Pasir Putih and Dum-Dum) are Christian and the other two (Akelamo Kao and Bobaneigo) are Muslim. The two Muslim villages are the most reluctant to join the administrative unit Kao Teluk with the Muslim Makianese. It is therefore highly unlikely that the refusal to merge is based on religion.

Research about this dispute mainly focused on the relationship between the Kao population and the migrants from Makian (van Klinken 2001; Duncan 2005; Wilson 2008). The motives of the inhabitants from Jailolo, who refused to join the new district called Malifut, were mostly subsumed to those of the Kao residents. Until this time, the residents of the six *desa* from Jailolo and from Kao appeared to be a community with common interests.

Historically, the Kao and Jailolo people had been subject to the Sultanate of Ternate since the decline of the Sultanate of Jailolo in the sixteenth century. During the first phase of that dispute, the inhabitants of the six *desa* from Jailolo formed a union with the Kao community, articulating their mutual refusal in reference to the social identity of their respective socio-territorial unit (*soa*).

Impacts of the mining company

In addition to claims based on social identity, resource-related motivations also played a key role. Goldmining made the territory between Jailolo and Kao highly contested. The PT Nusa Halmahera Mineral (NHM), a joint venture of the Australian Newcrest and the Indonesian PT Aneka Tambang, has operated in the border region between the districts of Jailolo and Kao since the 1990s. The Sultan of Ternate came to Halmahera to demand compensation for himself and for 'his people' of Kao and Jailolo, claiming that the mining company was operating on 'traditional land' (*tanah adat*) which belonged to him. Despite the efforts of the sultanate, the Makianese were supported by their numerous representatives in the regional government (Wilson 2008: 59), and when the mining company commissioned work in June 1999, the whole mining area was located in Malifut (Newcrest Mining 2011: 20).

The escalation of the conflict 1999–2001

After the law on the new district was passed, some small fights occurred between the Kao/Jailolo community and Makianese. In August 1999, violent disputes between these two groups resulted in the destruction of two Kao villages and the death of several people (Duncan 2005: 64). People from Kao and Jailolo were still trying to prevent the establishment of the new district, but as their attempts continued to fail, several thousand inhabitants of the districts Kao and Jailolo attacked Malifut, destroying all of their villages and expelling the Makianese from the area. They fled to Ternate, finding shelter in the southern part of the island, where many migrants from Makian were already residing. In the next months, this local dispute between communities in Halmahera over land use and district borders turned into violent conflicts between different groups, mainly along religious lines, that shook the province of North Maluku from 1999 until 2001 (van Klinken 2001).

Pemekaran in North Maluku 2003–present

After the conflict ended and most refugees returned to their former homes, the fragmentation of administrative entities continued. From 2003 onwards, the three administrative units *kabupaten* Maluku Utara, *kabupaten* Halmahera Tengah and *kotamadya* Ternate, were divided into eight new units.[9] From Maluku Utara emerged Halmahera Utara (North Halmahera), Halmahera Selatan (South Halmahera) and *kepulauan* Sula (Sula Archipelago). The remaining territory from the *kabupaten* Maluku Utara was renamed Halmahera Barat (West Halmahera). From the *kabupaten* Halmahera Tengah emerged Halmahera Timur (East Halmahera) and *kepulauan* Tidore (Tidore Archipelago). The remaining territory kept the name Halmahera Tengah (Central Halmahera) (UU 1/2003).

Administrative units are often fragmented to gain access to political power and financial as well as natural resources. These processes are further accompanied by significant corruption in the relations between regional and national governments. About 23.5 billion rupiah (*c.*1,465 million euro) were embezzled by the regional government during the 'blossoming' of administrative units in North Maluku from 2002 until 2003 (Media Indonesia 2005). Nonetheless, the shape of these new administrative units can mainly be recognised as a reformation of the old socio-territorial units referring to the four sultanates. The borders of the regencies Halmahera Tengah and Maluku Utara were based on the realms of the Sultanates of Tidore and Ternate respectively. After the second administrative divisions of 2003, the newly established regency Halmahera Selatan was referred to as the realm of the Bacan Sultanate. Even the territory of the district Jailolo was associated with the territory of its long abolished sultanate. Since North Maluku was declared a province, the Sultanates of Tidore and Bacan were both re-established in 1999. The Sultanate of Ternate was revitalised in 1986 (van Klinken 2007: 152). After several attempts to rebuild the Sultanate of Jailolo in the eighteenth and nineteenth centuries, it was finally revitalised in 2003, now claiming Halmahera Barat as its realm (Jäger 2015).

Redrawing district borders: Jailolo Timur a.k.a. Kao Teluk

The district Jailolo was assigned to the regency of Halmahera Barat and the district Kao to that of Halmahera Utara. Since Malifut was allocated to Halmahera Utara, the six *desa* from Jailolo were also included in that regency.

After the conflict ended and civil law was re-established in 2003, the five *desa* from the district Kao were integrated into the district Malifut without further violent outbursts. The inhabitants of the six *desa* from Jailolo, however, still refused to join this (administrative) unit. New communities of interests and new common social identities were constituted during this process.

After the law on the new territorial units (UU 1/2003) was passed by the central government, the inhabitants of Halmahera Barat were, again, highly malcontent. They claimed that the historical borders of their territory had been ignored and demanded the laws in question (PP 42/1999, UU 1/2003) be reviewed. As neither the national nor the regional parliament agreed to their requests, those *desa* of Jailolo that had been allocated to Halmahera Utara rejected this status and established a separate district belonging to Halmahera Barat. This district, called Jailolo Timur (East Jailolo), has not been officially recognised by the national parliament. Nonetheless, the district was proclaimed by the regional government of Halmahera Barat in 2005.[10] Jailolo Timur covers an area of 281 km² and its capital is Akelamo Kao (BPS Kabupaten Halmahera Barat 2013: 7). Besides the support of the regional government of Halmahera Barat, the Sultanates of Ternate and Jailolo were lobbying for the six *desa* to belong to Jailolo and thus, to Halmahera Barat.

Shortly after, in 2006, the government of Halmahera Utara passed a regulation to create the district Kao Teluk (Kao at the bay),[11] which consists of the six *desa* from Jailolo and five partly new created *desa* from Malifut covering an area of 135 km². The district's capital is Dum-Dum (BPS Kabupaten Halmahera Utara 2013: 8).

Figure 6.1 and Maps 6.1 and 6.2 illustrate these complex processes.

The situation is still unresolved. In the meantime, the inhabitants themselves have decided to split up each of the six *desa*. The large majority of the inhabitants declare that they belong to Jailolo Timur in Halmahera Barat; the remaining ones claim that they belong to Kao Teluk in Halmahera Utara. The inhabitants constitute two separate administrative bodies; they elect different regency heads and pay taxes to their respective regency. Additionally, each *desa* has two heads (*kepala desa*) and two versions of the Village Consultation Body (*Badan Permusyawaratan Desa*, BPD). The *desa* are not divided territorially. There may be neighbours, one claiming to reside in Jailolo Timur/Halmahera Barat while the other claims to reside in Kao Teluk/Halmahera Utara.

The province **Maluku Utara** was established in 1999 consisting of the *kabupaten* Maluku Utara, *kabupaten* Halmahera Tengah, *kota* Ternate

After *pemekaran in* 2003, the *kabupaten* **Maluku Utara** was segmented into the *kabupaten* Halmahera Selatan, Halmahera Utara, Halmahera Barat and *archipelago* Sula,

---

According to the *kabupaten* **Halmahera Barat** the six *desa* belong to the district **Jailolo Timur** within the regency Halmahera Barat (six *desa*)	According to the *kabupaten* **Halmahera Utara** the six *desa* belong to the district **Kao Teluk** within the regency Halmahera Utara (six *desa* + five *desa* from Malifut)
Desa: Bobaneigo, Tetewang, Pasir Putih, Gamsungi, Dum-Dum, Akelamo Kao	*Desa*: Bobaneigo, Tetewang, Pasir Putih, Gamsungi, Dum-Dum, Akelamo Kao, Tiowor, Makaeling, Tabonoma, Barumadehe, Kuntum Mekar

Figure 6.1 The *pemekaran* process 1999–2003.

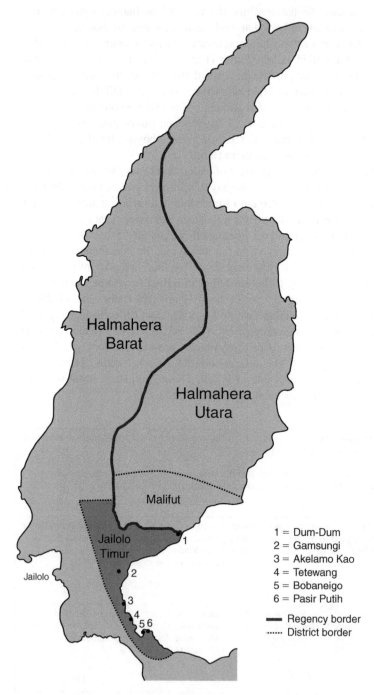

Map 6.1 Borders of regencies and districts, Version Halmahera Barat (approximate) (copyright Kirsten Jäger).

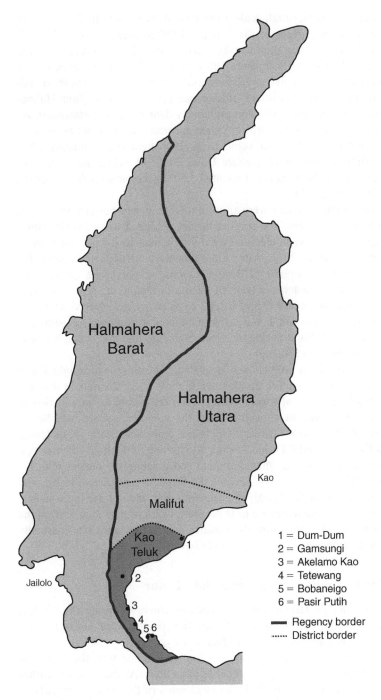

Map 6.2 Borders of regencies and districts, Version Halmahera Utara (approximate) (copyright Kirsten Jäger).

Throughout the years, small-scale riots have broken out. In 2010, a riot occurred when the employees of the Statistical Office (*Badan Pusat Statistik*, BPS) from Halmahera Utara tried to take a census in Jailolo Timur, registering the citizens as belonging to Halmahera Utara. People who claimed to belong to Halmahera Barat refused to give any information to the BPS team sent from Halmahera Utara. Finally, the Statistical Office requested another team from Halmahera Barat to interview those who had previously denied giving a statement. As a result, different population figures circulate according to different censuses.[12] The most recent census for Kao Teluk from Halmahera Utara counted 4,775 inhabitants (BPS Kabupaten Halmahera Utara 2013: 8), while the census for Jailolo Timur from Halmahera Barat counted 3,508 inhabitants (BPS Kabupaten Halmahera Barat 2013: 41).

The citizens in Jailolo Timur were allowed to vote in previous elections at the national and regional levels. The conflict further escalated when Jailolo Timur was no longer registered as an electoral ward for Halmahera Barat in the provincial governor election of 2013. After the announcement of this decision, the people of Jailolo Timur organised demonstrations, uproar broke out and the regional government dispatched a team to Jakarta to remind the central government to review the laws 42/1999 and 1/2003 so as to avoid further violent conflicts. Nonetheless, Jailolo Timur was, against national instructions, registered as a district in Halmahera Barat during the election in June and the second ballot in October 2013 (Malut Post 2013).

Besides their precarious political and legal status, the citizens of Jailolo Timur have also experienced economic disadvantages. Only those districts in the area of the PT Nusa Halmahera Mineral (NHM) which fall within the jurisdiction of Halmahera Utara receive an allocation from the company's Corporate Social Responsibility (CRS) funds. These districts are Kao, Kao Barat, Kau Utara, Malifut and Kao Teluk. NHM organises the distribution of the funds themselves. Each district has a CRS-team, managing and coordinating the budget with the 'village team' (*tim desa*) in every *desa* of the respective district (d'Hondt and Sangaji 2011: 8). In Kao Teluk, only the five *desa* from Malifut and the residents of the six *desa* who claim to belong to Halmahera Utara receive money from the funds. As a result, the economic discrepancy within the *desa* has markedly increased – a development which may lead to new disputes.

Articulating a common identity in Jailolo Timur

The shared identity of Jailolo Timur's residents emerged during the (failed) process of *pemekaran*. Before these processes, the six *desa* were part of the district Jailolo. As aforementioned, the inhabitants are quite heterogeneous.

In 1999, the inhabitants of the six *desa* formed a union with the five *desa* from Kao that were not willing to join Malifut either. At the time of further administrative fragmentation in 2003, the inhabitants of the six *desa* articulated their common identity mainly in terms of the four sultanates and the decentralisation laws. As the Sultanate of Jailolo was revitalised in 2003, Jailolo, including

Jailolo Timur, is seen as a social unit belonging to and deriving its specific identity from that sultanate model, allowing for the heterogeneous population of Jailolo Timur to be unified. Remarkably, the Sangirese immigrants were perceived by the inhabitants of Jailolo Timur as different from the Makianese. The Sangirese have been unified with the local inhabitants through marriage, therefore being integrated into the existing social organisational structures instead of establishing a district of their own designation. This illustrates that integration is not determined by one's origin, but by the willingness to be included into the other's socio-territorial concepts and to form a common social identity.

The refusal of Jailolo Timur's residents to merge with the Makianese is based on a fear of subordination by (assumed) Makianese social and political dominance. They are further convinced that taking a Makianese name for the district would indicate an assimilation of the Makianese identity (cf. Wilson 2008). Moreover, the inhabitants have tried to preserve their socio-territorial concepts as they underline their historical relations to Jailolo by naming their district Jailolo Timur. The Makianese migrants' wish to establish a new district also results from their desire to maintain their distinct identity as Makianese. Accordingly, the district's name Kao Teluk can be understood as a compromise, provided by the regional government in Halmahera Utara, neither emphasising Jailolo nor Makian as an identity marker. The name Kao Teluk rather indicates that the territory is mostly taken from the original district Kao and is located at the bay (*teluk*) which constitutes the natural border.

New centres

New centres of power, which are highly intertwined, (re-)emerge within the socio-political dynamics of the fragmenting state. The following section aims to identify new powerful centres which influence the socio-political dynamics in the region and explore how the inhabitants of Jailolo Timur, Malifut and Kao Teluk are able to relate with and benefit from these centres.

Regional governments

Regional governments have become more influential and are able to pass and implement regional regulations.[13] Since the implementation of the decentralisation laws, regional governments have more opportunities to gain allocation from the central government and they are responsible for negotiating contracts and compensation with companies working on the regencies' territory.

The regional government in Halmahera Barat reacted to the demands of residents who wanted to belong to Halmahera Barat by creating Jailolo Timur. This regional regulation contradicts the national law. Although the district is not officially recognised, the inhabitants of Jailolo Timur established an electoral constituency and a public infrastructure exclusively belonging to Halmahera Barat. This regional government has provided an opportunity to link the six *desa* with the former district Jailolo and Halmahera Barat.

Halmahera Utara passed a regional regulation to establish the district Kao Teluk according to national law, but this law has not been fully implemented and is being prevented by the refusal of Jailolo Timur's inhabitants to accept this declaration and the government's fear of prompting new conflicts in the region.

Adat *institutions*

The process of decentralisation has led to a revival of 'traditional ways' (*adat*) throughout Indonesia (Davidson and Henley 2007). The nationally operating organisation AMAN (*Aliansi Masyarakat Adat Nusantara*: Indigenous[14] Peoples' Alliance of the Archipelago), which tries to empower *adat* communities (*masyarakat adat*) was established as well as many *adat* councils on *desa*, district and regency levels. Some *adat* institutions were recreated by inhabitants after the conflict in hopes that further violence may be prevented (Duncan 2009). Furthermore, the sultanates returned to Maluku Utara claiming rights to their former land and access to political offices (van Klinken 2007). An example of this is when the Sultan of Ternate claimed without any judicial legitimation, that the mining company operated on 'his' land demanding compensation for himself and his subjects in 1999.

After the revitalisation of the Sultanate of Jailolo in 2003, this sultan claimed Halmahera Barat including Jailolo Timur as his 'traditional' realm. Despite the lack of acceptance for the Sultanate of Jailolo among the inhabitants and regional politicians in Halmahera Barat at first, the very same people argued in favour of this sultanate to stress the continuity of the region's socio-territorial entities and the need for the whole area of Jailolo, including Jailolo Timur, to stay intact (Jäger 2015: 260–262).

These processes led to a situation where the system of the sultanate and the government are intermingled with each other: government officials contribute within the organisation of the sultanates and the sultans get involved with government issues.

International companies

Another powerful agent has been the internationally operating mining company in Halmahera. Officially, the gold mine is located in Halmahera Utara, but due to ongoing exploration activity and unclear marking of borders, the company also explores within the regency of Halmahera Barat. According to my informants, the company is trying to influence the decision-making process over the six *desa* in favour of Halmahera Utara, in order to have to deal only with that regency's government.

New margins

The formation of new centres results in new margins. In the decentralised state, the definition of who is in the centre and who is at the margins shifts depending on the applied discourse and context. Communities may emerge as margins, suffering from political, economic and/or social disadvantage in one context, or they may locate themselves in the centre, being able to relate to a source of power in another context.

Malifut

For many years the Makianese migrants were marginalised in Northern Halmahera – being without legal status concerning land rights and their own representation on a district level. In the course of decentralisation, however, the well-connected Makianese elite was able to constitute the district Malifut in 1999. The Makianese managed to reconcile their concept of a distinct social identity by founding a new administrative unit. In the case of Malifut, the desire to maintain a distinct social identity was congruent to economic and political interests. The residents of Malifut profit from their relations to the empowered regional government.

Kao Teluk

In 2006 the regulation 5/2006 was passed, enacting five *desa* from Malifut to unite with the six *desa* from Jailolo. The partially new-founded Makianese *desa* all bear a Makianese name and the inhabitants emphasise their relations to Malifut. Although Kao Teluk has legal sanction as an administrative unit, it does not create a unity of people who share a common identity. Being separated from the Makianese in Malifut, Makianese in Kao Teluk perceive themselves as socially marginalised.

The government in Halmahera Utara has encountered difficulties democratically legitimising public offices in Kao Teluk. Whereas in Jailolo Timur citizens have directly elected their village head (*kepala desa*) since 2005, residents of the six *desa* related to Kao Teluk have only voted for their representatives since 2012. Before then, the *kepala desa* had been selected by the regency head (*bupati*) of Halmahera Utara. Additionally, the local government at the district level is neither transparent nor running effectively. Most of my informants in Kao Teluk state that they feel ignored by the government in Halmahera Utara because, for example, public buildings and health care are not provided by the government but instead is funded mainly by the mining company.

Therefore, those inhabitants of the six *desa* from Jailolo, who were willing to merge with Halmahera Utara, feel politically marginalised.

Jailolo Timur

In 2005, the regional government in Halmahera Barat established the district Jailolo Timur consisting of the six *desa* from Jailolo. The inhabitants' desire to belong to the district Jailolo Timur in the regency Halmahera Barat is based on the concept of specific socio-territorial units. Jailolo, including Jailolo Timur, is supposed to be the realm of the Sultanate of Jailolo. Thus, the inhabitants have tried to combine the new power of the regional governments and the returned sultanates so as to gain support to translate their socio-territorial concepts into the republican structure. The inhabitants of Jailolo Timur emphasise the historical ties to Jailolo/Halmahera Barat by establishing a new district. In contrast to the Makianese in Malifut who established a new district to underline their distinct social identity, political and economic interests do not correspond with those of social identity. Due to the district Jailolo Timur, the inhabitants have managed to obtain an identity as citizens of Jailolo/Halmahera Barat, distinct from the Makianese migrants.

However, the unofficial status of their district has resulted in their right to vote being questioned, and coupled with a lack of compensation from the mining company means that they find themselves politically and economically marginalised.

Concluding remarks

This chapter has outlined the *pemekaran* process in Halmahera that has resulted in the intersecting districts of Jailolo Timur and Kao Teluk, while focusing on the continuity of socio-territorial concepts and the changing power relations which these processes initiate. The aspect of agency becomes more important in the decentralised state. The possibility for people to refuse the national government's orders and to insist on and shape their own social identity was enhanced with the emergence of multiple centres.

Besides competing economic and political interests between the groups of Makianese residents and the inhabitants of Jailolo Timur, it is remarkable how the inhabitants try to relate their socio-territorial concepts to the (re-)emerging centres of power. The Makianese demand for their own district expresses their desire to uphold their distinct identity and provides them with access to political power and natural resources. They profit from the new power of the regional government in which they are strongly represented. Therefore, the Makianese tap into the discourse of decentralisation laws to articulate their interests.

People like the inhabitants of the six *desa* in Jailolo may refuse to merge with others to avoid becoming new margins. In order to articulate their refusal to be associated with the Makianese and to stay within the borders of Halmahera Barat, the inhabitants of Jailolo Timur tap into the discourse of newly re-established sultanates so as to identify themselves with Jailolo, one of the 'four mountains of Maluku'. Furthermore, they use the support of the regional government in Halmahera Barat to maintain their connection to Jailolo, even if this results in economic and political drawbacks. It seems therefore, as if Jailolo Timur's residents, above all, use the possibility to relate to these centres of power in order to translate their 'traditional' socio-territorial concepts into republican administrative terms. Therefore, the longue durée of socio-territorial concepts is still powerful in North Maluku. The conditions for the articulation of these social identities surface in the context of decentralisation and the fragmentation of the Indonesian Republic.

New sources of power (re-)emerge within the socio-political dynamics of the post-Suharto era, establishing complex relations to each other. *Adat* leaders are politically active, regional governments argue on the basis of socio-territorial concepts that have been in existence since long before the founding of the Indonesian Republic, and international operating enterprises influence regional decision-making. As this chapter shows, on the one hand, these multiple centres of power have provided people with new opportunities to connect themselves to this web of power relations in order to improve their social, economic and political status. On the other hand, these new centres have reshaped marginality, which implies economic disadvantages, a lack of democratic institutions on the district or *desa* level, or the sense of losing a distinct social identity.

Notes

1 These laws were replaced by UU 32/2004 and UU 33/2004 respectively.
2 Tradition is defined '[...] as a set of rules of social practice which adapted historically altered conditions through surreptitious adaptability so that although they changed, they also typically tried to conceal the evidence by an ideological rhetoric of immutability' (Kaviraj 1997: 5).
3 I understand *desa* in the sense of village; I will use the Indonesian term to avoid confusion.
4 The data for this research were collected through fieldwork conducted from August 2010 until July 2011, and for another month in June 2012 financed by the German Research Foundation. I thank Martin Rössler, Michaela Haug, Anna Grumblies and the participants at the 2013 Conference 'Transforming the Margins: Contesting and Reformulating Centre–Periphery Relations in Post-Suharto Indonesia' for their comments and questions, as well as Jos Platenkamp and two anonymous reviewers for their helpful comments on previous versions of this chapter.
5 From 1999 until 2003 Maluku Utara was the name of the whole province and the name of a regency (*kabupaten*) within this province.
6 Desa Bobaneigo, Desa Tetewang, Desa Akelamo Kao, Desa Gamsungi, Desa Dum-Dum, Desa Pasir Putih (PP 42/1999 (1c)).
7 Desa Tabobo, Desa Balisoang, Desa Sosol, Desa Wangeotak, Desa Gayok (PP 42/1999 (1b)).
8 Following Kao concepts of land use and ownership, the immigrants from Makian could only receive titles to land after four generations, and only on the condition of giving up their Makian identity and becoming Kao (cf. Platenkamp 1988: 94–96). This new district would invalidate their 'traditional' concept of land ownership and its associated identity formation. For further information about the conflict between Kao residents and Makian migrants (see van Klinken 2001; Duncan 2005; Wilson 2008; Jäger forthcoming).
9 By now, there are ten *kabupaten/kotamadaya* in the province. Morotai split from Halmahera Utara (UU 53/2008) and Taliabu from the Sula Archipelago (UU 6/2013).
10 Kabupaten Halmahera Barat, 2005. Peraturan Daerah (Regional Regulation) No. 6 tahun 2005 tentang Pemekaran Kecamatan Jailolo Timur. Perda 6/2005.
11 Kabupaten Halmahera Utara, 2006. Peraturan Daerah (Regional Regulation) No. 1 tahun 2006 tentang Pembentukan Kecamatan dan Desa. Perda 1/2006.
12 http://halbarkab.bps.go.id/substat-penduduk.html (accessed 31 January 2014); http://halutkab.bps.go.id/substat-penduduk.html (accessed 31 January 2014).
13 The central government is mandated to review all regulations from the regencies and provinces throughout Indonesia to guarantee they are in accordance with the national law (International Crisis Group 2012: 3).

14 The activists who emphasise the movement's international connections use the translation 'indigenous' for '*adat*' (Acciaioli 2007: 314).

References

Acciaioli, G. (2007) From Customary Law to Indigenous Sovereignty: Reconceptualizing masyarakat adat in Contemporary Indonesia, in J. Davidson and D. Henley (eds), *The Revival of Tradition in Indonesian Politics*, London: Routledge, pp. 295–318.
Andaya, L. (1993) *The World of Maluku: Eastern Indonesia in the Early Modern Period.* Honolulu, HI: University of Hawaii Press.
Baker, J.N. (1988) *Descent and Community in Tidore.* Ann Arbor, MI: University of Michigan Press.
Booth, A. (2011) Splitting, Splitting and Splitting Again: A Brief History of the Development of Regional Government in Indonesia since Independence, *Bijdragen tot de Taal,- Land- en Volkenkunde* 167(1): 31–59.
BPS Kabupaten Halmahera Barat (2013) *Halmahera Barat dalam Angka.* Jailolo: Badan Pusat Statistik Kabupaten Halmahera Barat.
BPS Kabupaten Halmahera Utara (2013) *Kecamatan Kao Teluk dalam Angka.* Tobelo: Badan Pusat Statistik Kabupaten Halmahera Utara.
BPS Propinsi Maluku Utara (2013) *Maluku Utara dalam Angka.* Ternate: Badan Pusat Statistik Propinsi Maluku Utara.
Bräuchler, B. (2007) Ein Comeback der Tradition? Die Revitalisierung von Adat in Ostindonesien, *Zeitschrift für Ethnologie* 132: 37–57.
Bubandt, N.O. (1991) *The Soa: The Organisation of Political and Social Space in the North Moluccas*, Unpublished Master Thesis, University of Copenhagen.
Bubandt, N.O. (2004) Towards a new Politics of Tradition, *Antropologi Indonesia* 74(28): 11–30.
Davidson, J. and Henley, D. (eds) (2007) *The Revival of Tradition in Indonesian Politics.* London: Routledge.
Duncan, C. (2005) The Other Maluku: Chronologies of Conflict in North Maluku, *Indonesia* 80: 53–80.
Duncan, C. (2009) Reconciliation and Revitalization: The Resurgence of Tradition in Postconflict Tobelo, North Maluku, Eastern Indonesia, *The Journal of Asian Studies* 68(4): 1077–1104.
Fox, J. (2011) Re-considering Eastern Indonesia, *Asian Journal of Social Science* 39: 131–149.
Fraassen, C.F. van (1987) *Ternate, de Molukken en de Indonesische Archipel. Van soa-organisatie en vierdeling: Een Studie van traditionele samenleving en cultuur in Indonesia.* 2 volumes, Unpublished Dissertation, University of Leiden.
Hall, S. (1986) On Postmodernism and Articulation: An Interview with Stuart Hall, *Journal of Communication Inquiry* 10(2): 45–60.
Hall, S. (1990) Cultural Identity and Diaspora, in J. Rutherford (ed.), *Identity, Community, Culture, Difference*, London: Lawrence & Wishart, pp. 222–237.
Hall, S. (1996) Introduction: Who Needs 'Identity'?, in S. Hall and P. Du Gay (eds), *Questions of Cultural Identity.* London: Sage, pp. 1–17.
Hauser-Schäublin, B. (ed.) (2013) *Adat and Indigeneity in Indonesia: Culture and Entitlements between Heteronomy and Self-Ascription.* Göttingen: Universitätsverlag.
d'Hondt, L. and Sangaji, M.S. (2011) *Environmental Justice in Halmahera Utara: Lost in Poverty, Interests and Identity.* Van Vollenhoven Institute Working Papers.

International Crisis Group (2012) Defying the State, *Asia Briefing* 138: 1–24.

Jäger, K. (2015) *Die Revitalisierung von 'traditionellen' politischen Gemeinwesen. Das Sultanat Jailolo in den Nord Molukken*, Dissertation, Westfälische Wilhelmsuniversität Münster.

Jäger, K. (forthcoming) Conflicts in North Maluku, Indonesia: Refusal to Exchange, Refusal to Establish Relations, in L. Prager, M. Prager and G. Sprenger (eds), *The World of Exchange*. Festschrift für Prof. Dr. Jos Platenkamp.

Kaviraj, S. (1997) Introduction, in S. Kaviraj (ed.), *Politics in India*, Delhi: Oxford University Press, pp. 1–36.

Klinken, G. van (2001) The Maluku Wars: Bringing Society Back In, *Indonesia* 71: 1–26.

Klinken, G. van (2007) The Return of the Sultans, in J. Davidson and D. Henley (eds), *The Revival of Tradition in Indonesian Politics*, London: Routledge, pp. 149–169.

Li, T. (2000) Articulating Indigenous Identity in Indonesia: Resource Politics and the Tribal Slot, *Comparative Studies in Society and History* 42(1): 149–179.

Lucardie, G. (1983) The Geographical Mobility of the Makianese: Migratory Traditions and Resettlement Problems, in E. Masinambow (ed.), *Halmahera dan Raja Ampat sebagai Kesatuan majemuk Studi-Studi terhadap suatu Daerah Transisi*, Jakarta: LEKNAS/LIPI, pp. 333–346.

Magenda, B. (1989) *The Surviving Aristocracy in Indonesia: Politics in Three Provinces of the Outer Islands*. 3 volumes. Ann Arbor, MI: UMI.

Malut Post (2013, 8 November) AHM unggul 10385 Suara.

Media Indonesia (2005, 25 November) Bupati Halmahera Barat diperiksa Kasus Korupsi Dana Pemekaran Wilayah. www.antikorupsi.org/id/content/bupati-halmahera-barat-diperiksa-kasus-korupsi-dana-pemekaran-wilayah (accessed 18 February 2014).

Newcrest Mining (2011) *Annual Report*. www.newcrest.com.au/media/annual_reports/FINAL_NCM_2011_Annual_Report_2011.pdf. (accessed 12 March 2014).

Platenkamp, J.D.M. (1988) *Tobelo: Ideas and Values of a North Moluccan Society*. Leiden: Repro Psychologie.

Platenkamp, J.D.M. (2013) Sovereignty in the North Moluccas: Historical Transformations, *History and Anthropology* 24(2): 206–232.

Schulte Nordholt, H. and Klinken, G. van (eds) (2007) *Renegotiating Boundaries: Local Politics in Post-Suharto Indonesia*. Leiden: KITLV Press.

Visser, L. (1989) *My Rice Field Is My Child: Social and Territorial Aspects of Swidden Cultivation in Sahu, Eastern Indonesia*. Dordrecht: Foris Publications.

Wilson, C. (2008) *Ethno-Religious Violence in Indonesia: From Soil to God*. London: Routledge.

Part III

Resources, power and inequality

7 Perceiving neoliberalism beyond Jakarta

Laurens Bakker

Indonesia is rising fast in the global economy.[1] Having joined the G-20 in 2008 and realising a steady yearly economic growth, expectations of its future economic performance are high.[2] With the global financial industry watching Indonesia, the nation's dedication to joining the global market and its ability to do so have become central issues in its economic policies. Observers point out that Indonesia's rise to global prominence is mainly hampered by internal bureaucratic and societal obstructions. Sukma (2012: 90), in discussing Indonesia's rise to global prominence, found the pace of economic growth to remain precarious. The development of the nation's democracy – 14 years after the ending of the dictatorial New Order regime – was opined to be a 'work in progress', threatened by defective democratic institutions, terrorism, communal violence, religious intolerance, corruption and weak law enforcement. Auditing company KPMG (2013: 7–8) nuanced a generally positive outlook with similar observations, emphasising that Indonesia's business environment suffers from poor infrastructure, weak institutions and considerable corruption.

In this chapter, I discuss perspectives on neoliberalism I encountered among the nation's 'ordinary people'. While Indonesia's economic progress can clearly be considered, as many analyses do, in terms of its attraction for global business, many Indonesian citizens tend to consider the effects of their nation's rise in terms of their own hopes, fears and experiences. The Indonesian people discussed the sovereignty that Indonesia as a state exerts over economic development within its national boundaries and while the control that they themselves, as citizens, exert over the government's policies are critical issues, of larger importance are the down-to-earth issues of who decides, who benefits and where the money goes. During research in some of Indonesia's outer islands, I frequently encountered the sentiments that 'Jakarta' was pocketing the nation's money, economic growth benefitted the rich only and that the national elite was squandering Indonesia's resources to foreign henchmen. Neoliberalism and neo-colonialism were frequently mentioned as facilitating these abuses, but whereas my interviewees – who ranged from university lecturers and students to *warung* guests, public transport passengers, taxi drivers, mall shoppers and such others as were willing to speak to me – could generally explain what they meant by 'neo-colonialism', neoliberalism turned out to be a vague concept. Generally, it was considered to effect a negative development in terms of societal cohesion, economic benefits and – importantly – a decrease of local influence in local affairs. Some pointed out that the close relationships that *reformasi* and administrative decentralisation had fostered between regional populations and their governments were now being uprooted by the indifference with which Jakarta 'dropped' its new projects on the regions. Others argued that it was in fact members of regional government falling over themselves to sell local riches to foreign bidders for their own profit. Neoliberalism, a theme seemed to be, damages the communal nature of Indonesian society and causes people to become more egoistic and more distant in their conduct, diminishing the importance of social ties.

I was surprised and intrigued. I made the study of these perceptions of neoliberalism a side-project in the areas where I worked (East Kalimantan, West Sumatra and the Minahasa). I tried to come to an understanding, first, of what people understood the concept to mean and, second, how the role of centre–periphery relations was seen to come to the fore in neoliberal practices. I thus approached the subject by focusing on perceptions of 'actually existing liberalism' (Wacquant 2012) and 'neoliberalism in practice' (Peck and Theodore 2012) in that I looked at what my interviewees saw as constituting neoliberal practices, as well as at practices that I, as an observer, considered to be neoliberal and on which I asked my interviewees to reflect. As such, I attempted to heed Gershon's (2011: 537) warning that local perspectives of neoliberalism require context to make them informative. Gershon argues for emphasis on agency, social organisation and people's epistemological differences in making sense of local particularities (2011: 537). I attempted to address these by applying a decidedly ethnographic perspective in order to seek out what Aihwa Ong (2006: 3), in discussing the spread of liberal calculation as a governing technology, described as 'specific alignments of market rationality, sovereignty and citizenship that mutually constitute distinctive milieus of labour and life at the edge of emergence' which, in this chapter, I mainly sought to understand in terms of local normative orders.

The chapter proceeds as follows. First, a brief discussion of neoliberalism in Indonesia, specifically paying attention to public debate and opinions. Then follow three sections based on ethnographic fieldwork. These describe three contextually different instances in which local actors explained their understanding of neoliberalism in specific economic and social contexts. The first section concerns the moral and religious dimensions of neoliberalism as perceived by restaurant owners in East Kalimantan and West Sumatra. This is followed by a section on an ongoing socio-political campaign in East Kalimantan to obtain special autonomy for that province. The last example brings ethnicity to the fore, looking at how a local ethnic militia in the Minahasa (North Sulawesi) took it upon itself to provide security to the area's inhabitants as it found the state's efforts to be insufficient.

Neoliberalism in Indonesia

Indonesia has fluctuated from almost complete disengagement with the world economy in the 1960s under Sukarno, to being very open to foreign capital and investment under Suharto's New Order. Under both regimes the national economy as well as the nation itself were strongly controlled by government ideologies emphasising the state as a unity, the members of which collaborated harmoniously to the benefit of all. The president's role was presented as that of a *pater familias*, a father-figure who has the needs and interest of his extended family at heart but also knows best what is good for them (cf. Reid 1998: 25–28). President Sukarno sought to unite the extended Indonesian family of national-ists, Islamist factions and communists in 'Guided Democracy', emphasising tra-ditional village-style discussion and consensus. His successor President Suharto professed to look after the Indonesian nation's wellbeing through *Pancasila* democracy, a broad political outlook that emphasised the principles of the national state philosophy of *Pancasila*, as well as the consensus and the family principle (*asas kekeluargaan*) introduced by Sukarno.[3] Suharto's regime took the family metaphor a step further through his nickname of '*bapak pembangunan Republik Indonesia*' – father of Indonesia's development – and professed to safeguard the nation's economic needs through *Pancasila* Economy, an eco-nomic policy based on the integralist elements of consensus, unity and the cul-tural, social and religious values of the Indonesian people.

It would be a farce to suggest that these principles were followed to the letter. An extensive literature exists on how Suharto's New Order regime developed into a system of crony capitalism, a 'business oligarchy' (e.g. Hadiz and Robison 2005), in which a small elite controlled government, the economy and the nation's wealth. The notion that the current democratisation of Indonesia's economy is hampered by the survival of networks of such 'predatory elites' who remain influential in pol-itics and the economy, and whose interests conflict with those of reformers seeking a more democratic state governed by the rule of law, is reported by many research-ers (e.g. Robison 2004; Dasgupta and Beard 2007). Indonesia's fast-paced reform allowed these elites to consolidate their positions by moving with the changes: from New Order regime into business, and from business into the boards and lead-erships of democratically elected political parties (Hadiz and Robison 2005; Aspi-nall 2013). Insofar as inclusive principles and harmonious collaboration came into play, we might conclude here, these concerned the 'regime family' rather than the 'extended family' of the nation. In terms of relations between the centre and the regions, the role of this 'regime family' in regional politics and economics has become an established subject of research (e.g. Aspinall and Mietzner 2010), while the increasingly manifest differences between individual regions in such matters as economic potential, society, development and migration (e.g. Hill 2014) are fast becoming one. Balancing these regional differences in terms of (dis)advantages for (individual) regions is framed in discourses including religious, political, ethnic and nationalist arguments. Neoliberalism is a regular element in these, but also considered against these standards in its own right.

Following the 1997 Asian financial crisis, the International Monetary Fund (IMF) and the World Bank imposed structural reform programmes to reorganise the Indonesian economy with a view to participation in the global market. This implied application of the dominant neoliberal market paradigm that sees unrestricted market access, unregulated competition and non-intervening governments as optimal conditions for trade. Reforms involved the privatisation of state enterprises, tariff abolishment and liberalisation of Indonesia's domestic market. These measures damaged elite business interests, but more so those of the population at large who suffered from the withdrawal of state subsidies on gasoline and basic foodstuffs. These harsh effects gave rise to a popular view that saw Indonesia as a victim of outside forces bent on establishing control over the nation. In the media the IMF was accused of being after foreign control over Indonesia's market and resources (cf. Budianta 2000: 121–122). Its conditions were compared to a return of the Dutch East Indies Company (Iqbal 1998: 44) and were said to be the cause of inhumane suffering for Indonesia's poor (e.g. Muttaqin 2003). Other – milder – authors pointed out that Indonesia had little alternative and in any case had not handed over its national autonomy (cf. Jusuf 1998).

With vast public support, the nation moved from regime-governance to a multi-party democratic system that emphasised decentralised governance and saw direct elections put into place for the three main levels of government. A new system of revenue sharing saw a more even redistribution among the regions of funds generated from – among others – income taxes, oil and gas production, mining operations and forestry and plantation products (all sectors containing considerable foreign interests). Despite unrest and local wars in various parts of the nation, these changes were achieved relatively peacefully. The nation remained stable and began to achieve steady economic growth. Development in rule of law, good governance and legal certainty did, however, lag behind as corruption, legal impunity and legal uncertainty indicated the persistent influence of power networks that managed to retain their positions and influence.

Indonesia's engagement with the global market wavered between a trade policy of opening up and limiting access, but showed a clear tendency towards global market involvement.[4] Then the 2008 global financial crisis took place and hit Indonesian export, manufacture and trade, causing the Indonesian rupiah to drop to its 1998-crisis level and spur a nationwide fear of a return to the dire circumstances of a decade earlier. The new crisis brought forth a wave of 'Suharto-nostalgia' and nationalism that recalled the low prices of basic goods at the time, as well as the quality of medical services and the security of society. Critical concerns over the powerful foreign firms and domestic business tycoons who were seen to control the economy and politics compounded fears over the future of Indonesian society. These fears resounded in a considerable and expanding literature on the dangers of neoliberalism (e.g. Rais 2008; Ridwan 2008; Aminuddin 2009; Notonagoro 2011) that emphasised inequality, loss of empathy and foreign take-overs of Indonesian firms and interests. Religious objections to neoliberalism included concerns that the individualism and competition of neoliberalism were incompatible with the piety, morality and economic justice that Islam pursues (cf. Fakih 2010; Hermawan 2012). Puns like 'too pig to fail' circulating on Facebook emphasised the un-Islamic character ascribed to neoliberalism. Also on Facebook, a 2005 fatwah by the *Majelis Ulama Indonesia* (Indonesian Ulama Council) that declared religious secularism, pluralism and liberalism forbidden (*haram*) for Muslims, was interpreted to include neoliberalism as well.[5] As these three principles had become popularly known by the acronym *sepilis* (syphilis), the argument on Facebook was that like syphilis, neoliberalism was a Western disease imported to Indonesia by foreigners and harming the nation and its people.

Some Indonesian intellectuals proposed *ekonomi kerakyatan* (people's economy) as a socially and nationalistically inspired alternative to neoliberalism. *Ekonomi kerakyatan*, they argued, embodies all those positive values that neoliberalism is said to lack: it is social, ethical, in line with Indonesian culture, traditions and religion. According to Mubyarto (2014: 5) the concept is similar to that of *Pancasila* Economy from the early 1980s, but with more emphasis on deliberation and unanimity in decision-taking.[6] It relates to the post-Washington Consensus anti-globalisation theories and emphasises morality, humanism, nationalism, democracy and social justice. It is, however, no longer possible to use '*Pancasila* Economy', as that concept was abused by the New Order to serve that regime's interests (Mubyarto 2014: 6–8). Before New Order interference the concept of *Pancasila* Economy combined elements of both liberal market economics (free market and individual enterprise) and socialism (state control of the market) while rejecting other elements of these ideologies, such as the free competition of liberal market systems and the lack of individual enterprise and ownership of socialism. *Ekonomi kerakyatan* featured in the media and gained some popularity among intellectuals and activists, but appears to have made little impact on society at large.

Objections to neoliberal policies thus included fear of increasing foreign influence in the domestic economy, fear of a loss of societal cohesion due to increasing competition and individualism, objections to an un-Islamic economic system and, combining all of these, objections to perceived forced alterations to Indonesian societal norms, culture and sovereignty. These objections thus take what is purportedly a reorganisation of the economy into the realm of inter-human relations: between Indonesia and the rest of the world and between different Indonesian citizens. As neoliberal qualities are seen as threatening to 'good' Indonesian values (patriotism, piety, consensus), they essentially ask how a neoliberal can be a good Indonesian person. This could indicate a dualism in that the denominator 'neoliberal' signals automatic disapproval of qualities that might be acceptable in other contexts, such as indicated by Rudnyckyj (2009). Writing on the restructuring of business management in an Indonesian steel plant, he found the concept of neoliberalism in Indonesia to have two facets: 'first, policies deployed to remake the country's political economy; and second, projects of individual ethical reform intended to elicit a type of subjectivity commensurable with neoliberal norms' (Rudnyckyj 2009: 106). These ethical reforms are presented under the denominator of religious values, not as related to neoliberal market ideology, although they clearly pertain to such labour regimes.

The inclusion of inter-human relations in terms of religion, patriotism and consensus takes neoliberalism decidedly beyond the sphere of the political and governance to include the personal and individual morality. As I seek to make clear in what follows, framing developments in terms of these qualities – or emphasising the lack thereof – are of considerable importance in the popular discourse identifying neoliberalism, neoliberals and such injustices as might be attributed to them.

Entrepreneurial ethics

Over the past ten years I have come to know 'Ahmad', a restaurant entrepreneur in the small city of Tanah Grogot in East Kalimantan, quite well. When we first met, Ahmad and 'Ida', his wife, ran a small *warung* on their house's porch, at the edge of the town centre.[7] Ahmad intended to specialise in *pecel*, a Javanese vegetable dish with a spicy peanut sauce. As a Javanese migrant Ahmad felt he had a claim to specialising in this dish while his wife's indigenous background would help to draw in non-Javanese customers. Strategically, the dish seemed a good bet: there was only one other *pecel* place in town.

Within two years Ahmad and Ida ran a large, dedicated *pecel* restaurant closer to the city centre. Portions were large, and a variety of side dishes such as fried chicken, fish and bean curd was available to go with the vegetables. They offered small discounts to returning civil servants and other office personnel, and during lunch and dinner the restaurant was packed. Unable to compete, the other *pecel* restaurant in town had closed down and its owner had returned to Java. Three years later the couple had expanded the restaurant to a 30-table venue with a branch across town. They were well-known locally for the quality of their food, the size of the portions and for their friendliness, but also for their participation in the local community. They contributed to charity and to the construction of a new mosque, helped their neighbours and paid the school fees of a number of local children. While Ahmad had told me before that he had undercut the prices of the other *pecel* restaurant until they went out of business, there now circulated a story that Ahmad had actually paid the owner's return trip to Java and was still sending money from time to time in order to ensure his wellbeing.

Upon my return the next year, they had opened a restaurant along the Balikpapan-Samarinda highway, having joined a collective of vendors lobbying bus companies to schedule stops at their location. Meanwhile, however, provincial government had given a local entrepreneur permission to build a large resting area some ten kilometres further on. The area disposed of ample parking space, toilets and shop space and included restaurants to let. Provincial government, referring to the layout of the new Trans-Kalimantan Highway, intended to declare this the only official spot for road-side restaurants. Ahmad and his colleagues attempted to prevent this through contacts in the provincial bureaucracy and among the bus companies, and by staging protests in front of provincial parliament. Some vendors – Ahmad insists this was not his group's doing – hired thugs to intimidate entrepreneurs willing to rent units at the new resting area by threatening to set the buildings on fire. Faced with such opposition, provincial government decided to halt the plans until things had calmed down. At the time of writing, the new resting area thus still remains unused and Ahmad and his colleagues remain in business.

I told Ahmad that I considered him a successful entrepreneur and strategist, but that I wondered whether his career did not illustrate the rise of neoliberalism in Indonesian business. After all, he succeeded because of free access to the market, because of coming out ahead of the competition and, when provincial government intervened in the market, by getting them out again. Ahmad became quite upset, and called over a number of his friends and customers to bear witness to his explanation as to why he was not a neoliberal entrepreneur. He argued that neoliberalism was about 'business only', that neoliberals had no concern for people or the human consequences of business decisions. Such an approach, he felt, was egocentric and could only be applied by those who had lost their attachments to the society – to humanity even. This, he felt, could hardly be the case for small entrepreneurs like himself, since he relied on the local community for survival: without his regular customers, he would go bankrupt. In Ahmad's opinion, big entrepreneurs control government and can afford to ignore the needs of ordinary people. They think of themselves, engage in corruption, and in doing so lose their humanity. Ahmad concluded, that as a common citizen and a devout Muslim, he should be mindful to never develop such an egoistic mindset.[8] Ahmad agreed completely, as did his friends, that free market access, fair competition and non-interventionist governments were good business conditions, but societal and religious norms should ensure the fairness and acceptability of it all, as business was after all only one aspect of life. Interestingly, Ahmad felt that provincial government's emphasis on the infrastructural layout of the Trans-Kalimantan Highway overruling the local entrepreneurs' interests typically illustrated this insensitivity of neoliberalism towards local circumstances. The highway, he felt, was a project developed by planners in Jakarta with no attention for local businesses in which big money was given the opportunity to take over local markets for no other apparent reason but greed and for profits. He praised provincial government for not following through with their initial course of action.

Ahmad's answers made me think further, and I decided to talk to some other rugged entrepreneurs in the same business, a family of Padang restaurant owners based in Padang, but with outlets in Java, Bali and Sulawesi. I asked them how they perceived neoliberalism to relate to the businesses of restaurant entrepreneurs. They argued that such market interventions by the government were often uncalled for where the restaurant business was open to new comers, but in many places access to the market was guarded by local officials, established entrepreneurs and gangsters, which Ahmad's story illustrated. That said, they agreed with Ahmad's statement that social responsibility and religious piety would prevent any decent Indonesian from willingly adhering to a 'neoliberal' outlook, regardless of what it entailed. For entrepreneurs such as themselves this was a matter of survival: publicly praising neoliberalism – even in reference to free market access and competition – would damage an entrepreneur's reputation. In Ahmad's case, the Padang restaurant owners suspected that his group had successfully monopolised the resting area and now tried to prevent entry to others. While unfair to aspiring restaurant owners, this guaranteed local jobs and incomes. The local population could be the judge of the decency of it all and treat Ahmad and his colleagues accordingly. It seems that local restaurant owners are only in favour of free market access as long as they stand to gain from it. The feared impact of the Trans-Kalimantan Highway made Ahmad and his colleagues take a decidedly protectionist stance which showed, as my friends in Padang suggested, that Ahmad's compassion did not extend to potential competitors.

For local entrepreneurs such as Ahmad, increased market access combined with a decrease of importance of local social relations is a worrying development, particularly because such developments may well be beyond their control if they are related to large, Jakarta-initiated projects. Ahmad and his partners prevented the use of the new resting area through local-level contacts and pressure, but they have no means to exert influence in the centre.

Demanding a larger revenue share

On 8 January 2015, during the celebrations marking the 58th birthday of the province of East Kalimantan, provincial governor Awang Farouk burst into tears while addressing the provincial parliament in the capital of Samarinda (Nara 2015). His anguish concerned the fact that the province still had not obtained special autonomy status, towards which he and others had been working for a considerable time now. Farouk told parliament:

'Now in East Kalimantan, what remains for us is to await disaster. Why not? East Kalimantan is ranked fourth in Indonesia in terms of greenhouse gas emissions. Our people only see the exploitation of our natural resources. Our environment is destroyed, we do not get anything. Let us just see, floods and landslides already haunt us.'[9]

(Nara 2015)

Farouk referred to the fact that East Kalimantan is among Indonesia's main producers of natural resources. The province disposes of reserves of oil, gas, coal, bauxite and gold, hosts large oil palm and pulp plantations, and is a major site for the farming of edible bird's nests. As these resources are being exploited, by far the largest share of governmental revenues end up in a revenue fund managed by central government. These funds are subsequently divided among all of Indonesia's provinces according to population size and the availability of other local revenues that benefit the respective provinces' treasuries.[10] East Kalimantan, many of its inhabitants feel, has been decidedly short-changed in the process.

Despite its riches and its important role in the national economy, the province is suffering from serious shortcomings that could, however, be solved fairly simply if a larger share of the revenue generated by the province benefitted the needs of its own population (cf. also Haug, this volume). Petrol is, for instance, often in limited supply in the province. As urban gas stations run dry, motorists are forced to buy their petrol at inflated prices from private sellers. Nevertheless, one of Indonesia's largest refineries is located in Balikpapan's harbour area. Its production is, however, largely exported to Java to fuel the island's staggering number of vehicles. Likewise, the province's electricity grid frequently suffers power failures. While the supplying power stations are located in Java, the coal that fuels them comes from Kalimantan. Government officials told me how power supplies to Kalimantan would be limited if demand in Java reached a certain level. A highly unfair situation, they felt, since Java needed East Kalimantan's coal to begin with. Plans exist for the construction of a dedicated power station near Balikpapan, but the sentiment that East Kalimantan's riches are used to sustain Java and Jakarta's economy is widespread.

Since the fall of Suharto and the introduction of decentralisation, exploitation by 'Java' has increasingly become an issue in the province's public discourse. Nowadays it is a mainstay that, as shown above, is used even by the governor. Within the province, NGOs, ethnic organisations, religious organisations and political activists put forward a discourse that emphasises the neo-colonial nature of mining, logging and plantations (cf. Bakker 2009a, 2009b) and argue for a larger share of the profits to benefit the local population. This discourse targets international and national companies alike. It refers comparatively to the exploitation of Papua as a spectre on the horizon, and sees 'Jakarta' or 'Java' as just as exploitative and disregarding of the interests of the population as multi-national companies, that lack nationalist ties to East Kalimantan.[11]

In 2011, a coalition of East Kalimantan NGOs, intellectuals, farmers, and provincial and regional members of governments supported a group of plaintiffs who attempted to alter the division of revenues in favour of the province. They argued that the division of natural resource revenues between the various levels of government as laid out in Law 33 of 2004 on Regional Taxes and Retribution violated their constitutional rights. They therefore requested the Constitutional Court to review the law and declare it invalid by declaring it as unconstitutional. The plaintiffs claimed that the percentages were unfair in that the largest share by far goes to central government although resources are regional, that the fluctuating prices of resources and hence of the funds available to the province did not provide legal certainty and that the percentages are discriminatory against the people of East Kalimantan and did not clearly contribute to the use of natural resources for the benefit of its people. In addition, they maintained that oil and gas exploitation did in fact cause social and environmental problems. The Constitutional Court found against the plaintiffs' request, declaring that centre–region financial relations and the percentages were constitutionally sound and that natural resources were the state's to exploit. Furthermore, the applicants' request would lead to economic instability in the nation, with especially dire consequences for those regions that had no oil or gas in place.[12]

The court's decision was a setback for the East Kalimantanese parties, but did not end their effort. Instead, provincial government began to prepare a request to national parliament for East Kalimantan to be given special autonomy (*otonomi khusus*) status based on its huge contribution to national development and the dire state in which its own infrastructure, educational system and population found themselves.[13] Provincial government argued that East Kalimantan was in dire need of development. Special autonomy status would provide the funds to realise this.[14] As provincial government was still preparing a scientific and judicial analysis of the feasibility of this proposal at the time of writing, the outcome is not yet known. The head of the National Development Planning Agency has already publicly declared that the plan does not make sense (*tak masuk akal*), which has been interpreted in East Kalimantan as a sign of Jakarta's unwillingness to share East Kalimantan's revenues more fairly (cf. Nara 2014). Another sign of Jakarta's attitude towards East Kalimantan's needs, supporters of special autonomy maintain, is the absence of a Minister of East Kalimantanese origin in the cabinet of President Joko Widodo (cf. Herudin 2014), for which extensive lobbying has taken place. If Jakarta would be willing to take East Kalimantan's troubles seriously and honour its importance to the nation, the reasoning goes, they could give its people a voice by taking one of them on as a minister. A member of Balikpapan's city parliament expressed to me that because this has not happened, it clearly demonstrates the national government's lack of attention to the province's human conditions, and shows how a neoliberal, uncaring attitude has overcome the family principle of Indonesia's governance.

Others, however, see things differently. 'That minister issue is only important to the political elite who were eyeing the job', argued student activists in the same city. 'Special autonomy would be good, but we really need to watch out for our provincial and regional governments who can be, well, just as neoliberal as national government.' These activists worried. They listed various senior politicians in provincial government who were said to be involved with natural resource exploitation companies and who, the students felt, would waste no time in involving these companies in the provincial economy once special autonomy was arranged. The students felt that there was little reason to assume that extra funds would benefit the population at large if no clear regulations would become available. 'Now it is all of East Kalimantan against the national government's neoliberalism', they told me. 'With special autonomy it is going to be the people against East Kalimantan's elite's neoliberalism.'

Ethnic market competition

The Minahasa, the northernmost part of the island of Sulawesi, is the home ground of Brigade Manguni Indonesia (BMI), an *ormas* (*organisasi kemasyarakatan* or societal organisation) that states the protection of the Minahasa and its inhabitants to be its reason to exist.[15] BMI uses discourses of democracy and regional interests to claim rights and resources for the predominantly Christian indigenous Minahasan population and threatens (and occasionally applies) violence to protect the interests of specific local, ethnic and religious groups, whom – they argue – the central government fails to sufficiently take into account. The organisation enjoys wide public support, including among local government officials, army and police personnel. As such, BMI's leaders, the *tona'as*, have considerable leeway in influencing economic and social affairs in the area, provided their actions are in line with popular sentiment.

Most of the *tona'as* are contractors, meaning that they may either run construction or business firms themselves, or act as brokers accepting projects and selling these on to third parties for actual implementation. Several *tona'as* run private security firms employing BMI members as guards and security personnel. As such, the influence of the *tona'as* in society is considerable and some of their operations and activities decidedly go against the interests of at least some locals. Possibly the best-known example of this is BMI's work for PT Newmont, an American mining company running operations in Buyat Bay, North Sulawesi, in the early 2000s. Buyat Bay is outside the Minahasa, in an area that BMI maintains is traditionally subservient to Minahasan leadership. BMI provided security services to PT Newmont at the site, which included keeping down protests from environmental campaigners and local fishermen worried about pollution caused by the mining activities. The *tona'as* maintained that the traditionally subservient status of the area and the jobs attributed to BMI members made the quelling of the protests legitimate. Only after the Indonesian government filed civil and criminal lawsuits against PT Newmont and its president on charges of environmental pollution, and the subsequent decision of the company to end its production in North Sulawesi, did BMI detach itself from PT Newmont which, until then, it had supported with a strong visible presence at the court's sessions.

Within the Minahasa, BMI's *tona'as* are influential in the provision of employment, the allocation of projects and the division of business. They categorically ensure that local Minahasans get a large share of any work, and keep Javanese and other non-local entrepreneurs out of the area if possible. Speaking to some of the *tona'as* about neoliberalism, it came as no surprise that they first mentioned moral corruption and the lack of humanity that characterised the negative consequences of such an orientation, but then they did surprise me by deciding that they themselves were somewhat neoliberal. By necessity, they hastened to explain.

BMI came into existence, the organisation maintains, because government's capacities alone were insufficient to secure the Minahasa. BMI established itself first as a private security force and went on to play an extensive role in local politics and the economy. They enjoyed local support because they paid well and hired locals. They felt that this made them, '*the* Minahasan firm'. BMI competed with the rest of Indonesia, which, popular opinion has it, has for decades been attempting to take over the Minahasa. Nowadays, they told me, BMI has people throughout Indonesia. Particularly in the big companies, ministries and cities that make up the centre of the nation. With such a network, they were well set for business competition. BMI, in addition to being an *ormas*, is developing as a business network based on a shared regional identity and united by a desire to resist the centre's influence in the Minahasa by – instead – building its influence in the centre.

While BMI is hardly a corporate business venture, the *tona'as* admission to being 'somewhat neoliberal' is noteworthy. They considered Indonesia a big, open market for BMI to engage in and establish themselves aggressively. Failure on the Minahasan side to do so, they feared, would certainly result in a take-over of their region by the powerful business tycoons of Jakarta.

Concluding remarks

This chapter has sought to show how local actors in different settings and regions in Indonesia perceived neoliberalism to influence their lives. Overall, the concept was considered negatively in terms of principles of nationalism, morality, religion and community and as constituting a threat to local interests by new, powerful forces from outside. What stands out in this are the issues of principles versus practices and the matter of scale. While the debate involved defining neoliberalism along an outline of principles, the designation of practices as neoliberal allowed room for context. The restaurant owners considered competition and market access feasible, provided it went along with local needs and morals, they mobilised locally to prevent a large new competitor from 'Java' from entering 'their' market. The Minahasan BMI displayed an almost textbook-like take on neoliberalism by taking up the provision of security in lieu of the state and establishing an aggressive and expansive style of approaching the Javanese business community. Conceptually, however, they phrased their activities in terms of 'ethnic unity' and 'protection of the region', and emphasised the need to protect the Minahasa from non-local business entrepreneurs. In both East Kalimantan and the Minahasa, competition and free market access were nominally favoured by my interviewees, but as privileged practices the benefit of which was to be determined by local needs and interests.

The importance of the local context involved a clear element of scale in designating neoliberalism. Regional perceptions strongly associated the threat of neoliberalism with national-level elitism and located it in Java 'Jakarta', and in foreign countries. They also associate neoliberalism with those powerful locals who link these (i.e. Java, Jakarta and foreign countries) to the region. In the national discourse, the neoliberal spectre awaits its chance beyond the national borders, in the global realm. This shared conceptualisation of what neoliberalism entails, but differing notions as to where it is to be found, illustrates an increasingly critical attitude with which the regions behold the centre. The case of East Kalimantan's government attempting to acquire a larger share of natural resource revenues indicates a challenging of 'Jakarta' that illustrated the complexity of the new national landscape in which local centres question their position as periphery.

Notes

1 I would like to express my gratitude to Manunggal Wardaya and Muhamad Nasir for their insightful advice and suggestions. This work was supported by the Netherlands Organisation for Scientific Research [grant number 463-08-003] as part of the research project 'State of Anxiety: A Comparative Ethnography of Security Groups in Indonesia' as well as by WOTRO [grant number W 01.65.334.00] as part of the research project '(Trans)national Land Investments in Indonesia and the Philippines: Contested Control of Farm Land and Cash Crops'.

2 For an overview of the development of the Indonesian economy and the role of foreign investment, see for instance the yearly reports of Global Business Guide Indonesia (www.gbgindonesia.com/) and the more detailed reports of the Indonesian Investment Coordination Board at www.bkpm.go.id/.

3 *Pancasila* is the national state philosophy of Indonesia. It consists of five basic principles: belief in One God, nationalism, humanitarianism, democracy and social justice.

4 This chapter lacks the space to detail the 'neoliberalization' of Indonesia's economic policies, but see Chandra (2011) for an overview.

5 See Keputusan Fatwa Majelis Ulama Indonesia Nomor: 7/Munas VII/MUI/11/2005 Tentang Pluralisme, Liberalisme, dan Sekulerisme Agama.

6 Surprisingly few outlines of the concept exist. Perhaps the most comprehensive is Mubyarto's and Boediono's (1981), who explain that in *Pancasila* Economy state enterprises and cooperatives take precedence over private enterprises, which are only allowed a major role in sectors where state enterprises are not effective. Furthermore, in contrast to the competition and individualism of the capitalist system, *Pancasila* Economy is based on higher motives: social and religious values in addition to economic ones. *Pancasila* Economy aims for greater social equality and egalitarianism, and unity of the population through such economic nationalism as is needed to build up sufficient economic strength to compete with foreign enterprises. Its functioning is guided by a balance between central planning and decentralised economic decision making, so as to optimise the possibilities of local cooperatives in relation to national needs and capacities.

7 Both Ahmad and Ida are pseudonyms.

8 I later found Ahmad's reasoning to be along the lines of a popular Hizbut Tahrir speaker based in Balikpapan, whom he may well have heard or read. See, for instance, *Jurnal Balikpapan* (2015).

9 Sekarang di Kaltim, kita hanya tinggal menunggu bencana saja. Bagaimana tidak? Kaltim berada di peringkat empat Indonesia, sebagai penghasil emisi gas rumah kaca. Masyarakat kita hanya melihat eksploitasi SDA (sumber daya alam). Lingkungan kita rusak, kita tidak dapat apa-apa. Kita lihat saja, sekarang ini banjir dan longsor sudah menghantui.

10 See Agustina *et al.* (2012a and 2012b) for an overview of revenue division.

11 Although few online reports on these manifestations exist, I was referred to KAMNI's (a national student organisation) anti-liberal manifesto a few times by student activists in Samarinda and Balikpapan. KAMNI Kaltim (2009) gives a good impression of the ideals and sentiments of the time.

12 See putusan Mahkamah Konstitusi Indonesia Nomor 71/PUU-IX/2011 tentang Pengujian UU No. 33/2004 tentang Perimbangan Keuangan Antara Pusat dan Daerah terhadap UUD 1945.

13 Special autonomy status awards far larger percentages of natural resource revenues to the province and district of origin. Currently only the provinces of Aceh, Papua and West Papua enjoy this benefit. The status is awarded by national parliament and confirmed in a national law drafted and passed for the specific province.

14 In the 8 January 2015 speech with which this section began, Faroek states that Papua

and Aceh receive 70 per cent of the revenues made from oil and gas in their territories. These percentages are somewhat lower in practice, but would, for East Kalimantan, raise considerable sums.

15 See Bakker (2015) for a more extensive discussion of BMI and similar *ormas*.

References

Agustina, C.D., Ahmad, E., Nugroho, D. and Siagian, H. (2012a) *Political Economy of Natural Resource Revenue Sharing in Indonesia*. Asia Research Centre Working Paper 55, London School of Economics and Political Science.

Agustina, C.D., Fengler, W. and Schulze, G. (2012b) The Regional Effects of Indonesia's Oil and Gas Policy: Options for Reform, *Bulletin of Indonesian Economic Studies* 48(3): 367–395.

Aminuddin, M.F. (ed.) (2009) *Globalisasi dan Neoliberalisme. Pengarah dan dampaknya pada Demokratisasi Indonesia*. Yogyakarta: Logung Pustaka.

Aspinall, E. (2013) The Triumph of Capital? Class Politic and Indonesian Democratisation, *Journal of Contemporary Asia* 43(2): 226–242.

Aspinall, E. and Mietzner, M. (eds) (2010) *Problems of Democratisation in Indonesia: Elections, Institutions and Society*. Singapore: Institute of Southeast Asian Studies.

Bakker, L. (2009a) *Who Owns the Land? Looking for Law and Power in Reformasi East Kalimantan*, PhD Thesis, Radboud University Nijmegen.

Bakker, L. (2009b) *Adat*, Land and Popular Democracy: Dayak Politics in East Kalimantan, *Borneo Research Bulletin* 40: 202–220.

Bakker, L. (2015) Illegality for the General Good? Vigilantism and Social Responsibility in Contemporary Indonesia, *Critique of Anthropology* 35(1): 78–93.

Budianta, M. (2000) Discourse of Cultural Identity in Indonesia during the 1997–1998 Monetary Crisis, *Inter-Asia Cultural Studies* 1(1): 109–128.

Chandra, A. (2011) *A Dirty Word? Neo-liberalism in Indonesia's Foreign Policies*. Winnipeg: IISD. Available online: https://www.iisd.org/ (accessed 1 December 2014).

Dasgupta, A. and Beard, V. (2007) Community Driven Development, Collective Action and Elite Capture in Indonesia, *Development and Change* 38(2): 229–249.

Fakih, M. (2010) *Bebas dari Liberalisme*. Yogyakarta: Insist Press.

Gershon, I. (2011) Neoliberal Agency, *Current Anthropology* 52(4): 537–555.

Hadiz, V. and Robison, R. (2005) Neo-liberal Reforms and Illiberal Consolidations: The Indonesian Paradox, *Journal of Development Studies* 41(2): 220–241.

Hermawan, H. (2012) Neoliberalisme dalam Perspektif Islam, *Media Ekonomi & Teknologi Informasi* 20(2): 33–43.

Herudin (2014) Orang Kaltim tak dipakai jadi Menterinya Jokowi, ini dia Foto-Foto Demonstrasi Protes!, *Tribun Jakarta*, 2 November.

Hill, H. (ed.) (2014) *Regional Dynamics in a Decentralized Indonesia*. Singapore: Institute of Southeast Asian Studies.

Iqbal, M. (1998) IMF dan Imperialisme Ekonomi, *Jurnal Kajian Islam* 1(3): 37–54.

Jurnal Balikpapan (2015) HTI Balikpapan: Indonesia kita Terancam: Neoliberalisme dan Neoimperialisme, 21 April. Available online: www.jurnalbalikpapan.com/2015/04/hti-balikpapan-indonesia-kita-terancam.html (accessed 6 July 2014).

Jusuf, M. (1998) Bila bukan IMF, lalu siapa?, *Tempo*, 30 January.

KAMNI Kaltim (2009) Kammi Pusat: Tolak Capres-Cawapres Pendukung Rezim neoliberal yang tidak pro Rakyat!, 27 May. Available online: http://kamdakaltim.blogspot.nl/2009/05/kammi-pusat-tolak-capres-cawapres.html (accessed 6 July 2015).

KPMG (2013) *Investing in Indonesia*. Jakarta: KPMG.

Mubyarto (2014) Ekonomi Kerakyatan dalam Era Globalisasi, in Mubyarto (ed.), *Ekonomi Kerakyatan*, Jakarta: Lembaga Suluh Nusantara/American Institute for Indonesian Studies (AIFIS), pp. 3–10.

Mubyarto and Boediono (1981) *Ekonomi Pancasila*. Yogyakarta: Fakultas Ekonomi Universitas Gajah Mada.

Muttaqin, H. (2003) Pencabutan Subsidi: Kebijakan yang tidak manusiawi, *Jurnal Ekonomi Ideologis*, 15 September. Available online: http://jurnal-ekonomi.org/pencabutan-subsidi-kebijakan-yang-tidak-manusiawi/ (accessed 5 January 2015).

Nara, G. (2014) Kepala Bappenas: Otonomi Khusus untuk Kaltim tak masuk akal, *Kompas*, 15 December.

Nara, G. (2015) Tuntut Otonomi Khusus, Gubernur Awang Farouk menangis histeris, *Kompas*, 9 January.

Notonagoro, W.H.K.P. (2011) *Neoliberalisme mencengkeram Indonesia: IMF, World Bank, WTO Sumber Bencana Ekonomi Bangsa*. Jakarta: Sekretariat Jenderal Gerakan Kebangsaan Rakyat Semesta.

Ong, A. (2006) *Neoliberalism as Exception: Mutations in Citizenship and Sovereignty*. Durham, NC and London: Duke University Press.

Peck, J. and Theodore, N. (2012) Reanimating Neoliberalism: Process Geographies of Neoliberalization, *Social Anthropology/Anthropologie Sociale* 20: 177–185.

Rais, M. (2008) *Selamatakan Indonesia*. Yogyakarta: PPSK UGM Press.

Reid, A. (1998) Political 'Tradition' in Indonesia: The One and the Many, *Asian Studies Review* 22(1): 23–38.

Ridwan, N.K. (2008) *NU dan Neoliberalisme. Tantangan dan Harapan*. Yogyakarta: PT LKiS Pelangi Aksara Yogyakarta.

Robison, R. (2004) Neoliberalism and the Future World: Markets and the End of Politics, *Critical Asian Studies* 36(3): 405–423.

Rudnyckyj, D. (2009) Spiritual Economies: Islam and Neoliberalism in Contemporary Indonesia, *Cultural Anthropology* 24(1): 101–141.

Sukma, R. (2012) Domestic Politics and International Exposure: Constraints and Possibilities, in A. Reid (ed.), *Indonesia Rising: The Repositioning of Asia's Third Giant*, Singapore: Institute for Southeast Asian Studies, pp. 77–92.

Wacquant, L. (2012) Three Steps to a Historical Anthropology of Actual Existing Neoliberalism, *Social Anthropology/Anthropologie Sociale* 20: 66–79.

8 Rich regency – prosperous people?

Decentralisation, marginality and remoteness in East Kalimantan

Michaela Haug

Introduction

The interior regions of East Kalimantan epitomise various forms and meanings of marginality. People living here are faced with the situation of being at the geographical periphery of the Indonesian state, far away from centres of power and decision making. These regions have further been characterised by political, economic and social disenfranchisement. Like other upland regions, they have been repeatedly constituted as margins by pre-colonial, colonial and post-colonial centres of power, as their marginal position and associated negative images of backwardness, ignorance and disorderliness were used to justify the imposition of central control and the exploitation of upland wealth (Li 1999). Consisting (at least partly) of dense forests, rugged mountains and areas with a poor infrastructure, the interior regions of East Kalimantan can further be characterised as remote places which often produce a feeling of 'being forgotten' or 'living on the edge' among its inhabitants.

However, regional autonomy has led to manifold changes in East Kalimantan during the last 15 years, challenging the image of its interior regions as being Indonesia's margins. Through an excessive *pemekaran* process, several new political and administrative centres have been created, endowed with new political authority and new economic opportunities. Five of Indonesia's wealthiest regencies are now located in East Kalimantan: Kutai Kartanegara, Kutai Timur, Kutai Barat, Berau and Pasir. The previously marginalised indigenous population of Kalimantan – commonly summarised under the term 'Dayak' – has on a whole been empowered and large efforts have been undertaken by local governments to increase service provision and transport connections. Taking the regency of Kutai Barat as an example, this chapter explores the processes of 'de-marginalisation' and examines to what extent new political authority and, more importantly, newly gained wealth have brought prosperity to the local population in the interior regions of East Kalimantan. The findings reveal an invigorated regional centre, which has clearly benefitted from decentralisation. However, spatial distance and remoteness are still major reasons why people feel poor, and new processes of marginalisation are taking place on regency and village level as new centres inevitably create new margins. The economic empowerment of

Kutai Barat has brought prosperity to the region, but while some people benefit, far too many continue to live on the edge of this newly gained wealth. This case study is thus related to the larger question of how natural resources and wealth in post-Suharto Indonesia are distributed. Democratisation and decentralisation did not automatically reverse ecologically destructive and socially unjust practices of natural resource exploitation that emerged during the New Order. Recent research demonstrates rather ambiguous developments. While in some areas 'political reforms have stimulated new forms of local resource management offering prospects for a more sustainable and equitable future', in others, 'political transformations have been accompanied by an acceleration of environmental decline and social disparity' (Warren and McCarthy 2009: 227). The example of Kutai Barat rather conforms to the latter.

Data for this chapter were collected during 22 months of field research in Kutai Barat between 2004 and 2007, and two shorter periods of field research in 2009 and 2011. My initial research was an integral part of a CIFOR-BMZ research project,[1] which analysed the impacts of regional autonomy on the well-being of forest dependent communities. One result of the co-operation between the project team and the government of Kutai Barat was a poverty survey organised by the Community Empowerment Service (*Dinas Pemerdayaan Masyarakat*) in February–March 2006. The survey assessed a total of 10,431 households from all 21 districts, in 222 of 223 villages.[2] I will draw on some of the results of this survey below. My field research concentrated on three Dayak Benuaq villages, which will be introduced below. My methods comprised a variety of qualitative and quantitative methods, e.g. participatory observations, formal and informal interviews and two comprehensive household surveys.

First, I look at how the concepts of 'marginality' and 'remoteness', as well as the related term 'periphery' have been used in this case study, the chapter will then show how regional autonomy has allowed Kutai Barat to emerge as a new regional centre, brimming with enthusiasm to challenge its marginal position. The following section then addresses the impacts of decentralisation on local livelihoods, exploring processes of marginalisation and the production of new inequalities on regency and village level. Based on these observations, the concluding section argues that Kutai Barat is characterised by a fragmented landscape of power relations, in which currently rather differentiated marginalities are being created.

Marginality, remoteness and periphery in Kutai Barat

Despite anthropologists' prevalent interest in marginal groups, marginality remains an under-theorised and rather a fuzzy concept, which 'has rarely been scrutinized conceptually beyond the particularities of its respective ethnographic setting' (Röttger-Rössler and Stodulka 2014: 16). As a consequence, various aspects of marginality come to the fore in different studies, and the delineation between marginality and related terms, such as 'periphery' and 'remoteness', often becomes blurred.

This case study, deploys the three terms to focus on diverse conditions, processes and experiences. I argue that a differentiated understanding of marginality, periphery and remoteness enables a more thorough analysis of the various aspects that are commonly subsumed within marginality, and how they are intertwined. The way in which the three concepts are used here exemplifies only one of several possible options. Therefore, the focus of this chapter is not upon the specific understanding of these concepts, but rather upon their differentiated application for analysis in general.

In this chapter, 'marginality' is used to refer to various processes of political, economic and social disenfranchisement by which certain groups of peoples, places or regions are constructed as marginal in relation to a (partly self-defined) centre. The focus lies thus on capturing the asymmetric power relations between a centre and its margin (Li 1999: 2), whereby the position of the two is neither naturally given nor fixed but constantly challenged and (re-)shaped (Tsing 1993: 90). The social distance, which is created between centre and margin, often corresponds with spatial distance, but, as demonstrated by research on the urban poor, this is not necessarily the case (cf. Hopper 2003).

The term 'periphery' is used here to capture spatial distance. Being located 'at the edge of a system' (Leimgruber 2004) and far away from the central point of reference within a political or economic entity constitutes a place, and the people living there as peripheral. Such regions are often marginalised, but there are significant exceptions. This is, for example, the case with border regions, which are sometimes of great importance and, as a result, receive special attention and investments. Each place must, of course, be seen in relation to several centres, and while it might be in a peripheral position to one centre, it can be close to another (cf. Dunne 2005).

'Remoteness', on the other hand, is used here to characterise places such as e.g. dense forests or rugged mountains, which are difficult to reach and lack appropriate infrastructure and services (Gurung and Kollmair 2005: 13). Such places are often, but not always, constituted as margins. They are not necessarily located far away from political, economic or social centres. However, their geographical characteristics provide their inhabitants with specific opportunities and limitations. While e.g. upland forests allow people to withdraw from state control (cf. Scott 2009) or to hide in dense woods (cf. Peluso and Vandergeest 2011), they also produce feelings of isolation and can have distressing consequences, i.e. when people die because they do not survive the long journey to the next hospital.[3] My understanding of remoteness stands in contrast to the idea of Harms *et al.* (2014: 362) who wish to detach the remote from its geographical moorings and instead understand it 'as a sociological concept of relative association or familiarity'. However, I do not want to express a fundamental disagreement with Harms and his co-authors. I merely see the processes they describe as closely related to marginality and its social constructedness, while I prefer to reserve the term remoteness to relate to the physical and infrastructural characteristics of a location and how they influence people's lives.

The rise of Kutai Barat as a new centre

(Re-)creating an upriver centre

Kutai Barat came into existence in November 1999 when the former regency of Kutai was split into three parts: Kutai Timur, with its new capital Sangatta, covers the eastern part of the previous regency. Kutai Kartanegara comprises the area of the lower Mahakam and stretches land inwards along the Balayan River. Its capital Tenggarong has been the centre of the former and meanwhile revived Sultanate of Kutai and the previous regency of the same name. Kutai Barat consists of the western part of the previous regency and stretches along the Mahakam River, including the lowland areas around the Mahakam lakes and the highland regions of the Middle Mahakam. The capital of the new regency became Sendawar – turning the rather remote Tunjung Plateau in a political, social and economic centre. This can be conceived of as the creation of a new centre insofar as a sleepy village has been turned into a lively hub of activity. From a historical perspective, which is ready to embrace the legendary and mythological, one could even argue that an old and nearly forgotten centre has been resurrected.

Today, Sendawar is a semi-urban area which encompasses several settlements of the districts Melak (located at the banks of the Mahakam), Sekolaq Darat and Barong Tongkok (both located further inland on the Tunjung Plateau). This area roughly correlates with the heartland of a former Tunjung kingdom called Kerajaan Sendawar, which was created between *c.*1360 and 1420 in the Middle Mahakam (Dyson 2002, 2008). According to Tunjung narrations, Sendawar has been part of a larger kingdom (Kerajaan Kudukng) which later became known under the name of Kerajaan Mulawarman or respectively Martapura (Venz 2012). The expansion of the Sultanate of Kutai upriver into the Middle Mahakam seems to have caused the decline of the Tunjung kingdom during the first half of the seventeenth century (Dyson 2008: 30). Due to limited historical sources, little is known about Sendawar and its extent, but it seems that the area of Kutai Barat by far exceeds the legendary kingdom. Furthermore, people in Kutai Barat barely relate to the former kingdom and it is not used as a socio-political entity to forge a common identity upon, as is the case, for example, with the former sultanates in the Moluccas (cf. Jäger, this volume).

Dayak become the ruling majority in Kutai Barat

Kutai Barat is home to many ethnic groups, comprising different Dayak communities, Malay-speaking groups like the Banjar and Kutai, as well as groups from other Indonesian islands, such as Javanese, Bugis and Batak. When Kutai Barat came into existence, the various Dayak groups together made up 63.9 per cent of the population, becoming the clear majority of the new regency (Gönner *et al.* 2007a). This marked a significant change, as the previous administrative division of East Kalimantan had contributed to the political marginalisation of

Dayak people by making them the minority population in many regencies and districts. Their chances to exert political power had further been limited through the allocation of government positions to predominantly Javanese or Kutai Malays. After the implementation of regional autonomy, the influence and representation of the various Dayak groups (mainly Benuaq, Tunjung and Bahau) within local government substantially increased (Andrianto 2006: 28). At the same time, ethnicity gained importance within local politics, just as in other areas of the Outer Islands, where 'resource competition and entitlement claims frame the identity politics that are driving regional administrative recon-figurations' (Warren and McCarthy 2009: 229).

In Kutai Barat competition and rivalry among the different Dayak groups increased, and even sub-group identity became relevant for seeking political support, gaining employment or access to higher education. From 2000 until 2006 a Dayak Benuaq was the first district head of Kutai Barat, who was suc-ceeded by a Dayak Tunjung-Rentenuukng (whose second mandate will end in 2016). Being one of the politically most powerful ethnic groups in East Kali-mantan, the Kutai Malays remained important in Kutai Barat, occupying several leading positions as e.g. the office of the deputy district head.

Like other regions of Indonesia, Kalimantan has experienced a 'revival of tra-dition' (Davidson and Henley 2007) and a (re-)construction of Dayak identities (Widen 2002). Dayak people enjoyed new pride in their indigenous identity after having experienced the devaluation of their culture under colonial and post-colonial rule. This new pride and a (sometimes rather rhetorical) reorientation towards an autochthonous culture have taken various forms. While this has pro-vided a hopeful atmosphere of departure in many villages, it has also been aimed against claims and demands of (trans-)migrants from other parts of Indonesia and fuelled violent conflicts in some parts of Kalimantan (cf. van Klinken 2002; Widen 2002; Davidson 2003; Peluso 2003; Oesterheld 2004).

In Kutai Barat, this new self-esteem of Dayak culture is expressed mainly in a revitalisation of local traditions and a folklorisation of *adat* dances, costumes and art. The local government provides e.g. support and funding for dancing groups, the production of traditional costumes, important rituals, and traditional arts and crafts. Further, a new centre for researching and documenting local Dayak culture, the 'Centre for Ethno-Ecology Research and Development' (CERD) was founded in 2004. This revitalisation and valorisation of *adat*, however, should not obscure the fact that Dayak culture is undergoing far-reaching changes in Kutai Barat as elsewhere in Borneo. While certain know-ledge and *adat* practices continue to be of great importance in everyday life, others fall more and more into oblivion (cf. Gönner 2001; Cahyat *et al.* 2005; Haug 2010; Venz 2012).

The pride and ambition of the new Dayak leadership of Kutai Barat finally become apparent in several prestigious buildings. One example is the spacious government building complex whose inauguration illustrates the introduction to this book. Another example is the Taman Adat Sendawar – a complex consisting of six newly built longhouses and a large stage for public events located in

Barong Tongkok. The concept of the Taman Adat Sendawar resembles the Taman Mini in Jakarta. Each of the impressive longhouses is supposed to represent one of the major ethnic groups in Kutai Barat, including the Kutai Malay, Dayak Tunjung, Dayak Benuaq, Dayak Kenyah, Dayak Aoheng and Dayak Bahau. The construction of the Taman Adat Sendawar, which was completed in 2012, has swallowed IDR40 billion[4] (approximately US$4.4 million).[5] It is thus not only a cultural monument but also a demonstration of Kutai Barat's wealth.

Rechannelling upland wealth

East Kalimantan looks back on a long history of downriver and coastal centres trying to capture upland wealth. The Sultanate of Kutai, as well as the colonial and post-colonial state, profited from interior natural riches mainly in the form of levies and taxes on trade with valuable non-timber forest products (Manning 1971; Magenda 1991). When commercial logging started to spread all over Kalimantan during the 1960s and 1970s, timber from East Kalimantan contributed to national economic growth and to the individual enrichment of Suharto and his cronies, while local communities' access to the forest was severely restricted.

East Kalimantan's natural resources – mainly oil, gas and coal – continue to contribute to the national economy. However, since the implementation of regional autonomy, a larger share remains within the region. Through fiscal decentralisation, the central government transfers a minimum 25 per cent of domestic revenues to sub-national governments. Revenues are transferred through the general and the special balancing funds (*Dana Alokasi Umum*, DAU and *Dana Alokasi Khusus*, DAK). Regencies further receive a share of the natural resource revenues generated within their borders and can additionally generate their own revenues (*Pendapatan Asli Daerah*, PAD). Although East Kalimantan profited from this new fiscal arrangement, there are strong voices that demand even larger shares of local resource revenues, based on the huge contribution of the province to national development (cf. Bakker, this volume).

Kutai Barat did fairly well under fiscal decentralisation. The district budget increased significantly under regional autonomy – from IDR372.4 billion (approximately US$37.2 million) in 2001 to IDR663.2 billion (approximately US$79.6 million) in 2003 (Andrianto 2006: 30). The district budget (*Anggaran Pendapatan Belanja Daerah*) for 2014 was estimated to reach IRD2.02 billion (US$162 million). PAD earnings also increased from IDR11.2 billion (approximately US$1.1 million) in 2001 to IDR24.8 billion (approximately US$3 million) in 2003 (Andrianto 2006: 30), but they accounted for a relatively small percentage of district revenues. The PAD for 2014 was estimated to reach IDR80.8 billion (approximately US$6.5 million) while for 2015 the PAD is targeted at IDR94.5 billion (US$6.6 million).[6] This shows that despite a further increase of the PAD in absolute numbers, locally generated revenues continue to contribute only a small percentage of the regency's budget. The main source of Kutai Barat's wealth comes from fiscal transfers from the central government.

Hence, reductions of shares from mining, oil and gas revenues by the central government can significantly impact the district budget of Kutai Barat.

The smallholder economy of the district is characterised by swidden agriculture, animal husbandry and small-scale estate crop production, for example coconut, coffee, pepper, cocoa and most importantly rubber, which constitutes approximately 84 per cent of estate crops in Kutai Barat. Rubber production increased continuously from 8,481 tons in 2000 to 15,831 tons in 2003 (Badan Pusat Statistik 2003) and further to 35,278 tons in 2013 (Badan Pusat Statistik 2014). During this time span, rubber prices have undergone significant variations. While traders bought rubber from the villagers for up to IRD16,000 per kg (US$1.6) during 2013, by the time of writing prices were down at IDR4,000 to 5,000 per kg (US$0.28 to 0.35).

Major economic sectors of the district are timber, oil palm and mining industries. Timber production started in East Kalimantan during the late 1960s, but it gained new importance during the logging boom triggered by decentralisation. Unclear task sharing and overlapping authorities of central and local instances within the forestry sector created a situation of great legal uncertainty (Resosudarmo 2004) in which the local government made eager use of their newly gained authority to hand out small-scale timber licences and villagers started self-organised logging operations in their village forests (cf. Casson 2001; Bullinger and Haug 2012). However, the logging boom was quickly ended by the new decentralisation legislation of 2004 and revised forest policies which drew back authority to the central government.

The development of oil palm estates in the sub-district Jempang looks back on a long history of conflict and controversy (Casson 2001; Gönner 2002; Haug 2014a). But over the recent years, palm oil production has grown continuously from 10,742 tons in 2008 to 203,705 tons in 2013 (Badan Pusat Statistik 2014). Meanwhile, a palm oil factory has been built in the district Jempang. This constitutes a significant step for the development of the palm oil sector in Kutai Barat and is likely to promote a further expansion of oil palm plantations in the regency.

However, Kutai Barat's most important economic sector is mining. PT Kelian Equatorial Mining (KEM) has operated one of the world's largest gold plants in Kutai Barat and has for a long time been the largest tax payer of the regency. During the time of my fieldwork PT KEM was closing the mine, and instead, coal mining gained increasing importance pushed by the Indonesian coal boom.[7] Kalimantan represents the centre of Indonesian coal mining – 83 per cent of Indonesia's proven coal reserves are located here (Lucarelli 2010: 40). The masterplan for acceleration and expansion of Indonesia's economic development (MP3EI) for the period 2011–2025 accordingly designates Kalimantan as the centre for the production and processing of national mining and energy reserves (Government of Indonesia 2011). The major mine site in East Kalimantan (and one of Indonesia's largest coal mines in general) is operated by PT Kaltim Prima Coal (KPC) in Kutai Timur. In Kutai Barat, coal production has increased continuously during recent years, and the coal mining sector roughly makes up half of Kutai Barat's gross regional domestic product.

In order to increase local revenues, policy-makers in Kutai Barat have so far mainly focused on the extraction of natural resources and the increasing conversion of forests. This readiness to risk long-term sustainability and intergenerational equity for short-term gains is prevalent in many regions of Indonesia (cf. McCarthy 2009; Hidayat *et al.* 2009; Lucas 2009) and a matter of serious concern.

Creating new peripheries

The local government of Kutai Barat invested a great portion of its new income into infrastructure development. Besides the above-mentioned splendid government building complex, this included the construction of a new hospital, several new schools, new roads and bridges and a small airport between Barong Tongkok and Melak. Instead of travelling up the Mahakam 22 hours by boat, Sendawar can now be reached in eight hours by car or in 45 minutes by plane from Samarinda. The local government further improved the availability of electricity, and through the extension of mobile reception and increasing Internet availability access to information has increased. However, most of these efforts concentrated on the area around Sendawar, while other areas, like the Upper Mahakam and some areas in the southwestern part of Kutai Barat, remain difficult to access. Vast parts of these districts continue to be characterised by a poor infrastructure. Public transport facilities are very limited and partly non-existent, which makes it extremely expensive to travel.

The above-mentioned household survey revealed that on average, about one-third of all households in Kutai Barat can be considered poor,[8] while 52.1 per cent feel that they live in poverty (Gönner *et al.* 2007a: 21). The area around Sendawar did not only benefit most from infrastructural development, it also represents the region where new economic opportunities brought about by decentralisation became most tangible for the local population. The best-off districts of the regency, namely Penyinggahan, Sekolaq Darat, Melak and Barong Tongkok are all located around Sendawar. The household survey further revealed that remoteness (measured in travel time needed to reach Sendawar) is an important factor influencing poverty in Kutai Barat: the more remote a village, the lower its results concerning health, household wealth, knowledge, economic opportunities and access to infrastructure and services (Gönner *et al.* 2007a: 45). At district level, material wealth strongly correlates with subjective wellbeing. While the inhabitants of the rather wealthy districts around Sendawar expressed the highest subjective wellbeing, it was lowest in the northwestern, southwestern and southeastern parts of Kutai Barat.

Interestingly, the Upper Mahakam region stood out in this respect. Despite material wealth comparable to that around Sendawar, people living here expressed a very low subjective wellbeing. The generally good condition of villages in Long Apari, Long Pahangai and Long Bagun can be explained by relatively high incomes from birds' nests, eagle wood and gold, a broad subsistence basis, and some special attention by local government, e.g. subsidised transportation and other welfare programmes provided by churches for many decades. But how do we explain the subjective feeling of being poor and unhappy? It might be that frequent conflicts about valuable forest resources negatively influence local wellbeing. But besides that, remoteness seems to play a major role. The Upper Mahakam is still characterised by large areas of dense forests where people feel 'cut off from the outside world'. The inhabitants of the Upper Mahakam repeatedly complained that infrastructural development, access to education and health care is lagging behind (their expectations). Additionally, they felt underrepresented in the local government of Kutai Barat, which was, and is, dominated by Benuaq and Tunjung while the Upper Mahakam is mainly inhabited by Kenyah, Kayan, Bahau, and Aoheng. All this contributed to the desire to form a separate regency, which finally was realised on 14 December 2012 when the five northwestern districts of Kutai Barat (Long Apari, Long Pahangai, Long Bagun, Laham and Long Hubung) split up and formed the *kabupaten* Mahakam Ulu.

Another area with extremely low subjective wellbeing lies in Kutai Barat's southeast. Besides increasing environmental degradation and economic dependencies, which will be elaborated below, the low subjective wellbeing of this area is closely linked to its peripheral position. The villages here are located relatively close to Tenggarong, the centre of the former sultanate, the previous regency Kutai and the new regency Kutai Kartanegara. For many villagers, especially ethnic Kutai Malays, Tenggarong constitutes the social and cultural centre to which they feel they belong (Bullinger 2008). Sendawar is thus perceived as being distant, and also as unfamiliar, as most households from this region of Kutai Barat lack family relations in and around Barong Tongkok. This makes the journey to the local government not only long but also expensive. After being located in the heartland of the previous regency of Kutai, the villagers – ethnic Kutai Malay and Dayak alike – find themselves now placed at the periphery of the new regency Kutai Barat.

Rising inequalities

Despite the concentration of development around Sendawar, new economic opportunities were felt throughout the district. Accordingly, 60.6 per cent of the households stated that they had new income opportunities compared to the situation five years ago (Gönner *et al.* 2007a: 30). However, while some of these new income sources promise a long-term perspective (e.g. a career as a civil servant), others proved to be highly temporary (e.g. income from logging fees). Furthermore, benefits from new economic opportunities were distributed unequally. The household survey shows a disparity of wellbeing distribution[9] in Kutai Barat which is higher than the disparity of poverty distribution measured by the Central Statistics Agency (*Badan Pusat Statistik*, BPS) for the whole of Indonesia and East Kalimantan (Gönner *et al.* 2007a: 20). The following section will provide a more detailed perspective on who flourished in these circumstances and who did not, by tracing how inequalities emerged between different village communities and between individual villagers.

Inequality between villages

Depending on their location, individual histories and the impacts of different industries, severe inequalities emerged between the villages of Kutai Barat. An example of this was in Engkuni Pasek, Jontai and Muara Nayan. The village Engkuni Pasek is located 11 kilometres away from the new district capital on the shore of the Idaatn River in the Western part of the sub-district Barong Tongkok. The larger proportion of the village area, approximately 55 per cent, is used for agriculture, including rice fields, fallow fields, rattan, rubber and forest gardens. Forest makes up 35 per cent of the village area and consists mainly of secondary growth with some small patches of old forest. The remaining area consists of fallow fields, gardens and forest patches which were destroyed by forest fires in 1982/1983 and 1997/1998. There are currently no private sector activities in the village area.

After the implementation of regional autonomy, Engkuni Pasek was characterised by a positive atmosphere of departure. Being located close to Sendawar, the villagers enjoyed many positive effects of decentralisation. The quality of the infrastructure increased significantly due to the construction of two roads and the refurbishment of two bridges. Half of the households reported that their economic situation had improved over the previous five years, mainly due to three new income sources: logging, rubber tapping and office jobs. Self-organised logging became a major income source during the early phase of regional autonomy and lost importance after 2005. Rubber tapping continues to provide an important cash income for many households in Engkuni Pasek, with revenues varying according to fluctuating prices. The most important and most stable new income source was a large number of office jobs that needed to be filled after the creation of the new regency. People of Engkuni Pasek profited from this opportunity as they live close to the new administrative centre and many people, although not all, possessed the necessary high level of formal education needed. At least 30 per cent of the households had members who got a new job in Sendawar, mainly as civil servants or teachers. These new job opportunities were also brought about by the close ethnic and personal links which exist between several families in Engkuni Pasek and the first district leader Rama A. Asia. Of the villagers, 41 per cent stated that they enjoy a good life, while 31 per cent felt they lived in poverty. As a consequence, Engkuni Pasek can be seen as a village where many people profited from regional autonomy and in general contributed well to the economic development of the region.

Muara Nayan is located in the new southeastern periphery of Kutai Barat described above, in the district Jempang at the confluence of the Nayan and the Ohookng River. The largest proportion of the village area (approximately 80 per cent) consists of rice fields, fallow fields, rattan, rubber and forest gardens while 15 per cent is covered with forest and 5 per cent has been converted to oil palm plantations. Extensive forest fires in 1982/1983 and 1997/1998 destroyed large parts of the village area. Therefore, the forested area mainly consists of young secondary growth. Muara Nayan has been impacted significantly by private sector activities since the arrival of an oil palm company in 1996, and a coal mining company in 1994/95 in the neighbouring district of Muara Pahu.

In Muara Nayan, nearly everyone complained about their new peripheral position. The villagers did not see a significant improvement in their living standard either. On the contrary, the large majority of households stated that their situation had remained more or less the same or fluctuated over the past five years (but not improved in any way). Only 17 per cent felt they lived a good life, while 72 per cent felt that they lived in poverty. Nearly all households have lost rattan, rubber and forest gardens through forest fires, logging activities and the land clearing activities of the palm oil company. The river water in Muara Nayan is affected by acidic rock drainage from upriver open pit coal mining and the use of chemicals (fertilisers, herbicides and pesticides) in the oil palm planta-tion. People complained about resulting skin irritations and increased costs as they either have to fetch drinking water from distant wells or buy bottled water. The villagers felt frustrated that their new local Dayak government was not taking more serious steps to control pollution, especially as decentralisation pro-vided it with more leeway and increased authority.

The villagers feel that their livelihoods are restricted and fear that the general situation in their village will continue to worsen (cf. Haug 2014c). The loss of natural assets reduces their economic alternatives and instead increases their dependency on additional cash income. They feel that the very industries that generate income at regency and national levels produce poverty for them.

Inequality within village communities

Being located 30 kilometres from Sendawar at the shore of the Nyuataatn River, Jontai also lies quite close to the new centre. However, the village is more remote than Engkuni Pasek because it is cut off from the road connection to Sendawar by the Nyuataatn. The largest proportion of the village area (approxi-mately 65 per cent) consists of old secondary and primary forest. The remaining area is used for agriculture, including rice fields, fallow fields, rattan, rubber and forest gardens. Commercial logging undertaken by different companies has played a major role in Jontai since the late 1960s.

The inhabitants of Jontai commonly stated that they were all poor as they knew about a survey conducted by the National Family Planning Coordination Agency (*Badan Koordinasi Keluarga Berencana Nasional*, BKKBN) which had designated the village as being 100 per cent poor. During my data collection in 2004, 22 per cent of the villagers said they lived a good life while 48 per cent felt that they lived in poverty. During the early phase of decentralisation, the economic situation in Jontai improved, mainly due to self-organised logging activities and increased fee payments from the local logging company which started operations under the new Forest Product Harvest Concession (*Hak Pemungutan Hasil Hutan*, HPHH). These new licences were not granted to the company but to the villagers (individuals, groups or cooperatives) who then worked together with logging companies as contractors. As a consequence, fees rose in Jontai from IDR3,000 (US$0.36) per m³ in 1999 under the previous concession system (*Hak Pengusahaan Hutan*, HPH) to IDR65,000 (US$7.15) per m³ under the new HPHH system in 2004.

However, inequality increased sharply among the villagers as people benefitted very differently from the logging boom. In order to partake in self-organised logging activities, one had to possess the necessary capital, equipment and adequate skills to operate a chainsaw. As a consequence, the majority of loggers were young and middle-aged men who either owned the necessary capital themselves or worked for someone who did. Income from logging further depended on ownership rights to forest areas. Men cutting their own trees received more money than those who worked within the forest areas of others, as they had to share the revenues with the respective owners.

The distribution of fee payments under the new HPHH scheme was also highly unequal and highly disputed. The villagers split into groups based on common ownership claims to certain forest areas (for a detailed analysis of this process see Haug 2014b). Most of these groups were represented by a (partly self-appointed) leader who had to control the actual amount of timber logged in the groups' area, make sure that the company would pay the correct amount and further was responsible for the distribution of the fee among all members of the group. This put young and rather 'tough' (BI *gigih*) men in a favourable position as it was no easy task to maintain good relations with the logging company and stay several nights in the forest if needed. Although 73 per cent of the households reported that they had received fee payments, the amount a person received varied between IDR200,000 (US$22) and IDR15 million (US$1,650) during 2004. This variation can be partly explained through differences in the amount of timber logged in the respective area, but it also was the result of dishonest group leaders and the unfair distribution of money within the groups. In summary, one can say that the (mainly male) village leaders and several 'tough' young men gained the largest profits. Nevertheless, high income from logging proved to be short-lived, as all logging activities in Jontai came to a halt with the expiration of the HPHH concession and the increased controls of illegal logging in late 2004. As a consequence, most households in Jontai had to revert to mere subsistence strategies, earning cash only through the selling of agricultural and forest products, or through wage labour. Some households have invested their logging money in small-scale businesses or higher education. But most of the money has been used for daily needs or blown away for short-term amusement. As a consequence, many people in Jontai expressed that after the logging boom had ended, they were at least 'all equal again'.

While the sharp inequalities that emerged in Jontai during the logging boom can be seen as rather temporary, much more persistent inequalities emerged in Engkuni Pasek. Two people are introduced here shortly to illustrate these new inequalities. Taman Sayan was born in Engkuni Pasek in the early 1970s. He attended the local catholic primary school, continued his education outside of the village, and graduated from a vocational school as a carpenter. He, his wife and their four children make their living mainly from agriculture and earn some additional cash through Taman Sayan's carpentry work and the occasional selling of rattan and rubber. The family owns a motorbike and lives in a modest and rather small wooden house in Engkuni Pasek. The living conditions of Taman Sayan and his family have not changed much due to decentralisation. They can fulfil their basic household needs and are not afraid to suffer from food shortage. However, they face difficulties in making larger expenditures or paying for medical care. They also worry whether they will be able to afford higher education for all of their children.

Tinen Niran was born in Engkuni Pasek during the late 1970s. She is the fifth and youngest child of the former village head. Despite her father's formal position the family endured much hardship in order to school their five children. But despite many obstacles all children graduated from high school and Tinen Niran was even sent to Samarinda to go to university where she studied economics. After the creation of Kutai Barat, when new government staff was needed, Tinen Niran came back to Kutai Barat and was employed at the Forestry Service of Kutai Barat. As her office is located in Melak, Tinen Niran has meanwhile moved with her husband, their three children and her mother to the new regency's centre. Tinen Niran's husband also gained an office job and their lifestyle resembles more or less that of an urban Indonesian middle-class family, including a one-family house, a car and being able to afford family vacations to Bali.

Taman Sayan and his family represent those villagers who neither profited from the logging boom nor gained an office job in Sendawar. They do not live in extreme poverty, but their life remains characterised by little material wealth and many insecurities. Tinen Niran and her family, on the other hand, represent those villagers who were lucky to get one of the highly valued office jobs and who became an active part of the prospering new centre of Kutai Barat. While many livelihoods in Kutai Barat resemble that of Taman Sayan and some that of Tinen Niran, there is a small number of extraordinary individuals from villages throughout Kutai Barat who have become part of its wealthy and influential elite, performing on the political stage, filling leading administrative positions or being deeply involved in local business activities. These individuals acquire huge parts of the regency's newly gained wealth. Some of them meanwhile reside in Samarinda, fly to Jakarta or even Singapore for medical treatment while serving as influential and respected patrons for their rural clientele.

Conclusion

In this chapter, Kutai Barat is used as an example to demonstrate that the interior of East Kalimantan can no longer be easily depicted as part of Indonesia's margins. Significant processes of 'de-marginalisation' are taking place, especially if one looks at the regency as a political and administrative entity and the various Dayak groups as a whole: Kutai Barat has become one of Indonesia's richest regencies, and Dayak, endowed with new political authority, have become the ruling majority. Additionally, large investments have been made in local infrastructure. However, it is shown that new processes of marginalisation are taking place on the regency as well as on the village level. As a consequence, only a small number of people prosper while a large proportion of the population in Kutai Barat remains empty-handed. In order to understand these new processes of marginalisation, and to assess emerging as well as persisting inequalities, it is argued that there are benefits to differentiating between processes of political, economic and social disenfranchisement, remoteness and spatial distance, as this allows one to trace how different processes and different kinds of experiences are intertwined.

As a political unit, Kutai Barat has gained power vis-à-vis Jakarta, representing one of the several new local centres in East Kalimantan, which self-consciously demand larger shares of what they perceive to be their natural riches and challenge the power relations that once established them as marginal regions. Jakarta remains an important point of reference and the major source of the regency's budget. However, Kutai Barat does not define itself exclusively in relation to Jakarta, as it is so closely related with other (re-)strengthened centres in Kalimantan. While Kutai Barat's spatial distance to Jakarta has not changed, new power relations and the increasing importance of multidirectional ties to other regional centres have placed the regency in a new position. This resembles the observation that strong regional links have evolved throughout Indonesia since the end of the *Orde Baru* which bypass Jakarta and which provide local political and economic elites with the opportunity to push jointly for regional ambitions (cf. Sakai and Morrell 2006; Kimura 2007).

With the creation of Kutai Barat and Sendawar as its new semi-urban centre, new peripheries have been created as well. In the Upper Mahakam, political marginalisation is closely intertwined with remoteness. The people living here did not feel well represented in the new local government. Besides that, they expressed an extremely low subjective wellbeing, despite material wealth comparable to that around Sendawar. It is their experience of living in a region that is difficult to access, with insufficient access to education and health care and of 'being cut off', which makes them feel unhappy and poor. In the southeastern part of Kutai Barat, on the other hand, processes of political, economic and social disenfranchisement are closely linked with spatial distance. After being located in the heartland of the old regency Kutai, the *pemekaran* process has placed these villages at the periphery of the new regency.

The contrasting village trajectories of Engkuni Pasek and Muara Nayan again demonstrate the intertwinement of marginality and spatial distance. The people of Engkuni Pasek benefitted from their unusually high level of education, their close relations to the first Bupati, but also from the proximity to Sendawar. The situation in Muara Nayan, on the other hand, is dominated by the negative impacts of the oil palm expansion, coal mining and related increasing environmental degradation. The inequalities experienced by them vis-à-vis large companies and the state are not new. While they felt that their natural wealth was being swallowed by Jakarta before, they now feel increasingly dispossessed by local elites. Describing evolving individual inequalities finally demonstrated how new local elites and a new semi-urban 'middle class' emerged in Kutai Barat. As in many areas of Indonesia, it is these (new) local elites who often become the primary beneficiaries of the redistribution of power and authority over natural resources (cf. Schulte Nordholt and van Klinken 2007; Warren and McCarthy 2009).

All things considered, one can say that previous processes of social and economic disenfranchisement of the interior regions of East Kalimantan and especially its indigenous population have been replaced by more complex processes of marginalisation and that former systematic political marginalisation has been replaced by much more differentiated power struggles among prominent individuals and local elites. With decentralisation, money poured into the regency, but the comprehensive development that seemed possible now did not set in. Becoming a rich regency has thus not brought prosperity to the large majority of the population in Kutai Barat.

Notes

1 The project 'Making Local Government More Responsive to the Poor: Developing Indicators and Tools to Support Sustainable Livelihood under Decentralization', was funded by the German Federal Ministry for Education and Research (BMBF) and carried out by the Center for International Forestry Research (CIFOR) in co-operation with the University of Freiburg, Germany.
2 Although this household survey seems a while ago, its informative value continues to be significant. Unfortunately no household survey of similar depth and comprehensiveness has been conducted since then.
3 During my field research I have been confronted with several cases where people died from injuries, complications during childbirth, or accidents. All of them would have had a fair chance to be saved without the long and exhausting journey to the hospital.
4 Badan Pelayanan Perijinan Terpadu Kabupaten Kutai Barat, http://perijinan.kubarkab. go.id/news31-taman-budaya-sendawar-mulai-berfungsi-telan-rp-40-m-pertama-di-kalimantan.html (accessed 23 September 2015).
5 In this chapter I use average conversion rates for each year as follows: 1999: 0.00013 – US$1=IDR7,879; 2001: 0,00010 – US$1=IDR10,250; 2003: 0.00012 – US$1=IDR8,593; 2004: 0.00011 – US$1=IDR8,945; 2012: 0.00011 – US$1=IDR9,329; 2013: 0.00010 – US$1=IDR10,395; 2014: 0.00008 – US$1=IDR 11,836; 2015: 0.00007 – US$1=IDR13,319.
6 http://apps.info-anggaran.com/index.php/ourdata/datadetail/2014/m/6402 (accessed 16 October 2015) and http://apps.info-anggaran.com/index.php/ourdata/datadetail/2015/m/6402 (accessed 16 October 2015).
7 Indonesian coal production has increased significantly during the last 15 years, and in 2011 Indonesia overtook Australia as the world's largest exporter of thermal coal.
8 Within the project team poverty was understood to have multiple dimensions, in contrast to approaches that focus merely on income or consumption. In order to capture the diverse notions and attributes of poverty, the project team conceptualised a poverty model consisting of several nested spheres (Gönner *et al.* 2007b). These included subjective wellbeing, core aspects of poverty like health, education, housing, food and wealth, and also the contextual enabling environment that represents the means to escape from poverty (e.g. availability and quality of natural resources, economic opportunities, infrastructure and services, social capital and cohesion as well as rights and participation).
9 The Gini Index (GI) is 39.3 for the core wellbeing values of the 2006 monitoring data (n=10,431 households), which is higher than the indices for Indonesia (GI=34.3; World Bank 2006) and East Kalimantan (GI=30.4; Badan Pusat Statistik 2003).

References

Andrianto, A. (2006) *The Role of District Government in Poverty Alleviation: Case Studies in Malinau and West Kutai Districts, East Kalimantan, Indonesia.* Bogor: CIFOR.

Badan Pusat Statistik (2003) *Kutai Barat dalam angka (Kutai Barat in Figures).* Kabupaten Kutai Barat, Indonesia: Pemerintah Kabupaten Kutai.

Badan Pusat Statistik (2014) *Kutai Barat dalam angka (Kutai Barat in Figures).* Kabupaten Kutai Barat, Indonesia: Pemerintah Kabupaten Kutai.

Bullinger, C. (2008) *Die Kutai in Kutai Barat, Ost-Kalimantan: Zu Auswirkungen der Dezentralisierung seit 2001.* Saarbrücken: VDM Verlag.

Bullinger, C. and Haug, M. (2012) In and Out of the Forest: Decentralisation and Recentralisation of Forest Governance in East Kalimantan, Indonesia, *ASEAS – Austrian Journal of South-East Asian Studies* (5)2: 243–262.

Cahyat, A., Iranon, B. and Edna, B. (2005) *Profil Kampung-Kampung di Kabupaten Kutai Barat. Kondisi sosial ekonomi Kampung-Kampung.* Bogor: CIFOR.

Casson, A. (2001) *Decentralisation of Policies Affecting Forests and Estate Crops in Kutai Barat District, East Kalimantan. Case Studies on Decentralisation and Forests in Indonesia.* Bogor: CIFOR.

Davidson, J.S. (2003) The Politics of Violence on an Indonesian Periphery, *South East Asia Research* 11(1): 59–89.

Davidson, J. and Henley, D. (eds) (2007) *The Revival of Tradition in Indonesian Politics: The Deployment of Adat from Colonialism to Indigenism.* London: Routledge.

Dunne, R.J. (2005) Marginality: A Conceptual Extension, in R.M. Dennis (ed.), *Marginality, Power and Social Structure: Issues in Race, Class, and Gender Analysis*, Amsterdam: Elsevier, pp. 11–28.

Dyson, L. (2002) *Sejarah Sendawar: Dari Mitologi hingga Histori suatu Kajian Sejarah lokal.* Surabaya: Airlangga University Press.

Dyson, L. (2008) *Sejarah Sendawar: Sebuah Sejarah Sosial.* Surabaya: Airlangga University Press.

Gönner, C. (2001) *Muster und Strategien der Ressourcennutzung: Eine Fallstudie aus einem Dayak Benuaq Dorf in Ost Kalimantan, Indonesien.* Zürich: ETH Zürich.

Gönner, C. (2002) *A Forest Tribe of Borneo: Resource Use among the Dayak Benuaq.* New Delhi: D.K. Printworld.

Gönner, C., Cahyat, A., Haug, M. and Limberg, G. (2007a) *Towards Wellbeing: Monitoring Poverty in Kutai Barat, Indonesia.* Bogor: CIFOR.

Gönner, C., Haug, M., Cahyat, A., Wollenberg, L., de Jong, W., Limberg, G., Cronkleton, P., Moeliono, M. and Becker, M. (2007b) *Capturing Nested Spheres of Poverty: A Model for Multi-dimensional Poverty Analysis and Monitoring.* CIFOR Occasional Paper No. 46. Bogor: CIFOR.

Government of Indonesia (2011) Masterplan: Acceleration and Expansion of Indonesia Economic Development 2011–2025. Jakarta: Coordinating Ministry for Economic Affairs. Available online: www.kemlu.go.id/rome/Documents/MP3EI_PDF.pdf (accessed 6 December 2015).

Gurung, G. and Kollmair, M. (2005) *Marginality: Concepts and Their Limitations.* IP6 Working Paper 4. Zürich: Swiss National Centre of Competence in Research (NCCR) North-South.

Harms, E., Hussain, Sh. and Shneiderman, S. (eds) (2014) Remote and Edgy: New Takes on Old Anthropological Themes, *HAU: Journal of Ethnographic Theory* 4(1): 361–381.

Haug, M. (2010) *Poverty and Decentralisation in East Kalimantan: The Impact of Regional Autonomy on Dayak Benuaq Wellbeing.* Freiburg: Centaurus.

Haug, M. (2014a) Resistance, Ritual Purification and Mediation: Tracing a Dayak Community's Sixteen-Year Search for Justice in East Kalimantan, *The Asia Pacific Journal of Anthropology* 15(4): 357–375.

Haug, M. (2014b) Disputed Normativities and the Logging Boom in Kutai Barat: Local Dynamics during the Initial Phase of Regional Autonomy in East Kalimantan, Indonesia, *Paideuma* 60: 89–113.

Haug, M. (2014c) What Makes a Good Life? Emic Concepts of 'Wellbeing' and 'Ill-being' among the Dayak Benuaq in East-Kalimantan, Indonesia, in T. Stodulka and B. Röttger-Rössler (eds), *Feelings at the Margins: Dealing with Violence, Stigma and Isolation in Indonesia*, Frankfurt and New York: Campus, pp. 30–52.

Hidayat, A., Ballard, C. and Kanowski, P. (2009) Forests for the People? Special Autonomy, Community Forestry Cooperatives and the apparent Return of Customary Rights in Papua, in C. Warren and J. McCarthy (eds), *Community, Environment and Local Governance in Indonesia: Locating the Commonweal*, London and New York: Routledge, pp. 145–166.

Hopper, K. (2003) *Reckoning with Homelessness.* Ithaca, NY: Cornell University Press.

Kimura, E. (2007) Marginality and Opportunity in the Periphery: The Emergence of Gorontalo Province in North Sulawesi, *Indonesia* 84: 71–95.

Klinken, G. van (2002) Indonesia's New Ethnic Elites, in H. Schulte Nordholt and I. Abdullah (eds), *Indonesia: In Search of Transition*, Yogyakarta: Pustaka Pelajar, pp. 67–105. Available online: http://papers.ssrn.com/sol3/papers.cfm?abstract_id=1127117 (accessed 6 December 2015).

Leimgruber, W. (2004) *Between Global and Local: Marginality and Marginal Regions in the Context of Globalization and Deregulation.* Farnham, UK: Ashgate.

Li, T. (1999) Marginality, Power and Production: Analysing Upland Transformations, in T. Li (ed.), *Transforming the Indonesian Uplands: Marginality. Power, and Production*, Amsterdam: Harwood Academic Publishers, pp. 1–45.

Lucarelli, B. (2010) *The History and the Future of Indonesia's Coal Industry.* Freeman Spogli Institute for International Studies, Working Paper 93.

Lucas, A. (2009) Berjuang di atas Perahu: Livelihood, Contestation and Declining Marine Resources on Java's North Coast, in C. Warren and J. McCarthy (eds), *Community, Environment and Local Governance in Indonesia: Locating the Commonweal*, London and New York: Routledge, pp. 59–88.

McCarthy, J. (2009) Where Is Justice? Resource Entitlements, Argarian Transformations and Regional Autonomy in Jambi, Sumatra, in C. Warren and J. McCarthy (eds), *Community, Environment and Local Governance in Indonesia: Locating the Commonweal*, London and New York: Routledge, pp. 167–196.

Magenda, B. (1991) *East Kalimantan: The Decline of Commercial Aristocracy.* Monograph Series, Publication No. 70. Ithaca, NY: Cornell University.

Manning, C. (1971) The Timber Boom with Special Reference to East Kalimantan, *Bulletin of Indonesian Economic Studies* 7(3): 30–60.

Oesterheld, C. (2004) *Scapegoaters, Avengers and Executioners: Oral History and the Kalimantan Riots*, MSc Dissertation, School of Oriental and African Studies (SOAS), University of London.

Peluso, N.L. (2003) Weapons of the Wild: Strategic Uses of Violence and Wildness in the Rainforests of Indonesian Borneo, in C. Slater (ed.), *In Search of the Rain Forest*, Durham, NC and London: Duke University Press, pp. 204–245.

Peluso, N.L. and Vandergeest, P. (2011) Political Ecologies of War and Forests: Counter-Insurgencies and the Making of National Natures, *Annals of the Association of American Geographers* 101(3): 587–608.

Resosudarmo, I.A. (2004) Closer to Peoples and Trees: Will Decentralisation Work for the People and the Forests of Indonesia?, *European Journal of Development Research* 16(1): 110–132.

Röttger-Rössler, B. and Stodulka, T. (2014) Introduction: The Emotional Make-up of Marginality and Stigma, in T. Stodulka and B. Röttger-Rössler (eds), *Feelings at the Margins: Dealing with Violence, Stigma and Isolation in Indonesia*, Frankfurt and New York: Campus, pp. 11–29.

Sakai, M. and Morrell, E. (2006) Reconfiguring Regions and Challenging the State? New Socio-economic Partnerships in the Outer Islands of Indonesia, in *Asia Reconstructed: Proceedings of the 16th Biennial Conference of the ASAA*. Wollongong, NSW, 26–29 June 2006.

Schulte Nordholt, H. and van Klinken, G. (eds) (2007) *Renegotiating Boundaries: Local Politics in Post-Suharto Indonesia*. Leiden: KITLV Press.

Scott, J. (2009) *The Art of Not Being Governed: An Anarchist History of Upland Southeast Asia*. New Haven, CT: Yale University Press.

Tsing, A. (1993) *In the Realm of the Diamond Queen: Marginality in an Out-of-the-way Place*. Princeton, NJ: Princeton University Press.

Venz, O. (2012) *Die autochthone Religion der Benuaq von Ost-Kalimantan: Eine ethnolinguistische Untersuchung*, PhD Dissertation, University of Freiburg.

Warren, C. and McCarthy, J. (2009) Locating the Commonweal, in C. Warren and J. McCarthy (eds), *Community, Environment and Local Governance in Indonesia: Locating the Commonweal*, London and New York: Routledge, pp. 227–253.

Widen, K. (2002) The Resurgence of Dayak Identities: The Symbols of Their Struggle for Regional Autonomy Are Self-evident, in M. Sakai (ed.), *Beyond Jakarta: Regional Autonomy and Local Society in Indonesia*, Adelaide: Crawford House Publishing, pp. 102–120.

World Bank (2006) *World Development Indicators 2006*. Washington, DC: The World Bank. Available online: http://data.worldbank.org/sites/default/files/wdi06.pdf (accessed 30 March 2016)

9   Concluding remarks

Michaela Haug, Martin Rössler and
Anna-Teresa Grumblies

Processes of democratisation and decentralisation have significantly changed the power relations that produced and maintained the marginality of the Indonesian periphery. Li (1999) has aptly portrayed the power relations between uplands and lowlands during the New Order:

> Although there are exceptions, to go upland, inland, towards forests, away from the coasts and from sawah cultivation is, in many parts of contemporary Indonesia to move from domains of greater power to lesser power and prestige, from centres towards margins.

(Li 1999: 3)

This picture has meanwhile changed – at least in many resource-rich upland regions which benefitted highly from regional autonomy. Moving inland in East Kalimantan for example, one runs across the revitalised Sultanate of Kutai Kartanegara and other new, splendid centres such as the government complex of Sendawar, described in the introduction of this volume, whose buildings outshine their provincial counterparts. The dichotomous image of an outer periphery against a powerful centre does therefore no longer conform to the changing appearance of the periphery. The hitherto existing image of a brilliant centre vis-à-vis a coarse periphery and related imaginations of uplands and lowlands therefore need to be replaced by a much more complex picture, which is quite challenging to draw.

This volume set out to explore such a picture from the perspective of the Outer Islands. Taking a comparative approach, case studies from the Riau Islands, East and West Kalimantan, North and Central Sulawesi, and the North Moluccas demonstrate how local actors have actively and creatively been engaged in creating new centres and new margins alike, thereby contributing to this complex political landscape, within which power relations between centres and peripheries are constantly reshaped. In this final chapter we summarise some major findings and examine patterns across the case studies, considering the four major themes that were highlighted in the introduction: the temporal and the territorial dimension of marginality, institutions and their role in shaping and (re-) creating centres and peripheries, as well as local actors and their agency. Finally, we will highlight some questions that we perceive as relevant for further research on Indonesia's margins.

The re-emergence of a complex landscape of multiple centres

For many centuries, the Indonesian archipelago has been characterised by the waxing and waning of various centres. This illustrates the temporality of centre–periphery relations, the fluidity of borders between different spheres of influence, and the fragility of power constellations that constitute certain places as centres and others as margins. It was only during colonial rule that Batavia – later Jakarta – emerged as the administrative, political and economic centre of the archipelago and finally became the hub of the highly centralised state during the *Orde Baru*. Since the downfall of Suharto and the implementation of regional autonomy, we can observe the re-emergence of a much more complex pattern of centres and peripheries, a pattern that is composed of regional centres, some of which were newly established, while others, often looking back at traditions spanning centuries, were revitalised. This picture in some respects reminds of pre-colonial conditions – albeit without direct reference to historical structures.

All case studies in this book portray fragmented landscapes of power relations, implying multiple centres and an increasing complexity of linkages between them. Yet the temporal dimension of marginality becomes most apparent in the cases of Long (Chapter 4) and Jäger (Chapter 6), both of whom describe the re-emergence of pre-colonial centres. Long reminds us that the Riau Islands were a major centre of commerce during the seventeenth century, and that the palaces on Lingga and Bintan were the epicentres of one of the Malay world's most important indigenous polities before the region was divided between the Dutch and the British in 1824, and henceforth located at the periphery of the Dutch East Indies. Being further dwarfed by the rise of neighbouring Singapore, it was regional autonomy and the formation of the new Riau Islands Province that made the Riau Archipelago re-emerge as a regional and administrative centre. Analysing the excessive *pemekaran* process in the North Moluccas, Jäger (Chapter 6) shows that the shapes of many new administrative units largely resemble the pre-colonial Sultanates of Ternate, Tidore, Bacan and Jailolo. Her case, therefore, demonstrates a considerable continuity of socio-territorial entities, as these until today have provided people with a strong sense of identity and belonging.

From changing power relations to new marginalities

Democratisation and decentralisation have provided the margins with new opportunities to challenge the hegemonic project of the Indonesian state. Power relations between Jakarta and the outer regions, for decades shaped by a clear-cut asymmetry, have changed in several ways:

a   Although a certain asymmetry between the centre and the regions still prevails, it is not as extreme as it had been for a long time.

b   The current asymmetries between Jakarta and the regions are much more heterogeneous; while some regional centres have gained more power vis-à-vis Jakarta, others have remained comparatively weak.

c   The position of a region within the Outer Islands is no longer exclusively determined by its relation to a single centre, Jakarta, but characterised by multiple ties with various centres at different scales, as linkages between regencies, between regencies and province, and between districts and regencies are gaining importance.

While this is illustrated by all case studies in this volume, it becomes especially evident in the case presented by Eilenberg (Chapter 5). He shows that the borderland of West Kalimantan is characterised by fragmented power relations that comprise multiple and overlapping semi-autonomous cores of power. The border movement, which pushes for a new border regency, is not only negotiating with the centre but also with influential actors at various governmental levels. Last but not least, these actors are carefully handling their relations with the 'mother regency' because through the establishment of a new border regency the 'mother regency' would run the risk of losing significant resources, and of becoming more isolated geographically. This case, as well as the excessive *pemekaran* process in the North Moluccas analysed by Jäger (Chapter 6), and the rise of Sendawar, the vivid new semi-urban centre of Kutai Barat examined by Haug (Chapter 8), further show how new centres inevitably create new margins. The latter case in particular, illustrates how new margins have been created on the outer fringes of Kutai Barat, as most development efforts have concentrated on the area around Sendawar. While the Dayak population has benefitted from regional autonomy as a whole, ethnic competition and rivalry have caused new inequalities. By promoting local Minahasans' business interests, the Brigade Manguni Indonesia (BMI) described by Bakker (Chapter 7) marginalises entrepreneurs with a different ethnic background, as for example migrants originating from other parts of Indonesia. This resembles some of the general consequences of regional autonomy described by Ziegenhain (Chapter 2), who shows how local politics tend to favour *putra daerah*, sons of the region, at the expense of other ethnic groups, and how religious minorities have been forced to comply with Islamic law (*shari'ah*) in terms of behaviour and dress in some regencies with a Muslim majority.

Grumblies (Chapter 3) takes the issue of land rights and the development of the agrarian legislation in Indonesia as the starting point for exploring marginalisation. She emphasises the central role that the territorialisation of the archipelago and its inhabitants has played for the expansion of state control and the construction of marginality in the Indonesian uplands. Many case studies presented in this volume show that in the Outer Islands spatial distance and remoteness are – in varying ways – closely intertwined with processes of social, political and economic disenfranchisement.

The importance of geographical closeness to centres beyond Indonesia is illustrated by Long (Chapter 4) and Eilenberg (Chapter 5). Being located far from Jakarta but close to Singapore, a centre that doubtless outshines Jakarta, or to economic centres in Sarawak, provides inhabitants of the border regions with opportunities to enhance their position vis-à-vis Jakarta. While the consequences of the *pemekaran* process and related processes of (re-)drawing borders and formalising socio-political entities play a central role throughout this volume, they become especially apparent in the North Moluccas (Jäger, Chapter 6), where the proliferation of new administrative units is used as a crucial process to re-arrange territorial claims and to build a much more fragmented landscape of intertwined power relations. The example of six villages that simultaneously came to belong to two different regencies shows how the location of a village and the course of a borderline are closely related to new processes of marginalisation. Eilenberg (Chapter 5) demonstrates how the remoteness of the border region in West Kalimantan and the sheer size of the regency Kapuas Hulu became major arguments to push for a new border regency. The significance of the territorial dimension of marginality is also put forward in the case of Haug (Chapter 8). Here it becomes apparent that subjective wellbeing in Kutai Barat is closely interrelated with specific geographical characteristics and that remoteness and spatial distance produce diverse feelings and experiences among the local people. The association of certain places with feelings is also addressed in the case of Jäger (Chapter 6), where identities and feelings of belonging are related to specific places, and in the context of West Kalimantan (Eilenberg, Chapter 5), where the infrastructural deficits of the densely forested borderland produce dissatisfaction and the feeling of lagging behind mainstream development. This is corroborated by Long who describes (Chapter 4) how images of the periphery as backward have been so deeply internalised by the Riau Islanders that feelings of inferiority still persist. Being located so close to Singapore and Malaysia, people simultaneously face the pressure of making a good impression to outsiders and equally, being figureheads for the Indonesian nation.

The role of institutions in the (re-)creation of centres and peripheries

Political and administrative institutions occupy most prominent positions, as they play a crucial role in shaping and (re-)creating centres and peripheries in post-Suharto Indonesia. The legislation of administrative and fiscal decentralisation provided the framework for a broad spectrum of changes discussed in this volume and several of the positive and negative impacts of regional autonomy outlined by Ziegenhain (Chapter 2) become apparent in the cases explored. However, it is often not merely the new legislation but rather the ambiguity of the laws as well as unclear and overlapping authorities that provide local actors with the critical room to manoeuvre. Long (Chapter 4) points out how 'administrative ambiguities' in the Riau Islands cause struggles over issues such as who can issue a mining licence, and Eilenberg (Chapter 5) demonstrates that it is the fuzzy character of decentralisation that provides leeway for local actors in West Kalimantan. It becomes apparent that new centres and peripheries are not simply produced by new laws, but that the ambiguous character of the legislation created a special situation in which local actors negotiate new power relations. Long (Chapter 4) accordingly argues that the administrative reform process has not created new centre–periphery relations in and of itself, but rather created new possibilities in which local actors actively engage to realise the images that are most desirable to them. This argument is confirmed by all cases presented here. New centre–periphery relations that emerge between Jakarta and the regions and also between regional centres and their margins are very much the outcome of processes of negotiation between local actors. Evidently the bargaining position of the respective actors determines who benefits and who does not.

Besides the new laws, various new, as well as old institutions at different scales play a crucial role in transforming the margins. In many places, *adat* institutions and local pre-colonial institutions of governance have regained political significance. For example, the North Moluccan Sultanates of Tidore and Bacan were revitalised in 1999, and the Sultanate of Jailolo in 2003 (Chapter 6). An institution of major importance, especially for ethnic minorities living in the Outer Islands of Indonesia, is AMAN. Since its formation in 1999, the *Aliansi Masyarakat Adat Nusantara*, having grown out of the indigenous peoples' movement in Indonesia, has advanced to an important institution of considerable size and influence, as it is well connected to the global indigenous peoples' network. Grumblies (Chapter 3) demonstrates how the Wana, by getting involved with AMAN, discovered their indigeneity as a means to challenge their marginal position within the Indonesian nation state. Bakker (Chapter 7) describes how the mass organisation BMI was founded on the basis of a shared regional identity, and was unified by the aim to challenge and alter the relations between the Minahasa and the nation's centre. The BMI can be seen as an example of a strong local institution pursuing political, economic and ethnic interests. Feeling dissatisfied with state institutions, they took matters into their own hands – a tendency which occurred in many parts of post-New Order Indonesia (cf. Warren and McCarthy 2009).

The agency of local actors

Many studies of post-Suharto Indonesia focus on local elites as crucial actors who often capture new powerful positions and, consequently, most of the financial benefits (cf. Schulte Nordholt and van Klinken 2007; Vel 2008; Aspinall and Mietzner 2010; and Ziegenhain, Chapter 2, this volume). By paying attention to local elites as well as to ordinary citizens and villagers on the Outer Islands, the case studies presented here attempt to provide a balanced picture. While local elites and their strategies are explored very vividly in the case of Eilenberg (Chapter 5), Long (Chapter 4) most explicitly focuses on 'ordinary people' and their feelings, motivations and aspirations.

The case studies reveal the crucial role of individual people and groups of actors for specific local outcomes as well as the great variety of these outcomes. The struggle for a new border regency in the case presented by Eilenberg

(Chapter 5) is strongly influenced by the leader of the border movement, a well-educated man holding an influential governmental position. The future of the whole *pemekaran* efforts along the border very much depends on the goodwill and personal goals of key individuals at various levels of the government. The border elite in West Kalimantan as well as the political elite of East Kalimantan described by Bakker (Chapter 7) demonstrate very well how local elites use (previous) state rhetoric of underdevelopment and backwardness which has for a long time been part of the marginalisation project of the state, to now claim more autonomy and larger shares of revenues from natural resources.

One of the most striking findings from all the case studies set forth in this volume and those presented in the workshop preceding it is the great creativity and zeal with which local actors engage in the possibilities created by decentralisation and democratisation in post-Suharto Indonesia. Various groups of actors, as well as individuals, engage in strenuous struggles to overcome past marginalisation, try to position themselves close to the centre of their choice and actively contribute to the creation of new centres and margins. This is well illustrated by the inhabitants of the six villages described by Jäger (Chapter 6). When they were assigned to the regency of Halmahera Utara, they refused by creating their own district which was part of the regency of their choice, Halmahera Barat. Although this new district has not been officially recognised by the centre, it was proclaimed by the regional government of Halmahera Barat. The means by which people have in this case resisted the national government's orders and formed their own administrative entity representing their social identity and feeling of belonging, reflects the increasing strength of local agency.

Several case studies show how the (re-)emergence of multiple centres of power provides the inhabitants of the Outer Islands with new opportunities to connect themselves to the centres of their choice in order to improve their social, economic and political positions. It is furthermore apparent that regional centres as well as individual local actors increasingly relate themselves to economic and political centres beyond the national borders. This is the case in border regions such as the Riau Islands (Long, Chapter 4), where people are increasingly oriented towards Singapore and Malaysia, or along the Indonesian-Malaysian border in West Kalimantan (Eilenberg, Chapter 5), where local elites maintain close ties with Malaysian businessmen. In a similar vein, the Wana living in the uplands of Central Sulawesi (Grumblies, Chapter 3) relate themselves to the global indigenous people's network through AMAN, while Jäger (Chapter 6) identifies an internationally operating mining company in Halmahera as a new local centre of power. These examples confirm the findings of Sakai *et al.* (2009: 11), who see international actors such as NGO movements and multinational resource corporations becoming increasingly incorporated into local processes of identity formation at the periphery. The case studies presented in this volume furthermore show that the engagement with centres beyond Indonesia plays a crucial role in enhancing local actors' situation vis-à-vis Jakarta. This is probably most effectively illustrated by the case of Pak Gunawan (Long, Chapter 4), a schoolmaster from Batam, who boosts the self-confidence of his pupils by making them feel familiar to Singapore before attending a school competition in Jakarta.

Ambiguous relations to Jakarta

Despite the re-emergence of a much more fragmented landscape of power relations, Jakarta remains the political centre of the Indonesian nation state and the major source of regional revenues, as has been shown in the example of Kutai Barat (Chapter 8). However, the ways in which the regions want to be related to Jakarta has changed, and, most interestingly, reveal considerable differences: while some regions want to get as much freedom from the centre as possible, others wish to relate to it more directly. Bakker (Chapter 7), for example, reports that he frequently encountered sentiments on the Outer Islands, according to which 'Jakarta' is pocketing the nation's money and selling Indonesia's resources to foreign companies. As a result, people in East Kalimantan are campaigning to obtain special autonomy for their province, or feel encouraged to take matters into their own hands, as does the BMI in the Minahasa. In a similar vein, the wish to achieve greater autonomy from Jakarta is a major motivation behind the struggle for a new border regency in West Kalimantan (Eilenberg, Chapter 5), as local communities have so far seen their forests being plundered for the benefit of the centre while they have remained empty-handed.

Long, on the other hand, reminds us that 'decentralisation can be as much about the desire for connection as it can be about autonomy' (Chapter 4). His case study shows that the Riau islanders do not wish to get rid of Jakarta, they rather want to be related to it more directly and on more equal terms. Several scholars such as Booth (2011), Quinn (2003) and Kimura (2007, 2010) have pointed out that the proliferation of new provinces and regencies was in some cases driven by the wish to escape the domination from regional centres or locally dominant groups rather than from Jakarta. Kimura (2007) further argues that neither the centre nor the margins are homogenous entities and that both national and local actors often do cooperate to achieve common goals. He thus states that 'power does not flow in one direction, from the centre outward, in Indonesia today' (2007: 95). The example from the Riau islands, described by Long (Chapter 4), further shows that local people often look hopefully towards Jakarta: they expect the centre to control local misuses of power and to provide justice. The centre is, therefore, especially by ordinary citizens, seen as vital for the control of local leaders.

Perspectives for future research

The case studies presented in this volume provide a glimpse of the unfolding complexities in the so-called Outer Islands. But as processes of contesting and reshaping centre–periphery relations are ongoing projects that are constantly challenged, more case studies on a broader variety of regions are needed to understand the intricacies of these processes. A perspective from Nusa Tenggara

Timor (NTT) and the provinces and regencies of western Papua would be especially desirable, not only because of the Christian majority in both regions. NTT, for example, has suffered from a general decline since the implementation of regional autonomy (cf. Bräuchler and Erb 2011), while Papua is still considered the region with the lowest human development indicator and GDP per capita in Indonesia (The Jakarta Post 2014). Interestingly, with respect to Papua a contrasting view of *pemekaran* has been reported, since in that region, it is associated with an expansion of state control rather than with a higher degree of autonomy (McWilliam 2011). In addition, the incorporation of the western part of New Guinea into the Indonesian nation state continues to be challenged by an indigenous movement, which has just recently received international attention by acquiring the status of an affiliated observer for the Melanesian Spearhead Group, an intergovernmental organisation of Melanesian states (The Jakarta Post 2015).

Changing power relations, the revival of *adat* institutions, the re-emergence of local institutions of governance and the rise of old as well as new local elites result in new processes of marginalisation and the (re-)production of social inequalities. While much attention has been paid to ethnicity and religion as major factors underlying differences, conflicts and rivalry, the issues of gendered and inter-generational inequalities have hardly been addressed.

Infrastructural development has long focused on Java and Jakarta, but this is changing. In his recent speech at the Rapat Kerja Nasional of the PDI-P held in Jakarta in January 2016, President Joko Widodo proclaimed a fundamental change of course when he said, 'Now we do not want to be Java-centric in the development of infrastructure but Indonesia-centric'.[1] His speech was accompanied by the presentation of major construction projects, including roads, railways, airports and harbours all over the Outer Islands. Although infrastructural development and increasing access to governmental services are perceived as proceeding too slowly by many inhabitants of remote places, rising investments have been made in the infrastructure of the Outer Islands since the implementation of regional autonomy, and this trend is – the president's vision ahead – likely to increase. However, road construction, increasing mobility and access to new media already offer manifold new opportunities to the people of the Outer Islands, even in the most remote regions. But how new infrastructures are appropriated locally, and the desired and undesired consequences that come with them, is still very little understood.

Processes of social, political and economic disenfranchisement evoke specific feelings (cf. Stodulka and Röttger-Rössler 2014). Long (Chapter 4), for example, used the term 'mindset of marginality' to describe how people have internalised images of being backward, ignorant and possessing a less valuable culture. Do such feelings disappear with the construction of new infrastructure or splendid centres? Obviously not automatically and not everywhere, otherwise the school master from Batam would not have needed such remarkable efforts to build up his students' self-esteem. The (re-)emergence of new fragmented landscapes of power relations provides local actors with new chances and opportunities to pursue the lives that are most desirable for them. Long consequently argues that 'the question of what mode of life is desired and why stands out as a pressing matter for ethnographic investigation'. What aspirations do the ordinary people of the Outer Islands have for their future? What kind of developments do they fear and what kind of futures do they envision for their children?

Finally, the examination of changing power relations from the perspective of Indonesia's margins revealed that the perspective of the centre is largely unaccounted for. It would, therefore, be highly interesting to analyse how the centre perceives the changing periphery and its position within an emerging fragmented landscape of multiple centres and peripheries.

Note

1 The original quote in Bahasa Indonesia 'Sekarang kita memang tidak ingin Java-sentris dalam membangun infrastruktur, tetapi Indonesia-sentris' can be found under the following link at sequence 15:50–16:03: https://m.youtube.com/watch?v=NSICvUxBpaY &feature=share (accessed 12 January 2016).

References

Aspinall, E. and Mietzner, M. (eds) (2010) *Problems of Democratisation in Indonesia: Elections, Institutions and Society.* Singapore: Institute of Southeast Asian Studies.

Booth, A. (2011) Splitting, Splitting and Splitting Again: A Brief History of the Development of Regional Government in Indonesia since Independence, *Bijdragen tot de Taal-, Land- en Volkenkunde* 167(1): 31–59.

Bräuchler, B. and Erb, M. (2011) Introduction: Eastern Indonesia under Reform: The Global, the National and the Local, *Asian Journal of Social Science* 39: 113–130.

Kimura, E. (2007) Marginality and Opportunity in the Periphery: The Emergence of Gorontalo Province in North Sulawesi, *Indonesia* 84: 71–95.

Kimura, E. (2010) Proliferating Provinces: Territorial Politics in Post-Suharto Indonesia, *South East Asia Research* 18(3): 415–449.

Li, T. (1999) Marginality, Power and Production: Analysing Upland Transformations, in T. Li (ed.), *Transforming the Indonesian Uplands: Marginality, Power, and Production*, Amsterdam: Harwood Academic Publishers, pp. 1–45.

McWilliam, A. (2011) Marginal Governance in the Time of Pemekaran: Case Studies from Sulawesi and West Papua, *Asian Journal of Social Science* 39: 150–170.

Quinn, G. (2003) Coming Apart and Staying Together at the Centre: Debates over Provincial Status in Java and Madura, in E. Aspinall and G. Fealy (eds), *Local Power and Politics in Indonesia: Decentralisation and Democratisation*, Singapore: Institute for Southeast Asian Studies, pp. 164–178.

Sakai, M., Banks, G. and Walker, J. (eds) (2009) *The Politics of the Periphery in Indonesia: Social and Geographical Perspectives.* Singapore: NUS Press.

Schulte Nordholt, H. and van Klinken, G. (eds) (2007) *Renegotiating Boundaries: Local Politics in Post-Suharto Indonesia.* Leiden: KITLV Press.

Stodulka, T. and Röttger-Rössler, B. (eds) (2014) *Feelings at the Margins: Dealing with Violence, Stigma and Isolation in Indonesia.* Frankfurt and New York: Campus.

The Jakarta Post (2014) www.thejakartapost.com/news/2014/05/12/reducing-decentralization-s-dysfunction.html#sthash.jR0ek10f.dpufPapua (accessed 22 January 2016).

The Jakarta Post (2015) www.thejakartapost.com/news/2015/09/29/papua-now-pacific-radar.html (accessed 22 January 2016).

Vel, J. (2008) *Uma Politics: An Ethnography of Democratization in West Sumba, Indonesia, 1986–2006*. Leiden: KITLV Press.

Warren, C. and McCarthy, J. (eds) (2009) *Community, Environment and Local Governance in Indonesia: Locating the Commonweal*. London: Routledge.

Index

Page numbers in *italics* denote tables, those in **bold** denote figures.

cross-border: hinterlandisation 67;
relations 87
cultural diversity 10, 44, 50, 52
cultural marginality, concept of 47

Dana Alokasi Khusus (DAK) 137
Dana Alokasi Umum (DAU) 137
Dayak communities: competition and
rivalry 136; indigenous identity 136;
political marginalisation of 135–6; as
ruling majority in Kutai Barat 135–7
de-marginalisation, processes of 19
decentralisation process, in Indonesia 108;
consequence of 12–13, 16; dark side of
35–8; democracy and 32–5;
democratisation and 31–2; governance
and administrative structures 29; impact
of 39; political decision-making 31, 34;
reforms in 11–14; tax-raising and public
expenditures 31; weaknesses of 40
decision-making, political 31, 34
Department of Social Affairs (DEPSOS),
Indonesia 53
desa government 12, 98
devolution, principles of 31
Dewan Perwakilan Daerah (DPD) 30
Dewan Perwakilan Rakyat (DPR) 29, 37,
38
Dewan Perwakilan Rakyat Daerah
(DPRD) 29, 34, 37
distribution of wealth, patterns of 17, 34
domeinverklaring, principle of 50
dress code, for women 38
Dutch East India Company 4–5, 65, 120

East Kalimantan 118, 124, 128, 137;
interior regions of 132; natural resource
exploitation 133, 137; social and
economic disenfranchisement 146
economic crisis of 1997–98 13
ekonomi kerakyatan (people's economy)
121
election campaign 33
entrepreneurial ethics 122–4
estate crop production 138
ethnic conflicts 35
ethnic market competition 126–8
ethnic minorities 1, 10, 38, 154
ethnic nationalism 8
ethnoreligious tensions 14

Facebook 121
Farouk, Awang 124
foreign direct investment 73

Forest Product Harvest Concession 142–3
Forestry Law of 1999 55
Forum for Border Community Care 83
Free Aceh Movement 82–3
Free Iban Movement 82
free market 121, 123–4, 128
free trade zone 84

Gerakan Aceh Merdeka (GAM) *see* Free
Aceh Movement
Gerakan Bersama Maju (GBM) *see* Jointly
We Prosper Movement
Gerakan Iban Merdeka (GIM) *see* Free
Iban Movement
German Society of Technical Cooperation
(GIZ) 31
global financial crisis (2008) 120
global financial industry 117
goldmining 101
governance performance, quality of 34
Gowa, empire of 4
'Growth Triangle' scheme 67
'Guided Democracy' 119

Habibie, President 30
Hak Pemungutan Hasil Hutan (HPHH) *see*
Forest Product Harvest Concession
Halmahera Barat 18, 96, 102–3, 106–10,
155
Halmahera Utara 18, 96, 102–3, 106–8,
155
Hindu–Buddhist culture 3
Human Development Index 73
human resource quality 72–3, 75–6

indigenous communities, territorial claims
of 51
indigenous religions 11
Indonesian Central Statistics Agency 13
Indonesian Constitutional Court 55
Indonesian Ulama Council 121
Indonesianization, processes of 10
inequalities: gendered and inter-
generational 157; rise in 140–4; within
village communities 142–4; between
villages 141–2
inter-ethnic rivalry 82
inter-human relations 121–2
international companies 108
International Monetary Fund (IMF) 120
international resort area 67
Islam 3, 6, 10–11, 14, 49, 119, 121

Jailolo Timur (East Jailolo) 103, 109–10;

constituting margins during 51–3;
constructing marginality during 9–11;
patrimonial power structure of 39
otonomi daerah 30, 36
Outer Islands 2, 5–6, 9, 14, 34;
construction of marginality on 10;
cultural diversity of 10; political
marginality 51; status as inhabitants of
70
ownership rights, to forest areas 143

Pancasila, principle of 10, 51, 119, 121
*Panitia Pembentukan Kabupaten
Perbatasan Utara* (PPKPU) *see*
Committee for the Establishment of the
North Border Regency
pater familias 119
*Pembinaan Kesejahteraan Masyarakat
Terasing* (PKSMT) 53
pemekaran 18, 84–6, 90–1, 96–7, 110–11,
132, 145, 152–3, 157; in North Maluku
99–106
Pendapatan Asli Daerah (PAD) 137
pilkada 17, 32, 33
political authority, devolution of 12
poverty distribution, disparity of 140
poverty rate, measurement of 13
power relations, to Jakarta 156
preman (gangsters) 36
PT Newmont 127

regencies and districts: borders of 16, **104,
105**; minority population 136
regional autonomy 12, 30, 86–8;
implementation of 141
regional governments 12, 14, 52, 69, 96,
101–3, 106, 107–8, 109–11, 118, 126,
155
Regional Taxes and Retribution 125
relative association, sociological concept
of 15
religious affiliation 11, 55, 58n12
religious beliefs, equality of 38
religious freedom 11
religious minorities, discriminating against
14
religious secularism 121
remote areas, concept of 15
Riau Archipelago 65, 151; affective life of
a periphery 70–6; centre–periphery
relations 66; Gunawan's story 73–6;
human resource quality 73, 75; Sri's
story 71–2
Riau Islands Province 17, 65, 151

Riau Merdeka separatist movement 68
Riau-Lingga sultanate 77n2
rubber tapping 141

Sailendra dynasty 4
security and sovereignty, state rhetoric of
85–6
self-government 31
sepilis (syphilis) 121
sexes, equality of 38
shari'ah 37, 152
Sinar Mas Group, Indonesia 89
social disenfranchisement 15, 132, 134,
145
social identities, constructions of 98–9,
101–2, 107, 109–11, 155
social stratification 3
society, security of 120
socio-political campaign 118
socio-territorial organisation, in North
Maluku 18, 97–8
Southeast Asian nationalisms 7
Special Administrative Zone 84
Special Authority Region 84
Srivijaya, Buddhist kingdom of 4, 7
state enterprises, privatisation of 120
state sovereignty 80–1
Suharto, President 11, 51, 81; downfall of
53; New Order regime 1, 11, 119;
pembangunan, agenda of 52; resignation
of 29, 96
swidden agriculture 10, 50–1, 53, 138

Taman Adat Sendawar 136–7
Ternate, Sultanate of 101–2
territorial sovereignty 80, 91
territorialisation, process of 9
timber logging 143; illegal 143; licences,
issue of 14; self-organised 141
Trans-Kalimantan Highway 122, 123–4
transmigration programme 10
transnational: corporations 13; networks
89

unemployment 35
United States of Indonesia (USI) 8
Unity in Diversity (*Bhinneka Tunggal Ika*),
principle of 10, 38
upland marginalisation processes 55
upland wealth: exploitation of 132;
rechannelling 137–9

Vereenigde Oostindische Compagnie
(VOC) *see* Dutch East India Company

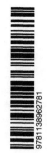